Finding Celia's Place

Finding Celia's Place

CELIA MORRIS

TEXAS A&M UNIVERSITY PRESS : COLLEGE STATION

Excerpt from "Too Young," by Nat King Cole, reprinted by permission of The Songwriters Guild of America. Excerpt from "Let's Do It," by Cole Porter, copyright 1928 (renewed) Warner Bros., Inc., used by permission of Warner Bros. Publications U.S. Inc., Miami, Fla., 33014. All rights reserved. Excerpt from "Leda and the Swan," by W. B. Yeats, reprinted with the permission of Scribner, a Division of Simon & Schuster form *The Collected Poems of W. B. Yeats,* Revised Second Edition, edited by Richard J. Finneran, copyright 1928 by Macmillan Publishing Company, copyright renewed 1956 by Georgie Yeats. First stanza from "Thousand-and-First Ship" from *F. Scott Fitzgerald Poems, 1911–1940.* Copyright 1972, 1978 by Frances Scott Fitzgerald. Reprinted by permission of Harold Ober Associates Incorporated. First ten lines of "Lullaby," by W. H. Auden from *W. H. Auden: Collected Poems,* edited by Edward Mendelson, copyright 1940, 1968 by W. H. Auden, reprinted by permission of Random House, Inc. Excerpt from "You're the Top," by Cole Porter, copyright 1934 (renewed) Warner Bros. Inc., used by permission of Warner Bros. Publications U.S. Inc., Miami, Fla., 33014. All rights reserved. Excerpt taken from the MARY McGRORY column by Mary McGrory. Copyright 1997 Dist. by UNIVERSAL PRESS SYNDICATE. Reprinted with permission. All rights reserved. Excerpt from *The Great Tradition,* by F. R. Leavis, published by Chatto & Windus, reprinted by permission of The Random House Archive and Library. Quotes from *Man's World, Woman's Place* and epigraph from Suzanne Langer courtesy Elizabeth Janeway. Excerpt from *North Toward Home,* by Willie Morris, courtesy Vintage Books, a Division of Random House, Inc. Four lines from "The House of Quiet and the World Was Calm," from *Collected Poems* by Wallace Stevens, copyright 1947 by Wallace Stevens, reprinted by permission of Alfred A. Knopf, a Division of Random House, Inc.

Library of Congress Cataloging-in-Publication Data

Morris, Celia, 1935–
      Finding Celia's place / by Celia Morris. — 1st ed.
          p.   cm.
      ISBN 0-89096-963-9 (alk. paper)
        1. Morris, Celia, 1935–.   2. Women—United States—Biography.
   3. Sex role—United States—History—20th century.   I. Title.
   HQ1413.M66 A3   2000
   305.4'092—dc21   00-037804
   [B]   CIP

IN GRATEFUL MEMORY OF

My Mother & Father

WHO WORKED SO HARD IN SUCH GOOD FAITH

CONTENTS

ILLUSTRATIONS

following page 122

The snug bungalow where it all began for me
Our gang, my first
Daddy and his little girl on Galveston beach
Huddling next to my favorite uncle, Mickey, with Grandma
With Mama, before the hard times came
The big house on Buffalo Speedway
With Mama and Glenn, hoping for the best
E. A. Snapp, Jr., and his girls' swimming team
A typical moment in the elegant life of River Oaks
With Madeline, Jayne, and others acting silly
With Willie at the Theta house
With Barry Bishop after polio confined him to an iron lung
Receiving an armful of roses as Sweetheart of the University
With Willie after he received his degree at Oxford
John Sullivan in my New York apartment, with David and Ichabod
David at seven, in a petulant moment
Mother and adolescent son, cutting up on winter holiday
With Bob Eckhardt, enjoying one of our favorite pastimes
Daddy reading my Christmas promise of a lavish dinner
With Bob and Andy Young
With Shirley Garner and Sally Leach
Friends for more than forty years

ACKNOWLEDGMENTS

Most of the people I call special friends in *Finding Celia's Place* have read one early draft of this book or another, and some have read them all. Each has responded with the rigor, forthrightness, and generosity I value most in the friendships that sustain me, and for this, as for the friendships themselves, I am permanently in their debt. I also want to thank Merrill Skaggs, the first person to read the manuscript, and with a delight that kept me going; Anne Barstow and Tom Driver, who gave it their meticulous attention and spent a long New England day with me exploring the issues it raised; Bob Sherrill, who goaded me into writing a book that would pass his inspection; Elizabeth Janeway, whose careful notes were almost as long as the manuscript itself; Jane Garrett, who believed in it; Betty Fischer and Barbara and Isaac Green, who watched over me tenderly as I waited; the autobiography working group of the Society for Values in Higher Education, which spent two lively sessions grappling with key questions; my son David, who read even the painful passages and responded, "I'm proud of you for having the courage to write it"; Martha Carroll, who insisted with such zest on getting the pictures right; John Egerton and Susan Ford Wiltshire, who committed themselves to finding the right publisher; and Julie Ford, who struggled to keep me from putting my head in a noose. Finally, my thanks go to the people at the Texas A&M University Press, who have shown me publishing at its best, and especially to its director, Charles Backus, whose initial letter was so fine it would have made a hardened author weep.

Finding Celia's Place

The story that follows springs from what I call my pagan mystical experiences—sudden illuminations that come unbidden and change me. Subtly, to be sure, but forever. Though commonly spoken of as religious, they appear to many of us who feel presences and dimensions in the world that rationality cannot account for. I had the first one I remember in Houston, Texas, when I was nine, but the one that prompted me to begin this book came not long after my sixtieth birthday.

It was early one morning on the streets of the nation's capital, and only minutes before, at the weekly meeting of a twelve-step group, a man I admire had said emphatically, "If I took *one* drink, I'd die!" Meaning that once he started, he would slide into a binge that could lead only to that one end. As I walked up Pennsylvania Avenue toward my home on Capitol Hill, mulling over his stark message, I suddenly saw my danger differently: if I took a drink and began that dread, irreversible slide, I'd marry another liberal folk hero—*my third*. And I felt as stricken as my friend had been at the specter of death.

Still, a fresh cup of coffee and a few moments watching the hummingbirds flicker through the trumpet vine in my small back garden gradually trumped my panic, for yet another misadventure along those lines seemed unlikely. Not long before, I'd been startled to realize not only that I am now a happy woman, but that if this unwonted serenity lasts, I'll have had a far richer, more resonant life than anyone could have predicted when I was fifteen or twenty. And I will have beaten the

3

family odds, for although, by the standards of the American Dream, my hardworking, upright parents were stunningly successful, happiness had eluded them, and behind the public image of charmed lives were days shot through with suffering.

When my mother was the age I am now, she had only a year to live before she drank herself to a gruesome death—after more than a decade of courting oblivion in a quart of vodka a day. Not long afterward, my father gambled on finding happiness at last with a woman across the road—and lost—and within another two years, he was dead of cancer. The anxieties that had ripped my parents apart and pitted them against one another had been so deeply imprinted on my own psyche that until I was well past fifty I thought you couldn't be authentically human unless your life was laced with pain. And an hour with the *Washington Post* or the *New York Times* can still bring on acute attacks of guilt; in a world where millions live and die wretchedly, my own life is so filled with blessings that after decades of unbelief, I sometimes wonder if Grace isn't working gently in my life.

Being happy, to be sure, turns out to be different from what I thought when I saw it from the outside. It doesn't rule out feeling melancholy for those who did *not* beat the odds, for instance, or being outraged and indignant from time to time, and even most of the time. Or hurt, confused, anxious, frustrated, bored, or even sodden with grief. Being happy doesn't blot out—it scarcely even dims—the abiding sorrows. Nor does it mean always getting what you try for, though I *do* think being happy depends on a more modest understanding than I had at twenty of one person's power to address the world's wrongs.

If happiness came late, the adventure, excitement, fulfillment, and glee did not, and even some of my luckiest peers, I'm told, have envied me. But during long decades the good times were interwoven with heartache and humiliation, for women who grew up, as I did, in the 1940s and '50s were taught to define ourselves in marriage. It didn't matter that I had an adored grandmother who learned to knit while riding horseback herding a thousand sheep and who seemed to have passed her frontier spirit virtually intact to me. *For our times were different;* as adolescents in perhaps the most aggressively domestic period in history, my friends and I had known only *one* story for women, really, and it ended with "and they lived happily ever after." So we'd set out expecting to be wives and mothers first and then community volunteers, though by the time we graduated from college, some of us were also mulling over the prospect of work we might actually be paid for.

But if a handful of contemporaries would find themselves in marriages that were good and lasting, and scores of others in relationships they could tolerate, many of those I knew best—women who'd won the prizes the University of Texas offered and married men they admired and thought they loved—would find themselves in marriages that shattered their confidence and undermined their self-respect. Ordinary human frailties aside, the institution of marriage, we discovered, had worked at cross purposes with our basic values. It had stunted our hearts instead of opening them; it had threatened our capacity to know and tell the truth; it had made us lesser people.

And our problems in marriage had not arisen because, by the standards of our culture, we had been dispirited or unprepared, for in a white, middle- and upper-middle-class world of privilege, we'd been luckier than most. With superb health, good brains, decent looks, enough money, gregarious instincts, and disciplined habits, we'd had choices a lot of other women did not. You would *never* have caught us sitting back and letting the boys star; we competed with them as well as with each other, and any guy who expected us to kowtow to his superior purchase on the world was in for a decided shock.

In fact, at twenty-two I could have made a good case for "family values" myself. Like my friends, I took it for granted that wives were as important as their husbands and that the enterprise we embarked on together mattered in the scheme of things. Descending from people who had tamed a frontier, we women expected to do *at least* as much and probably more than our share. Nor did we mind doing everything backward and in high heels like Ginger Rogers when she danced with Fred Astaire; the odds that it might be harder simply heightened the challenge.

But all of us had counted on a partnership like that of Astaire and Rogers—tender, juicy, and playful. For I suspect that all those years of watching them joined at the fingertips, matching step for step, swirl for swirl with never a stumble, seeing them swing apart and come back together with so much zest left me thinking that that's what the whole business was about. I *too* would have a partner who moved with flair, who liked and respected and needed me, and together we would dance with thrilling verve until the grand finale. (In addition to watching the couple with the patent leather tap shoes, we had seen Hepburn with Tracy, and Bogart with Bacall, and will *never* underestimate the degree to which those images of saucy, sexy men and women together had ignited our young imaginations.)

Well, it hadn't happened that way, and it wasn't just that our lives had fallen short of the Hollywood glitz and glamour. For the hard truths we would discover were fundamental: all of us had been astonished when we smacked into what Jane Kramer, writing in the *New Yorker*, called the "shattering invisibility" of women in a man's world. The will turned out to have less power and life to be more confusing and frightening than our culture had suggested when we were twenty.

In fact, we turned out to be part of a bridge generation; born into traditional expectations for women, we had lived into a time when they can be astronauts, jockeys, governors, and stockbrokers—and people expect them to be. *Never* had the prospects for women—personal and professional—changed so fast or so dramatically than in the years after we married, and we were the generation that felt those contradictory tugs most acutely: *while we never lost faith in women's traditional role, we also knew we had to do other things as well.* So we had to identify and then struggle with received ideas about women's "natures" that would loosen their hold on the generation that followed us but that worked to stifle our spirits. These ancient notions were fodder for both men and women who insisted we stay in our "place."

In retrospect it is easy enough to see that my friends and I were grotesquely unprepared for marriage. Not only had we not experimented with sex, we'd never even *talked* frankly about it—or about our fears and confusion, or the *real* lives of the people we came from. In the 1950s, brightness was all. Shaped by a culture that exalted the individual and prescribed a stiff upper lip, we would discover that the pull-your-self-up-by-your-bootstraps rhetoric had been dangerous twaddle, for the women's movement that began when we were in our twenties would change our lives profoundly. It would teach us that problems we'd thought unique were anything but—and, at the same time, would give us a language to help us understand them. But before we began to discover ways out of the despair for which nothing had prepared us, some of us had been brushed by the ebony wings of the Angel of Death.

6

Since I now live in the nation's capital, I sometimes take its rituals to heart, and so, during the presidential inaugural after the 1996 elections, I gave an open house. As the official ceremonies ended and the crowds drifted away from the West Front of the Capitol, the usual suspects began to gather in my home across from the Library of Congress — journalists, political operatives and analysts, more than our share of lawyers, but also artists, economists, the occasional historian, and even a couple of Republicans.

It was a gaudy afternoon, and in what seemed a remarkably short time, the noise level was very nearly impenetrable; the shrimp were little more than a pile of translucent coral shells; the ham had lost its appealing heft and shape; the boxes of empty bottles in back had begun to bulge indecently. And finally the front door burst open and the guest I'd awaited most impatiently ran down the hall and into my arms. She is a sweet-faced, brown-eyed woman named Sydney Brammer, who had cast her spell over me when she was three years old and still looks like an ingenue from the silent movie era — a cross between Claudette Colbert and Marion Davies. Sydney was then living with folk singer Peter Yarrow, of Peter, Paul, and Mary fame, and he, along with a small entourage, followed her into my long hallway as she and I made up in hugs and exclamations for a separation that had lasted more than twenty years.

At last, sensing that my friends — and hers — were mildly curious about all this glee, I led Sydney into my living room, tapped on a glass for silence, and then said, "This is my second husband's second wife's eldest child — whose brother is my first husband's namesake." The woman nearest me, who had started the Washington Family Therapy Practice Center, laughed uproariously and then asked me to repeat that litany. I did so to the crowd's general delight — and then added to my therapist friend, "That's how we do families in Texas!"

As everyone knew, that last quip is not precisely true, much less the whole of the story, but as a spur-of-the-moment explanation, it would do. And as we stood there I marveled how preposterous life seemed at that moment. It had been a long, long way from my harsh encounter with those ebony wings to these moments of high hilarity.

For not only did many women in my generation discover that the ideas and stories about women that we'd grown up with were grossly inadequate to the realities we faced, but we also learned that it isn't always true that what you don't know won't hurt you. In fact, what we didn't know had hurt us quite a lot—whether it was ignorance about ourselves, or sex, or about the difference in power between men and women.

The story that follows, then, is about a woman whose highest values turned out to be incompatible with the marriages those values had led her into. Who came to realize that traditional families can be dangerous places, particularly for women and children, but also for men whose relative privilege blinds them to the ways they may abuse it. Who learned the hard way that making the best of things is often folly. Who discovered that her most serious mistakes came from her strengths, her hopes, her dreams—though weakness, terror, ignorance, stupidity, and bad luck obviously played a role, as they do in all merely human stories.

It is also about women who found that men who tell us to "Know thyself!" are often those who know themselves the least. Who discovered that the will is necessary, but insufficient by itself. Who found that only when we open ourselves to the whole range of human experience, from the humble to the grand, from the terrible to the sublime—and take *full* responsibility for what we do and who we are—can we enter into the spiritual life to which our traditions and our best literature bear witness.

Part of the problem for women, I'm convinced, comes from the plain fact that men historically have told the world's stories, since it turns out that many women would tell them differently if given the chance. For the men have left too many things out and have spoken, quite naturally, with bias. And in fact, I was drawn to the idea of telling my own story because *both* my ex-husbands have had their say in print. Indeed, my first told what he took to be our saga *twice*—initially in an essay in *Esquire* that prompted people from all over the country to call and say it made them cry. When a second version appeared in a widely noticed book, virtually all the reviewers singled it out as the most moving chapter. And I too was moved, for these accounts read rather like an apology and a peace offering. Still, his version of reality and mine were as similar as the stork version of childbirth is to the natural process.

In a 1994 *Texas Monthly* article, my second husband said his three marriages had been fine while they lasted, but he gave me a few extra words of praise: I'd been very good to him after he had a stroke, he said, but then we'd fallen into a "terrible dispute." He "gave [the writer] a helpless look, over the ages, man to man. 'Well. You know.'" When I wrote to see if the author had asked what the dispute was about, he replied that he hadn't but now was awfully curious. So the next time I was in Austin, Texas, we had lunch and I told him.

With such goading then, I decided to try reconstructing my own experience, yearning to understand finally how I had moved from a life that merely *seemed* blessed to one that really is. I would do it even though I would have to write things about myself and others that some would shudder to hear. Even though I'd have to violate a code of privacy in which I believe, since without a certain minimum revelation, the story would lose its point—being, as it is, about the tangled lives of men and women in our generation.

So what follows is *my* version—the product of a long struggle to get it right—though flecked, no doubt, with bias nonetheless, like any intensely human story. But unless we tell our hard truths to one another—unless we pass along these lessons for which we have paid so dearly—the ground we gained will be lost, and generations to come will repeat the grim cycle.

CHAPTER ONE

To the untutored eye, and on paper, I had an idyllic American childhood, with the accent firmly on "American." I was born in the midst of the Great Depression and grew up in West University Place, a small incorporated town on the edge of Houston, Texas. Until I was thirteen, we lived in a brick bungalow with three bedrooms on a street that had maybe twelve houses, some frame, some brick, two or three of them two-story but all basically the same except for a huge brick house on the corner that had a four-car carriage house with servants' quarters above it as well as a tennis court. My neighborhood gang and I didn't really count that house as part of our block because it faced another street and an elderly couple lived there whom we scarcely ever saw. Our life was about kids.

The only thing in the world around us that whispered of mystery, the corner house was living on past grandeur; the grounds were ill kept, the garages and servants' quarters empty, and the surface of the tennis court so pocked and eroded that on the rare occasion one of us managed to hit a ball over the imaginary net, it was likely to bounce sideways and sail over the scraggly wire fence into a weed-choked lot to the back. I've blamed that court ever since for turning me permanently off tennis, for everything about it was so warped and broken that only a fool or masochist would have kept trying.

But the corner house was surrounded by almost an acre of land and scores of trees that made the property shady in the hot summers, and our gang would sometimes park our bicycles and sit on its patchy grass to regroup. The bicycle accident I remember most vividly happened there: while doing figure-eights on the wide concrete apron in front of the garage, I lost control, smashed into a door, and shattered a glass pane—a disaster so humiliating that I ran to get my mother and held her hand all the way back. At the door, a wispy lady accepted my abject apology along with my mother's pledge to pay for the damage, and then, in the fall, with the gentle lady's blessing, I gathered windfall pecans and took them home for Mama's pies.

Apart from the aging lord and lady of the manor, the rest of us were not very different. Of the three other girls about my age, Ellen's father was a butcher, Theresa's worked for some company or other, Marie's was a salesman, and mine was an engineer for the Humble Oil Company. There were two boys a little older than we—Mike and Gillian O'Connor, who were both going to be doctors. Four were a little younger: Theresa's brother Tom and Marie's, whose name I forget; Jake, who lived on one side of me; and Harold, who lived across the street and once, when we were playing strip poker, showed us tricks with his penis. (My friends' names—though not my friends—are figments of my imagination.)

I think that was the first penis I ever saw, and though it could do nothing but wiggle a little, Harold seemed inordinately proud of it. Gillian initiated me into the mysteries of sexual intercourse by way of a line drawing, which struck me as interesting, albeit surely irrelevant. To entertain some schoolmates, Mike and Gillian once bet me a dollar I wouldn't chase Jake and kiss him. Though Jake flew off, I caught him anyway and smacked him on the cheek, but Mike and Gillian tackily reneged.

We were healthy and full of energy and mischief. We played with trucks, cars, and erector sets more often than dolls, and I held my own at marbles and jacks. Theresa was the neighborhood champion with bubble gum; her bubbles would puff astoundingly until they exploded all over her face, and she'd have to use alcohol to scrub the gum away. Little bits stuck in her hair nonetheless, and behind her ears, but Theresa wasn't a stickler for cleanliness.

She was also the neighborhood yo-yo champ, for she could do seventy-five loop-the-loops without stopping, and once she even won a contest at the Village Theater, where we went for weekend matinees.

The Village, which abutted Rice Institute a mile or so away, was our shopping and recreational center, and winning a talent contest there was making it into the big time. Six months older than I, Theresa was a mass of freckles and I adored her.

If I had to pick an image of our gang's life there, it would be a fast blur. We ran or skated or rode our bicycles up and down the block; played kickball and rover-come-over and crack-the-whip; jumped off roofs and climbed high in trees; teased and yelled and taunted. Hurricanes were fun because the flood waters backed up and we could swim in the street and catch crawdads in the bayou. We went to the beach in Galveston in the summers and got awful sunburns, though we already spent most of our time outdoors. There were rivalries and feuds and hurt feelings, of course, but mostly we had fun and were pals in the totally unsentimental way of children.

My mother, Inez Fix Buchan, grew up in a little town outside Dallas called Terrell. After getting a degree in interior design from CIA, the College of Industrial Arts, in Denton—now Texas Woman's University—she had come to Houston to work in a furniture store where she drew ads for newspapers. After a couple of years, she quit to marry Daddy, and almost five years later, she had me. Until my brother was born nine years later still, my father and I were the focus of her life.

She told me once that sometimes I would be mainly her girl and sometimes mainly Daddy's; first she'd get her feelings hurt or feel left out, and then he would. But after a while, there was no contest.

Mother wore her hair, which was prematurely gray, in a bun at the nape of her neck, and I remember her mainly in shorts or pedal pushers and starched cotton shirts that buttoned in front. She'd sit in the back-yard shelling bushels of peas or snapping beans, and then she canned most of the vegetables and fruit we ate through the winter. We kept chickens in a big pen behind the garage—I fed them and gathered the eggs when I got old enough—and Mama's chicken and dumplings could have won a prize at a fair. More often, she fixed steak well done and baked potatoes because that's what Daddy liked, and for dessert, wonderful apple or pecan pies.

For a while we had a maid named Cecil, a stocky black woman who somehow inspired my first real ambition: I would be a doctor, and she would keep house for me. But one day Cecil disappeared—moving on, rumor had it, to California or Chicago—and I was so desolate that my dream vanished with her. Daddy couldn't stomach the women who tried to take her place, and as the years went by, things kept getting harder for Mama. I remember her scrubbing clothes on a corrugated washboard and ironing for hours when it was over 90 degrees, which it usually was in a Houston summer.

Ellen's mother worked as a nurse, and we thought it a pity she had to. But the rest of the neighborhood women got together every week for coffee around somebody's breakfast table, and now and again another couple would come over for Friday night bridge. Sunday mornings people scattered to worship: Theresa's family was Catholic; Harold's were Jews; Ellen's were Methodists, and so was Mother, vaguely. Daddy, however, had no truck with churches, so Mama and I didn't go very often.

Late most weekday afternoons I'd go up to the corner across from the bus stop and climb my favorite tree and wait for Daddy. He'd get off waving and cross the street, and until I got too big, I'd drop onto his shoulders and ride home. He'd change into his khakis, and I'd watch impatiently while he drank a beer and read the *Houston Chronicle*. Almost every night after I was supposed to be asleep, I'd call for a glass of water, and he'd bring it and kiss me goodnight again.

Most of all I liked being Daddy's helper, and on weekends I'd carry the hammer or nails and hold the screens or whatever he needed me to do while he fiddled. When he hit his thumb with the hammer, which was pretty often, I would be the rescue squad. He thought I was really something, and the feeling was mutual.

When I got to be six, I started walking the half mile to West University Elementary School, sometimes alone, sometimes with one of the gang. Whenever the public schools had a holiday I'd go with Theresa to parochial school and be thankful the nuns didn't smack *my* hand with a ruler. Except for the sour tomato soup our buildings reeked of, I loved school and counted on being the teacher's pet.

So that was mainly it: Fibber McGee and Molly on the radio one night, the Shadow, the Lone Ranger, the Thin Man, and Amos 'n Andy on the others. Football in the fall, Galveston beach in the summer, the matinee and sometimes the midnight show at the Village Theater on Saturday, the funny papers on Sundays—especially Popeye and Olive. We didn't lock the front door much less the back at night.

Until I was five or six, my worst problems seemed to be that Daddy hogged the bathroom, I had nightmares about The Mummy who rose up from quicksand with a claw-like hand reaching out for naughty girls, the birds usually beat us to the figs in the backyard, and sometimes I was afraid of Ellen. Oh yes, and Boris Karloff scared Theresa and me to death. We all had mumps, measles, and the rest roughly on schedule.

Daddy was six feet tall and lanky, with heavy bones and outsized joints. His name was Rudolph Carl Buchan, and though, like many Germans, he could do a mean schottische, his favorite dance was the Charleston. When he hunched over and worked himself up, he turned into rubber, with elbows and knees flying. To pay his way through Texas A&M, he'd played a bass horn in a dance band, and he was usually whistling or humming. When I was older I discovered he was an awful racist, but he loved Louis Armstrong nevertheless, and I grew up listening to Louis sing "I've Got the World on a String" and "The Darktown Strutters' Ball," or playing Bix Beiderbecke and Paul Whiteman on the Victrola. George and Ira Gershwin pulled a lot more weight in our house than Bach, Mozart, and Beethoven together.

Daddy had a bony face with a thin, high-bridged nose and big ears that stuck out. He had a high forehead, sparse brown hair, and striking brown eyes, and whenever anybody asked me, "Where did you get those big brown eyes?" I'd say proudly, "From my daddy." I loved the way he walked, with an extra roll or undulation, and the way he'd fling his arms about as if conducting the big swing bands playing "Stardust" or "The Man I Love" on the radio. I even liked the way he smelled when he'd been working hard and sweating or had spilled creosote on his khakis.

The fourth child of eight—the third son—Daddy had grown up poor in Galveston, Texas, and, when he was nine, had started working. All the Buchan boys threw papers for the *Galveston News,* getting up before 4 A.M. to race downtown on their bicycles to get their allotted number and start off on their paper routes. While throwing newspapers, he'd memorize poetry and could do such a spirited rendition of the first twenty-two lines of Chaucer's *Canterbury Tales*—in Middle English— that I learned them too, to the astonishment of my first college English professor. When still in high school, he was made circulation manager of the newspaper, and a lot of people probably never saw his playful side.

In the fall of 1929, about ten days before the stock market crashed, Daddy went to work as a chemical and petroleum engineer for Humble at $125 a month. A few weeks later, everybody got a 15 percent cut in salary, so for a long time, things in our house were tight. But they didn't let him go and he was loyal. In the years to come, he invented oilfield equipment that made millions of dollars for the company but from which he got merely a fancier title and maybe a small bonus. But whenever anyone criticized Humble or Big Oil—and eventually, the somebody was usually me—he lashed out indignantly.

He had no patience with religion but rarely talked about it. His mother had grown up in Lutheran country, and once she'd heard a preacher declare that anybody bitten by a rattlesnake was bound to die. Since Grandma's uncle had survived such a bite by about forty years, that was the end of that. She never went to church but had no quarrel with people who did, and neither did Daddy. They thought nevertheless that virtually all problems could be solved by clean living, hard work, and education. So their religion was secular, but their faith was absolute.

This American idyll had its dark side, for it would turn out that I'd thrown myself into the street life of my block to seal off a heart irradiated with pain, though my sorrow stayed deeply buried until I was in my thirties, when it began to hemorrhage on a psychiatrist's couch in New York City. And there, in the midst of anguish I'd never imagined anyone could feel and survive, my analyst would ask patiently, "But where does your strength come from?" As I struggled with this question, I also wondered, given my troubled relationship with my mother and her miserable decline, why I had never felt ambivalent about being a woman. How was it that I could have such deep and abiding friendships with strong women? And the single most important reason, I came to believe, lies with my paternal grandmother, Emelia Reinke Buchan.

Grandma was a big woman, not given to lavish shows of affection, and I don't remember ever cuddling in her lap or collapsing on her large, sagging bosom. Years later, a picture of Gertrude Stein made me think of Grandma. She had a slight mustache and hairs springing from a mole on her chin, and once when I was about eight and she looked me over and said, "At your age, I looked just like you," my mouth fell open and my fright must have been so stark that my parents jumped up and bustled around to cover up for my bad manners. But nowhere did I feel more beloved than in Grandma's house. Nowhere did I feel more secure than in Grandma's presence.

We drove the fifty-odd miles from Houston to Galveston every six weeks or so when I was a kid, for Daddy loved his mother, though you had to know how to read the signs. I could hear it in the way he said "Mama" with a respect and tenderness he never used for my mother. Grandma spoke English with a heavy German accent, and at least once each trip she'd fondly rebuke him with "*Mein Gott,* Rudy!"

She lived a few blocks from the seawall in a two-story white frame house with a front staircase that led to a second-floor porch where her boarders would loaf and read trashy books or racing sheets. In a shady patch under the steps, Grandma's dog Pluto passed his summers. In another life, Pluto may have been a fine Dalmatian, but in this one he was a liver- and white-splotched mutt—the scrawniest, creakiest, pokiest creature you'd ever hope to see. So I'd scratch his belly while Daddy knocked on the door, and sometimes Pluto would open an eye and bop his tail before Grandma lumbered down the hall to unlatch the screen, and sometimes he wouldn't.

She seemed always to be wearing a shapeless print dress she'd made or perhaps bought out of the Sears catalog or at the nearest Woolworth's. She'd have a white bib apron over it, and her thin, gray-brown hair would be pinned up with tortoise-shell combs in flat braids she crossed on top and then tucked under. She smelled of strong, homemade soap with a hint of crab, trout, or lemon, and her house was like her—spare, solid, and clean.

The walls and woodwork of Grandma's house were white, and the floors were scrubbed pine or fading linoleum. The room we sat in had two chairs, a rocker, a stool, an old oak highboy with a shelf that had a cloudy rectangular mirror behind several large conch shells with purply gray and peach-colored throats, and a cast-iron Franklin stove she let me feed in winter. The rocker was for Grandma and the stool was mine. She made the word "plain" feel wonderful to me.

As a child from a German immigrant community in central Texas, she had seen her father shot dead in their corral by a man he'd fired, and she and her sisters had peddled sausages to tough guys in frontier saloons so their family would have enough to eat. At eighteen, she had come to Galveston to cook and clean in rich folks' homes.

She had survived the 1900 storm—the deadliest natural disaster in

American history—when six or seven thousand people out of thirty-seven thousand inhabitants drowned or disappeared, including her only kinfolk there. Then she'd married a barrel-maker and borne eight children, but Grandpa left her after one of his sons knocked him out with a cast-iron frying pan when he was about to slug her. So loath was our family to deal with failure or unpleasantness that I was told he was dead, though until I was seventeen he lived less than fifty miles away.

I heard these stories and others like them from Daddy and my favorite uncle—Mickey, Grandma's baby—who was only fifteen years older than I and still at home when I began knowing Grandma. These were the two most important men in my life—I adored them and, with the breathtaking egoism of childhood, didn't doubt that they adored me—and they both revered their mother. So I grew up convinced that the men I loved would love and respect strong women who, after all, clearly held things together.

Mickey was shorter than Daddy, with sandy-colored hair, periwinkle-blue eyes, a radiant, aw-shucks grin, and a swimmer's trim, muscular body. Though I couldn't have told you what "sexy" meant when I was three, I knew it when I saw it, and Mickey was sexy. Unlike Daddy, he was also sweet: an easygoing, laconic boy/man who let me watch him work at his lathe in the shop out back and took me downtown on the trolley to buy peanuts and saltwater taffy on the Strand.

More than half a century later I spent several days at Rehoboth Beach in Delaware with an ebullient, one-year-old named Emma and her mother and grandmother. And as I watched this round, chortling, sassy child toss sand about her in widening arcs and laugh at a surf-soaked Irish setter, I knew I was looking at a scene from my own past. I too had taken my shovel and pail to the beach, where my parents, my grandmother, and Mickey helped me make towers and castles; I too felt exultant in a world where the sun was hot and the sea gulls swooped and squalled, where sailboats tacked a few hundred yards offshore and giant tankers heavy in the water moved silently on the horizon. Where the fins in the middle distance were never sharks, but always porpoises at play. Without those first years, I doubt that I'd have made it to thirty.

More nearly her own person than anyone I knew until I went off to college, Grandma treated everyone with interest and respect—from Aunt Liza, the former slave who lived next door for almost thirty years, to the African American family who ran the filling station at the end of the street, the two Jewish families across the way, and the Baldassaris, who owned the little Italian grocery on the corner.

It was Mickey who told me about Aunt Liza, who'd been a tiny woman—not quite five feet—but strong until she was well into her eighties and stubborn enough to be the undisputed boss of the five people who lived with her. She'd go fishing with a hand line, using a railroad spike as a sinker, and once she came back with a red snapper slung over her shoulder that reached almost to her knees. So powerful was her presence that when my Uncle Fritz was almost ninety and senile, he still remembered Aunt Liza as a giantess.

She and Grandma helped each other out. On Juneteenth, the anniversary of the day Lincoln's Emancipation Proclamation was first read in Texas, Aunt Liza would dig a pit in the backyard and barbecue meat she'd gathered from groceries and markets all over Galveston, and all the former slaves in town would be her guests. Grandma would make some pies, and when the singing and clapping began to rattle the windows, she'd round up her children and join the party.

By the time I came along, Aunt Liza was gone and my favorite was Tina Baldassari, a thin, sallow woman who sat behind the cash register and gave me treats, for she had gone to school with Daddy. Being poor in their part of Galveston in the 1930s and '40s meant being part of a very mixed human family. Grandma and Mickey thrived there, though Daddy's reaction, I would discover to my everlasting regret, was much more complicated.

Nana and Dindaddy, my maternal grandparents, lived in Oak Cliff, a suburb of Dallas, and one of my childhood treats was getting on a train called the Dixie Special to visit them and all the kinfolk scattered within a twenty-mile radius. Each table in the dining car had a starched white linen cloth down to the floor, along with enormous linen napkins beautifully folded and a rose in a crystal vase, and as I sat there with the world spinning past and a courtly black waiter smiling beatifically, I might as well have been a fairy-tale princess. Once when I was seven or eight I went alone—a trip as venturesome and thrilling as trekking in Nepal would have been at forty.

Dindaddy got his whimsical name from my cousin Paula, and by the time I came along five or six years later, that's what all the children called him. Nana wore corsets with whalebone stays, and he smoked long, fat cigars. Because of the corset, Nana's lap was not very inviting, but Dindaddy's was. He had a fringe of gray hair and a soft, fleshy body, and everybody loved him—even Daddy. They'd had the first automobile in Terrell when Mama was a girl, but they had lost all their money in the Great Depression and now ran a feed store. Dindaddy still wore three-piece suits with a gold watch chain that dangled across his round belly, and Nana made me dresses I loved out of feed sacks.

During Prohibition, Nana was said to have poured a bottle of Dindaddy's whiskey down the drain, and there was not much question, even to a little girl, where the power lay in that family. She had been the oldest Pinson girl in a family of fourteen, so she'd had to take care of her brothers and sisters on their farm in Forney, about twelve miles from Dallas. The youngest, Clem, was born the day she got married at eighteen, so I had a large extended family with second cousins more nearly my age than Mama's. Although they grew up among farm people, Nana and her sisters all held themselves erect and groomed themselves impeccably like ladies of the old school.

Nana's kid sister, my Aunt Kate, lived in Forney in a big white two-story Victorian house where my Uncle Guyton had been born. Surrounded by a peach orchard, it had a wide verandah on two sides, stained glass panels in the front door, a back staircase, and an upstairs bathroom with a window down to the floor and a huge, claw-footed bathtub. Kate always wore starched cotton skirts with petticoats and drove to the store, which was only two blocks away. Every now and then she referred to the woman who worked for her as the "nigger maid," and almost half a century later when I visited her in a retirement home in Dallas, she said with her eyes wide, "Why, the niggers come in the front door just like people!" For decades, she was my favorite aunt.

My favorite cousins were Uncle Clem and Aunt Mary Alice's tow-headed daughters, Patricia and Sarah—one a little older, the other a little younger than I—who lived on the old Pinson homestead. Patricia was beautiful, with the air of a princess, but Sarah was a tomboy who rode horses bareback. We'd go fishing or climb into the hayloft of my great-great-grandfather's barn to tell ghost stories or throw rocks at rats and gigantic yellow-and-black spiders. Patricia and Sarah tried to teach me how to milk a cow but failed utterly. We took turns cranking the handle to make homemade peach ice cream that no treat since has ever surpassed, and late in the summer, Dindaddy would climb into the cab of Clem's truck and I'd ride in back with Patricia and Sarah, perched grandly on piles of cotton and giggling our way to the gin.

Best of all was Dindaddy and his jaunty cigar, which seemed to vanish only when it was time to eat. I'd sit on his lap in the swing and we'd play a game to see how long an ash he could hold on the cigar before it fell. I passed a milestone when he let me light it for him, and the smell of a strong cigar became, to my subsequent undoing, the mark of a tender soul.

When I was about five, Grandma Buchan grew obsessed with Adolf Hitler and my world began to darken. She came, after all, from a German community inclined to keep to itself. Her father, Paul Reinke, was an immigrant, and she'd spoken only German until she was nearly grown. Her father-in-law, Wilhelm Buchan, also came from Germany, making his way from New York down to Texas, and her first five children had Teutonic names: Frederick—called Fritz—Hans, Alma, Frieda, and Rudolph, all of whom spoke German at home until they went to school.

So Grandma had reason to take Hitler personally. In 1940, not long after he sent his panzer troops spreading through France, Holland, Belgium, and Luxembourg, she bought a hurriedly translated copy of *Mein Kampf*. And she would spend the next five years stuffing the volume with newspaper stories about Nazi atrocities and Hitler as a psychopath.

Daddy, on the other hand, was an isolationist—an "America Firster"—and so he and Grandma began to disagree openly. She thought the world had to be purged of Hitler, and as war began to inch closer, I'd hunch anxiously on my stool while they bickered. Rocking slowly, Grandma loomed with the bulk and solemnity of an Olmec temple sculpture. Daddy leaned over with his elbows on his knees and fidgeted. He had big hands with long bulbous fingers and ropy blue veins on the back, and he moved them a good deal—lighting a cigarette, fooling around with a toothpick. They barely noticed Mama, who mainly smoked.

Neither Grandma nor Daddy ever budged the other, for neither was given to nuance or negotiation. Each would make a flat statement, and then it was the other's turn. When Mama tried to mediate or make her own point, they'd look at her as though she wasn't quite there and then go back to their business. So it was not from Daddy, Grandma, or my mother that I would learn the arts of reflection and compromise.

On Sunday, December 7, 1941, not long after I turned six, my parents and I had just sat down to lunch with friends named Claudia and Aaron when the telephone rang and Claudia got up to answer it. Since these were not voluble people, the silence didn't seem ominous until she shattered it with a high-pitched "Pearl Harbor" or "Japs" or "Bombed" or "Pacific fleet." I can't remember exactly what she shrieked, but over the next few days those words would become interchangeable. Everybody jumped up from the table as a chair hit the floor, and they dashed for the big console radio where we all clustered for the next hour.

My generation had just been defined: we were children of World War II, and no matter what our many, various, and often intractable differences, we shared the experience of coming to awareness in a world gone insane and murderous on the grandest scale in history.

This was a time when the radio was our main link with the world beyond the purviews of West University Place, and from now on, the family gathered around it whenever we expected something important to happen. So the next afternoon we listened to President Franklin Delano Roosevelt tell a joint session of Congress about the day that would live in infamy, and when I saw the *Houston Chronicle* with its huge banner headlines and the picture of FDR at the podium with a wide black band on his sleeve, I took it to stand for the tragedy of war. His solemn dignity on that day won me forever, and under his tutelage, a child of six, and then seven, and so on, came to feel a part of history.

Daddy was so hostile to the president that he would call the dime with Franklin Roosevelt's picture the "American destroyer dime," and to the end of his life he insisted that during the Depression, banks were *not* failing and people were *not* starving. He thought, furthermore, that Roosevelt had set up the American fleet at Pearl Harbor. But before I was old enough to learn that this was nonsense—a neurotic projection, it may be, of his need to believe he had made it out of poverty solely on his own resources—I had learned to put my trust in FDR. In a part of Houston that would flirt with fascism, FDR and his wife Eleanor became my heroes, and my admiration may well have signaled the beginnings of my rebellion against my father. But one thing is sure: nobody can have been luckier in her first public objects of devotion.

Apart from the juicy figs and seductive smell of honeysuckle, then—apart from the skates, the jacks, the chicken pie, and my buddies—the good memories from the next five years have to do with the clarity of our cause and a sense of shared purpose. Even Daddy conceded that we had to fight after the Japanese attacked and Hitler declared war, and it was thrilling to grow up listening to the sweeping speeches of Winston Churchill: "We shall go on to the end, we shall fight in France, we shall fight in the seas and oceans . . . we shall defend our island, whatever the cost may be . . . we shall never surrender, and even if . . . this island or a large part of it were subjugated and starving, then our Empire beyond the seas, armed and guarded by the British Fleet, would carry on the struggle until, in God's good time, the new world, with all its power and might, steps forth to the rescue and the liberation of the old."

A child who hears words like these may count on hope and fortitude as a birthright, and more than half a century later, I look back on those amazing broadcasts as the time when words themselves became my inspiration and solace—and I began to use them as a narcotic.

We also listened to the high voice of Princess Elizabeth telling us that her sister Margaret was by her side at Windsor Castle and wishing all the children in the world a safe, good night. Her broadcasts came while the night skies over Britain were zigzagged with tracers seeking out Hitler's Luftwaffe—while sirens wailed, antiaircraft guns pounded, bombs shattered whole sections of cities, flames crimsoned the night air, and multitudes lived until dawn packed into bomb shelters. And if two winsome princesses not much older than I could be that brave, so, surely, could we.

The bad memories sprang mainly from terror. In the fall of 1941, my beloved Uncle Mickey began putting in twelve-hour days, seven days a week, as a pattern-maker at the Todd Shipyard in Galveston, where he worked in the dry docks repairing British ships the Nazis had strafed or torpedoed. But in 1943, he joined the Seabees, vanishing from my weekend life but not from my imagination. On top of Grandma's horror of Adolf Hitler and the disgrace of the Nazis' spread through Europe, she now had to worry about her favorite son, and the rocker began to move more slowly.

As an engineer in an essential industry, Daddy was not subject to the draft. But Mama's best friend Thelma Hamrick, the blithe spirit of my childhood, was married to a big, handsome doctor named Wendell who was like my second father, and he went into the Navy in 1942. Her son "Little" Wendell and I had been thrown into the sand pile together as soon as we could sit, and for the next few years we lived with the daily anxiety we already sensed it would be cowardly to mention—that "Big" Wendell and Mickey might not come back.

CHAPTER TWO

Since everyone in our neighborhood knew somebody off at war, it infected even our play. The radio brought us Edward R. Murrow with the latest from London, and when we watched gruesome newsreels at the Village Theater we whooped and hollered when planes emblazoned with swastikas or a big red sun exploded in midair. Our parents read choice bits aloud from the daily *Houston Chronicle*, the weekly *Saturday Evening Post*, the *Reader's Digest*, or *Life* magazine. Rationing meant that Daddy rode the bus to work and we cut down on trips to Galveston. Like my friends, I hoarded nickels and dimes to buy war bonds and got them for birthdays and Christmas. We killed more chickens, raised more fruit and vegetables, and, when we were told to, put blankets over the windows and practiced air raid drills. But none of that spelled personal hardship; most of it was exciting and some was even fun.

What was devastating was the terror that had no outlet and the way it seemed to shadow the darkening relations between my parents. Both had been profoundly scarred by the Depression—Mama by losing most of her money and Daddy by having so little. Like their frontier ancestors for generations back, they were people of few words: they did not talk things out, much less through, and their example was contagious. As Judith Paterson puts it in *Sweet Mystery*, "troubled families teach their children to keep their problems to themselves." So the bad things festered.

Fortunately for Daddy, he was superb at his work, and it challenged him. He may not have been well enough rewarded by my later standards—or even by his—but it was enough to give his family a security he himself had never had. Enough to pay for a snug brick bungalow on a sunny street, for swings in the backyard and a chemistry set for his little girl, for three hearty meals a day and treats on Sunday.

Unfortunately for Mama, though she was good at her work as she and Daddy defined it, it was the same thing over and over—nothing a grownup could get her teeth into—like living on Gerber carrots after you've turned thirty. And for all Daddy's virtues, he was also haughty and impatient. Anything tentative would drive him wild, sooner or later, and as the years passed, he grew more peremptory. Meanwhile Mama's head bent ever so slightly lower, her chin trembled, and a woman of grit and intelligence began to slip into a profound depression from which she would emerge only fitfully.

Her ebullient friend Thelma would bring Wendell over to play, but when Thelma said it was *her* turn to take care of the children, Mama always said no, her place was at home. So while Thelma was off organizing some drive or other, or simply having fun, Mama was bent over a hot iron or in the backyard snapping peas. The lash of compulsion was on her, and I wonder if she didn't work so hard to prove to her family—and maybe to herself—that Daddy had been "good enough" for her. Before the Depression hit, after all, her parents had been among the wealthiest people in town, and her Aunt Kate lived in the grandest house in Forney, with back stairs for the servants. But the harder she worked, the more vacant her expression became.

Since they were fanatic about saving money, pleasure in its more obvious forms was scarce. They seldom went out at night or had friends over. Daddy bought an upright piano, but his bulbous fingers kept sticking between the keys and nobody else's playing passed beyond the stage of good intentions. Books seemed neither a stimulant nor a solace, and the only ones I remember on their shelves were Dale Carnegie's *How to Win Friends and Influence People,* Will and Ariel Durant's *History of the World,* and a set of encyclopedias they bought from a traveling salesman. They took the usual magazines and bickered over politics.

Otherwise Mama deferred to Daddy in everything. Any secret I told her, however private or embarrassing, she passed along to him—which hurt my feelings and made me distrust her, while winning her little if any credit with the boss. Though she had a college degree in interior design, *his* taste prevailed, and a man who insists on steak well done is likely to be insensitive to the finer points of shape and color. For decades I thought that khaki, gray, and chocolate brown were primary colors.

The chasm between them seemed widest at dinner. Mama would ask a question like "How was your day?" and Daddy would answer with a monosyllable. Mama would make a comment about the war and Daddy would ignore her. Mama would tell him about some minor victory of mine and Daddy would grin, fiddle around with a toothpick, lean back, and wink at me. Then he would get up and jerk his head in the direction of something that needed fixing, and I'd run off to be his helper. Mama would do the dishes alone, and later we might listen to the radio or sit on the front porch in the summer, where they would smoke and kibitz with neighbors while I swatted mosquitoes, counted fireflies, and longed for peace.

Day after day we got reports of bombs flattening London or U-boats blowing Allied ships out of the water. In the papers and on the newsreels, we saw the empty shells of buildings where people like us had worked and lived and loved, and blank spaces on a calm ocean where a ship had been an hour or a day before. Without anyone's saying it, I knew that Mickey might have been there, and as it turned out, he *was* on a support ship in the English channel during the Normandy invasion. Nearly seven thousand men were killed on Omaha Beach in a few hours on that overcast morning, and almost every day, Murrow would report a new disaster; the numbers of American dead skyrocketed and the waiting was awful.

I had a recurrent nightmare: a man's head, disembodied and floating up near the ceiling, was mocking me. His laugh was slow, sardonic, and menacing. I had no way to stop him except to wake up, and by the time I was seven or eight, I knew *not* to tell my parents because they couldn't help.

After I turned thirty and my life spun finally out of control, I spent hour after hour on a psychiatrist's couch in mid-Manhattan, wracked with sobs that seemed unlikely ever to end. Eventually my doctor would tell me that for the first three years we hadn't even been doing analysis; he'd been putting on bandages. He'd been holding my hand, emotionally speaking, while for the very first time I let myself *feel* the pain of my childhood.

I don't know what happened to alienate my parents from each other, for they scarcely knew themselves, and in lieu of finding words to address their problems, or bring understanding and solace, they threw themselves into their work. In my teens Mama's buried anger inspired her to frame a William Steig cartoon of a man stuffed into a small box with a caption that read, "I am blameless." And so fiercely did Daddy repudiate the implication that *he* might bear some responsibility for their impasse, or that he might find gentler and more constructive ways to deal with others, that whenever someone says "I'm doing the best I can," as he did repeatedly, my hackles *instantly* rise and I assume the worst.

But like most couples of their generation, they stayed together. Practicalities aside, Mama may not have left because she was too proud to admit that she'd made a mistake. In my late thirties, when she was drinking herself to death, I asked Daddy why he hadn't left her. And he said he'd thought about it when I was six or seven but hadn't been able to bring himself to leave me—and especially to leave me with her. I was the joy of his life, as he was the joy of mine.

For weeks at a time, though, Daddy would be off in the East Texas oil fields, and I would be alone with Mama. When I was in college, she told a friend we'd never liked one another, and that comment reignited the corrosive mix of hurt and anger I grew up trying to hide, especially from myself, because, like my parents, I didn't understand my pain and had no idea how to express it without blowing our lives apart. Never have I been able to push back in memory to the inner life of the girl I was before I learned to try to be fair—before I saw that Mama was in a vise that was squeezing her life out and that I hadn't designed the instruments of her torture.

I cannot remember the howling loneliness in the heart of a child who longed to be cuddled—much less the self-loathing of a girl who believes her mother is miserable because she herself is disgusting. What I recall are mainly the blanks: no soft breasts to rest on, no playful games, no teasing, no shared secrets, no moments of silliness or glee. What I recall most is a woman with a pinched laugh who was dutiful and distant. And because I spent decades trying fiercely to please—and often to please people for whom nothing and no one would ever be enough—I know that doomed struggle was there from the beginning.

My mother's picture in the college annual shows a pretty woman, with wavy hair and rather delicate features, and the fact that she got a college degree in an era when few women did marks her as able and tenacious. Nor would many of her contemporaries have taken a job two hundred miles from the place where they were raised, for the world was much more parochial then, and she would be leaving behind a large extended family of people who liked one another and were easygoing and genial. Trusting her own judgment and marrying for what she no doubt thought was love, she chose a man whose upbringing had been far less privileged than hers, but who was a hard worker and responsible. Up and coming. So she was bold for her time—well mannered and game.

The shocking scenes came very much later: the evening she sat at dinner and vomited quietly into her plate; the day she pitched drunkenly down a flight of stone stairs and split her head open; the many occasions when she lost her way in a conversation and looked out blankly from blistered eyes. But my childhood memories are of a woman who was turned away—scrubbing clothes on an old-fashioned aluminum washboard, or ironing shirts from a pile that never seemed to get smaller. No music attaches itself to a picture of her, no fragments of song, and the laugh I remember was more like a hoot, with no merriment in it.

My father didn't make love to her on their wedding night, and this withholding marked their marriage. I suspect that he was as inexperienced as she, or nearly so, and I doubt that he was being deliberately cruel. But she expected something of him that he never gave, and the sorrow marked her early. On the eve of my first marriage, when I asked how often people made love, she said matter-of-factly, "About once a month." They left their bedroom door open, and only once in seventeen years did I hear the panting sounds I realized years later went with sex.

Daddy, in turn, assumed that if he were a good provider, unlike his own father—and if, as the old Russian proverb would have it, he ate bread and salt and spoke the truth—then he would find happiness. When he didn't—when the reward eluded him, though he'd done more than his share—he grew defensive and hard, and his anger simmered only just below the surface. I think of the two of them as George Segal sculptures, sitting upright next to one another on a stone bench, not touching and looking straight ahead.

The memory that best evokes my love and need for them both comes from a time when I was seven or eight. Mama and I were walking down our driveway when I asked, with a knot in my throat that I still can feel, "Do you love Charlie better than Daddy?" Charlie was a gentle man whose wife had left him, and he had turned from time to time for solace to my parents. I was terrified that Daddy might leave and that my mother would give the affection I knew by then was in short supply to somebody else. But she laughed and said "Don't be silly," and then went and told my father. I was of course relieved but also humiliated, for she'd seemed to mock my anxiety and expose my grief.

My mother and I ate at least two meals a day together for seventeen years, and she was as responsible in her job as Daddy in his. She took me to the doctors, the dentists, the dance lessons. She bought my clothes and gave me permanents, talked to my teachers and coaches, watched me practice and perform. She was always home when I got there. As far as I can recall, we never had a fight, but the dislike she later admitted shot its poison all through what looked to be a remarkably pleasant life.

The only sin for which I blame my parents is the sin of being unhappy. For I became a substitute — the means by which they would find happiness — and nothing I could do was ever enough. I don't blame Mama for hating the bald fact that Daddy preferred me, but it isn't a competition a little girl should have to win. I locked her into a life that was devastating to her self-esteem. I did well in school so the teachers would praise her for it, but her pride in me was mixed with rage that Daddy gave me love she wanted for herself, and then with guilt that she resented her own little girl, who clearly loved her. And gradually her clothes got dowdier, her eyes more vacant and bewildered, her way with her chores more listless and mechanical. Almost every gesture and intonation began to say "I hate this!" Translated into little girl language, this meant "I hate you!"

So from the time I was six or seven, an awful chasm began to grow between the happy surface and the hurt inside. My mother was obscurely sad and unreachable. My father looked to me for proof that he had succeeded in life, and I threw myself into winning the prizes that would please them. Meanwhile, I felt guilty and confused, and all I knew how to do was look away and keep busy.

Sometime in the midst of my eighth year, Mama and Daddy sat on the edge of my bed and said a baby was joining us, and I fell back on the pillow whooping with delight. Though I had never been particularly interested in dolls, I thought a mascot would be nifty, and perhaps I thought a baby might make my mother happy.

My brother Glenn was born in mid-December, 1944, during the Battle of the Bulge—a verbal irony Thelma playfully made the most of. Daddy burst into my schoolroom with a grin and a stage whisper: "It's a boy!" Nana came down from Dallas to help out for a week; we took turns cuddling this wiggly new creature, and the house grew silken with tenderness.

Two days after Nana went back to Dallas, our telephone rang. I was a few feet away when Mama answered, and I watched curiously as she stood there listening with a strange, blank expression I'd never seen before. And then she screamed. Daddy ran in from the other room as she fell on the bed crying, and in the midst of the jumble I finally heard: Dindaddy was dead.

All during the war, I hadn't worried about Dindaddy. I hadn't known that I had to, and now that it was too late to protect him, I couldn't even cry. Frightened and ashamed, I went into a state of shock that in some sense didn't end for a quarter of a century. Only then, on the analyst's couch in New York City, could I afford to give him up at last, as I lay sobbing for my beloved grandfather.

When Mama got back from the funeral, she told me that if Nana hadn't come to Houston to help with the baby, she'd have been taking care of Dindaddy as usual, and he wouldn't have died. Though he'd had a cerebral hemorrhage nothing could have prevented, at nine years old I took what my mother said at face value. Glenn too grew up believing that he had been responsible for his grandfather's death, and the burden of that guilt must have been heavy enough. But he hadn't known Dindaddy. I knew what we had lost, and I blamed my brother.

I had gotten a dangerous sibling and perhaps my first real sign that my mother might be quietly crazy.

The pillars that propped us up kept falling. In mid-April, a harsh voice broke into a soap opera on the radio, and a few seconds later I was running down the sidewalk shouting, "The president is dead!" In memory, I'm reduced to a little girl, no more than three or four, fat arms and legs churning. I *knew* there had been presidents other than Franklin Roosevelt but didn't believe it, and it felt like the world had cratered. The worst by far was yet to come.

Less than a month later, in the first week of May, I was sitting alone on the living room sofa facing the open front door, through which the late spring sunshine flooded. The wind had blown away the last blossoms from the azaleas, but the redbud trees were still blooming and the bees were frolicking. I was thumbing idly through the latest issue of *Life* magazine when everything changed utterly. Half a century later, perched on a high stool in the Library of Congress with a copy of that issue, I retched as I saw the pictures again and remembered.

Some thirty pages in, a headline blazed "ATROCITIES" in big letters. I caught the phrase "German Concentration Camps" and then a subtitle that ended: "Barbarism That Reaches the Low Point of Human Degradation." Above and below the headline were photographs from places called Belsen and Buchenwald, and the whole of the facing page was taken up with a huge picture of a little boy about four or five walking up a curved road, staring at the photographer, while on either side of him were rows of corpses. Some were laid alongside one another, while others were in heaps. Some were naked. On the right, about fifteen feet from the road, was a copse of trees, and through their spindly trunks were more piles of bodies.

The pictures from Buchenwald showed stick-like men lying or sitting on bunks and staring out, most of them with blank expressions, and one caption said, "They were so hungry that the first U.S. food rations made them sick." I turned the page to see men who had been burned alive in a wooden building the Nazis had set ablaze, picking off those who tried to escape with rifle fire. One corpse was kneeling as though in prayer. Another bald, blackened head protruded from under a wall. I turned the page again.

The last full-page picture was the worst. The photographer was standing a little above a man and woman in Nazi uniforms knee-deep in a mass grave tugging at a corpse. Her sleeves were rolled up. His head was bald and he wore epaulets on his shoulders. Above them near the far edge of the pit was the twisted body of a naked man, thin like razor wire, with his head thrown back and his mouth open in a horrible grimace. Bare shin bones and knees and crumpled clothes surrounded him. The caption referred to "decaying flesh."

A month later, the *Saturday Evening Post* ran a story called "Journey to a Shattered World." Suddenly old long before my time, I read the whole seven pages, sitting in the same place. One photograph showed a man lying on a floor with legs so thin you knew they wouldn't hold him. Beneath that picture was one of two dead children, one of them a girl not much younger than I, with a caption that said they were "victims of deliberate starvation by the Nazis." The bottom picture was of Red Cross workers standing slack-armed and blank-faced in an open boxcar full of corpses.

After another grim session on the sofa bent over a description of lampshades made of human skin and soap distilled from human fat and whole rooms full of eyeglasses, the nightmares began. In the most vivid, I dangled from the ceiling with a hook through my vagina.

In ways far beyond my powers to calculate or express, the Holocaust would change my life. I can't fully account for the moral and emotional chemistry, but this was the first of what I came to call my pagan mystical experiences. For after that jolt, I became someone rather different.

I was only nine years old when I learned how savage men could be, and perhaps I felt an echo of that savagery somewhere deep inside myself that I resolved to fight. For in the face of such horror, a child whose emotional heritage was anything but subtle had to make common cause either with the one side or the other. With the oppressor or the oppressed. The determination was buried deep in my subconscious, and if anybody had accused me of messianic presumption, I'd have hastily denied it. But in retrospect, I see that instinctively I cast my lot with the victims and decided to contrive somehow to connect my life with theirs.

For the time being, though, my fear of this savage world was compounded by my sense that I too was wicked and ugly. My great-grandfather had immigrated to the United States from Buchenwald, which Grandma thought meant "Buchan's Wood." And so, when the horrid stories came pouring out of southern Germany, she felt personal guilt that I managed to take on my own shoulders.

Not that I told anybody then or, for that matter, knew myself. Instead, I started misbehaving. By late summer, 1945, when the United States dropped an atomic bomb on Hiroshima and then another on Nagasaki, and we found out that Mickey was safe, I had almost lost the capacity to feel. I ran away from time to time, though only a few blocks to the homes of people who would call my mother, and the cute little girl with brown eyes and curly hair became a brat.

Though I'd been a favorite pupil, my dancing teacher asked my parents to take me out of her school, for I was complaining loudly of this and that and spreading discontent. They started me on piano lessons, for which I had neither the affinity nor the hands, so I neglected to practice and bounced on the stool during lessons. During my first recital, I mangled a duet so badly we had to start the whole piece over, and the teacher glowered as I came off stage. (Gradually, through long periods of sullenness and fitful bursts of temper, I managed to behave badly enough to liberate her and myself from this mutual torture.) In the fifth grade I led a gang that cruelly shunned another girl, and instead of being thrashed or sent to a counselor, I got double-promoted.

Mama and Daddy would have hotly denied their own misery had anyone accused them—for being unhappy was thought to be a moral failing, like torturing animals. So nobody knew what was wrong with me, and nobody asked.

One day when I was about twelve, Mama caught me masturbating and called for Daddy, who stood in the doorway with a stricken expression and said, "Oh, don't do *that!*" When I asked Mama what "fuck" meant, she—and then Daddy—just said *never* to say it.

No doubt this turmoil in my soul had something to do with Glenn, who was easier by now for Mama to love and seemed to need her more. He was born with his eyes crossed, and when they didn't straighten, he had two operations and had to be fussed over. He wore glasses before he could walk and, for a long time, a patch over one eye. Because of the patch, the doctors told Mama he shouldn't cry, which meant she had a reason to hover and spoil him.

So my brother was never the mascot I'd hoped for and I would never really know him: with nine years' difference in our ages, we both grew up like only children. Since Mama and Daddy didn't go out at night, I was never asked to babysit, and when I wasn't in school or doing homework, I spent my time with my own friends, who were much easier to please. Glenn and I turned out to be very different people with too few interests in common to seek each other out, and in a family that never cohered, we passed in the night.

I remember so little about him. A baby who peed on me while I was changing his diaper. A toddler with a patch on his eye. A boy who threw a tantrum on the front porch one Christmas Day because he got a wooden train instead of the electric one he longed for. Much later, Little League baseball practice, muscle-building, and loud music. But very little more.

So Glenn could scarcely be blamed for thinking me a lousy sister. Long after I'd left home, teachers would ask, "Are you Celia Buchan's little brother?" suggesting expectations he could hardly welcome, and my aloofness may well have hurt him. Decades later, his resentment surfaced, and though I don't recall ever being deliberately cruel, I had missed the chance to be tender and would eventually try to make up for it by loving my friends.

This, then, was the reality behind one family that seemed to live idyllically in the mode of the 1950s, and the reason my course would be set on flight.

CHAPTER THREE

*W*hen I was thirteen, we left our bungalow and my neighborhood gang to move six blocks to a ten-room, two-story, corner brick house on Buffalo Speedway, one of the boulevards, so to speak, of West University Place. The lot, like the house, was about twice the size of the one we were leaving and blessed with an impressive oak tree, along with a respectable number of waxy-leafed bushes and a handful of azaleas. It also had a two-car garage with an apartment above it where a middle-aged school administrator lived quietly.

We moved because Glenn needed more room and Mama could use some help, so Nana was coming to live with us. Daddy's paternal grandfather had lived at Grandma's while he himself was coming of age, and he reasoned, I'm sure, that if Grandma could manage that bursting household on a pittance, he could handle one more person on a generous and reliable salary. Somewhere in the recesses of his heart, no doubt, he still needed to prove to Nana that he had been good enough for her daughter, and I suspect she was invited to give me the extra attention everyone hoped would turn me again into a sunny child.

So we bought this big, handsome house with high ceilings and even a butler's pantry, and Mama framed a cartoon of a couple in a tiny, beat-up car staring at a mansion and wondering how they could afford it. I was given a second-floor room at the front with a bath attached, along with a second room opening onto it and filled with light from windows on three sides. Nana got a darkish room at the back and a bath, while

Mama and Daddy had the master bedroom, with the side room opening off it assigned to Glenn. This arrangement meant not only that the last three shared a bathroom but that neither my parents nor Glenn had much privacy.

It also meant I was the designated family star—though nobody said so—and for four years, I was never asked, much less required, to help with chores. I was expected to keep my own space clean and tidy, but I seldom even set the table, much less learned to cook. It would be a long time before I saw that what passed for luck meant that I would never share whatever pleasure Mama and Nana took in each other's company. And beyond that, my exemption from domesticity was a way of saying that women's traditional lives were tedious and dull.

In fact, by this time the whole business of growing up and becoming a woman had begun to seem problematic. Adolescence had splintered my neighborhood gang even before we left our bungalow for fancier quarters, for the carefree play was over. Mike and Gillian had lost interest in the little kids; Jake had turned silent and Ellen grown sultry. Boys had been disappearing into her house for hours at a stretch, and she'd begun to look like a dime store Lana Turner and to slow and slur her words. As puberty came on, I'd fallen even deeper into my game of let's-pretend-this-isn't-happening, but Ellen's game was evidently different. When I started menstruating, Mama told Daddy, who patted my shoulder awkwardly to signal, I'd discover, the end of that wonderful physical closeness. No more snuggling, or horsing around on the Galveston beaches, or riding on his shoulders. So I was lonely.

For sex was mysterious and frightening. About that time, the news of Ingrid Bergman's liaison with Roberto Rossellini hit the stands, and she turned, virtually overnight, from America's favorite actress to the most notorious and despised adulteress since Hester Prynne. She was attacked even in editorials and from pulpits as a corrupter of the young. And my fear of sex, whatever that might turn out to be, was heightened by the stories my mother told about Ella, Daddy's kid sister. According to Mama, Ella was wild and Grandma had told her to shape up or get out. Ella had gotten out, married scandalously, and died young of tuberculosis. Whenever Mama told those stories, she would be at her most sanctimonious, and then she'd invariably say how much I reminded her of that particular aunt.

Ella turned out to have been a delicate, blue-eyed blonde with dimples

36

and spit curls, but since I didn't even see a picture of her for almost fifty years, I was late in understanding just how hurt and angry Mama must have been to link two such different people. But the message I *did* get was that good looks could kill you. At the very least, a pretty, sexy girl who didn't behave was likely to sink in Grandma's esteem. And though the old tomboy life was over, I was not about to risk Ella's fate.

So I stopped misbehaving and turned to a very different life. While I kept getting the A's that puffed out my father's chest and gave me something concrete to cling to, I also got swept up in school activities; joining became a way of muffling fear and confusion, a kind of whistling in the dark. Getting along with my peers was immeasurably easier than making my mother happy in any more direct way, and once the pattern was set, I could *not* back down. For the next seven or eight years, life became a blur of too many things to do and the prizes I won for doing them; in the ninth grade, for instance, I edited the school newspaper, got elected Most Popular Girl, and won the American Legion Award.

Not that my authentic self was wholly buried under the camouflage of good-girlism, for the mischievous spark still burned somewhere. When a teacher warned my mother that I was hanging out with rowdy boys, I refused to desert them. In the ninth grade, I took my name off the ballot for the May Fete court, though May fetes were big-time affairs in Texas in the 1950s. Instead of being a duchess or whatever, I wanted to be a jester and do a silly dance with a tall, rubber-limbed guy who looked a little like Tommy Tune. And he and I—and the audience too— had a grand time.

So on the one hand, I was a deeply troubled adolescent who stayed frenetically busy to stave off the impertinent matter of sex and hide the void inside. On the other, I was a spirited teenager given to taking small risks. And the combination would persist long past adolescence, chronologically speaking.

Almost by accident, I fell into swimming competitively when a white-haired man named E. A. Snapp spotted me at a local pool and asked if I'd swim on his team at the Golfcrest Country Club. So the summer between junior high and high school I spent doing laps in long pools all over our part of Texas.

The old man had a son, E. A., Jr., who'd been training for the Olympics in the mid-1940s when he'd gotten polio. His arms and lungs were not affected, but the doctors had said he'd never walk again. So father and son worked with the grit they'd earlier brought to the Olympic competition, and by the time I knew him in 1950, E. A., Jr., could not only walk but even run a little. "Junior" was officially our main coach, but since he worked full time as a physical therapist, we spent our days with E. A., Sr., who was a sweet, laid-back guy.

There were about eight girls and ten boys swimming for Golfcrest that summer, several a year or two younger, most of them slightly older than I. The fact that the boys could swim faster didn't mean they were more important; they could just get to the other end of the pool sooner. They were from schools all over Houston and families with modest incomes, so I fell into an older version of the gang I'd grown up with.

I'd sworn I wouldn't be caught dead in a tank suit, but when the time came, I wore one like everybody else, and though they could hardly have been more revealing, they were not erotic. Perhaps we worked off our adolescent energies in the pool, or maybe we were just phenomenally repressed. But boys and girls managed an easy camaraderie as teammates—laughing and talking and hanging out together—and when a race was on, our loyalties were ferocious. One of the boys, Dave McComb, would become a noted Texas historian and a lifetime friend.

The first meet of the 1950 season, sponsored by the Gulf Coast American Athletic Union, was scheduled for the Shamrock Hotel in late June, and on a whim, E. A., Jr., decided that I should swim the 800-meter freestyle. Since I'd never swum more than 300 consecutive yards in my life, I was dumbfounded and aghast in equal measure.

But when I tried to weasel out, E. A. got on one side of the Golfcrest pool, put a minion on the other, and told me to swim forty widths. Whenever my hand lingered on the turn, they would pop it with a wet towel. After finishing, I could hardly pull myself out of the water, and when I did, E. A. made me bend over and gave me some licks on the behind, blistering me so badly I rode home sitting backward. But my anxiety was far worse than the pain.

The 800-meter race was sixteen lengths of the Shamrock pool, and somehow E. A. got me into a coveted middle lane. On one side would be a sixteen-year-old from College Station named Patsy Bonner, who had won all the prizes the year before. On the other would be Dolores Anderson from the Shamrock, who was about a year younger than I but already had the shoulders and lanky build of a champion.

When I get nervous, I yawn, so I spent the hour before our race yawning every few minutes, convincing everyone that I was a monster of self-confidence. Katie Hunter, my best friend on our team, threw up when she was nervous, and since Katie usually looked and sounded awful, I had good reason not to regret my own peculiar response, however misleading.

Still, I sat yawning on the starting block feeling stupid and wondering how I'd ever got myself into this, while E. A., Sr., hovered and talked soothingly. But finally the starter called us to toe the line, the gun sounded, and we sliced into the water.

Patsy Bonner set the pace, and for the first three laps, she, Dolores, and I swam virtually stroke for stroke together. But Patsy and I came out of the third turn slightly ahead and kept building our lead. I breathed on my right, while Patsy breathed on her left, so that from the shallow end to the deep, we were looking right at one another.

Old E. A. bent down to shout and cheer me on whenever I turned at the shallow end, and by the sixth lap, young E. A., who'd come in late, was doing the same when I turned at the deep. The guy on the loudspeaker was haranguing the crowd to pull for the hometown girl from Golfcrest, the roar was stupendous, and E. A., Sr. and Jr., were working themselves into a frenzy.

Patsy and I stayed together stroke for stroke until the turn on the thirteenth lap, when I began to pull ahead. Way beyond pain, I kept increasing my lead until I made the last turn and the starter's gun went off to signal only one to go. Patsy put on a big sprint, but I wasn't about to let her close.

Hitting that bank at the end of the sixteenth lap was one of the great moments of my young life. Flashbulbs were popping, E. A., Sr., fell into the pool, and Dave McComb and a couple of others followed. Daddy was standing on the bank yelling and waving his arms, and E. A., Jr., whom I could see running alongside the pool while I was making my last push for the gold, finally rounded the end and made it to my lane. He leaned down to shake my hand with a smile almost as beatific as Daddy's.

The photographer from the *Houston Chronicle* took a picture of me sitting on the diving board between Jane Kneip, who had won all the shorter freestyle races, and Mignon Martin, who'd won the diving. The picture made me look rather like Elizabeth Taylor, and late the next afternoon the telephone rang. When I answered, a man asked an obscene question about his finger and a part of my young anatomy. The voice was muffled, and I wasn't sure I'd heard correctly, so I asked him to repeat it. When he said it again, I hung up. I didn't really know what his words had meant, but I had an idea, and it was decades before I could bring myself to tell anyone what had happened.

CHAPTER FOUR

*L*amar was the hot-shot public high school in Houston, as academically rigorous as they got in Texas in the 1950s. At a time when most people, no matter how wealthy, still trusted their children to the public schools, Lamar was Houston's jewel in the crown, Highland Park in Dallas being its near equivalent in the rival city two hundred miles to the north. By every measure of scholastic excellence that counted in Texas, Lamar was either number one in the state or at least among the top three.

About two miles from my home, it was on the fringes of River Oaks, the most exclusive section of Houston, where Secretary-of-State-to-be James Baker grew up and would meet President-to-be George Bush, and those who envied us liked to quip that River Oaks Boulevard was the only street in the world with a country club at either end. Multimillionaires such as Hugh Roy Cullen, Jim West, and Frank Sharp had mansions that spread over whole blocks of that boulevard's short distance, and Sharp's daughter Frances would be my classmate.

Kids like us from Pershing Junior High felt like country cousins with muddy oxfords and outgrown pinafores next to teenaged sophisticates from Lanier Junior High or St. John's, an Episcopal prep school a couple of blocks away. To my wide eyes, the girls looked like they'd been dressed by Neiman Marcus, and some had been.

So Lamar was to be my introduction to the life of Texas' super-rich, and for a time I was dazzled. When I went home with my new friend

Susan Black, I tried not to gape when I found that her *whole house* was air-conditioned, and since it was approximately 98 degrees outside on my first visit, I wanted to stay forever. Even the humblest room seemed to have at least one porcelain vase with a flower arrangement *Town and Country* might have photographed. Her mother dressed in cashmere suits with impeccably tailored silk blouses and wore a perfume called Femme, which to this day spells elegance to me. Here was a new world where the crystal was Baccarat and the silversmith was Jensen.

Though a lot of romantic drivel has been written about the 1950s, part of the rosy picture is true. At a school like Lamar, most of us were healthy and well cared for, and class differences, which nobody acknowledged, were not insurmountable; a girl who lived in a bungalow and sang like Judy Garland or played a good game of tennis was just as welcome in any group that mattered to her peers as a girl whose father was president of Shell. At a time when able women who needed or wanted to work had few options, the teachers were first rate, and their classrooms were orderly, busy, and sometimes fun. (The only appalling teacher I remember was in chemistry; he spent inordinate amounts of class time bragging about a device he'd invented that made cheating impossible, and since the challenge in his course seemed to be to cheat successfully, most of us did.)

While I was there, both the girls' and boys' swimming teams were city champions every year; the football team was always one of the best in Houston and, the year after we graduated, won the state championship; the debaters invariably made it to the state finals; and so on down the list of virtually every sport or skill adolescents are likely to engage in. The drama club was excellent, and a boy one year ahead of me, Ted Van Griethuysen, went on to become a mainstay of Washington, D.C.'s Shakespeare Theatre. The choir was one of the best of any description in the city, and the band was great. Everyone in Houston knew that Lamar would be a serious contender in whatever category, and the thrill of being on top was worth the envy we generated.

So strong was our competitive spirit that on a questionnaire preceding our fortieth reunion, when asked what we remembered most vividly, Susan Black wrote with asperity that Celia Buchan had won all the prizes. For once more, my mode was total immersion; I signed up for an outlandish number of activities and half the clubs, so that by the time I was a senior, the identifying list by my picture in the yearbook hogged the page. I was a duchess and then a princess in the May Fete, treasurer of our sophomore class, president when we were juniors, and sweetheart of my favorite boys' club. I was a cheerleader in our senior year, and rumor had it that I'd gotten the most votes but the principal wouldn't hear of a girl's being head cheerleader. (He was a dour old man who wore his Phi Beta Kappa key on a chain that hung across his vest, and so this apparent bias against girls in high positions could be written off as outmoded priggishness. Or so we imagined.)

But the hard emotional truth behind this frenzied pace and my compulsion to make the headlines lay in what was happening at home. The triumphs did not cancel the pain and relieved it only fitfully. For its source lay in my family, and until I could grapple with the basic causes, the pain would stay. And if anyone in my family had known how to grapple, we might not have gotten into such a hideous tangle in the first place.

In the summer between my sophomore and junior years, I swam again for Golfcrest, and since, the year before, I'd come very close to beating the San Antonio superstar Jane Kneip in the last 100-meter freestyle race of the season, I was revved up to start this one by knocking her out of the water. Our first meet was in Tyler, and as they were wont to do, Daddy and Mother drove me and several teammates into deep East Texas. But I felt wretched and, by the time we got there, had a fever. Daddy took my temperature, which he told me was 100.2, and a doctor gave me a shot of penicillin.

A boy on our team named Charlton Haddon warned me not to swim; if I did, he said, I could set myself back six months. He was a stellar athlete but a tough guy I never knew quite how to take, and since my fever seemed nothing to speak of, I ignored him. But Charlton turned out to be right; I came in fifth in the race for which I'd earlier set a record, and it wasn't until the last meet of the season that I was swimming as well as I had the year before.

And sometime that summer my mother told me my father had lied. My temperature hadn't been 100.2; it had been 102.

Daddy's betrayal was devastating to me. He put his faith in the naked will, and I knew that he himself would have swum under the circumstances. But knowing that did not help, for by the standards of fairness he had brought me up to honor, I—not he—had the right to make that decision. My apparent exemption from his tyranny had come to an end, and the idea that my father would not only lie to me but put winning before my well-being was unspeakably horrible.

We did not, in fact, speak of it for years, and then only in passing. Nor did I ever ask my mother why she stood there silently while Daddy lied. For by then the problem at home was very nearly unbearable, intensified as it was by a triangle; the two of them were clearly at odds, and the proximate cause was Nana. Daddy was convinced she looked down on him, and though this may have been true, I suspect it was a fantasy bred from his fierce resentment at growing up poor. At any rate, both Nana and Daddy were accustomed to getting their way, and each of them counted on bossing Mama.

Their conflict had turned dinnertime into a nightmare of grimaces, dumb show, timid questions, and curt monosyllabic responses. Nana, who sat opposite me and next to Glenn, would eat quickly and then start clearing the table. Though he moved fast by nature, now Daddy would loiter as long as he could and even lean back when he was done and pick his teeth. Once he actually slapped her hand when she reached for a dish that still had a small potato in it.

Not long after she arrived, Nana had virtually turned her life over to me, so their feud was like a vicious beak tearing away at my heart and spirit. When I was editor of the junior high school newspaper, she had learned to type so she could help me do the copy. She made all my clothes, including the May Fete dresses with their huge skirts and acres of ruffles, each of them taking easily a month to create. Every week, she washed, starched, and ironed the cotton skirts and blouses I wore every day.

So the two women who had shaped their lives around mine were being emotionally bludgeoned day after day by the person I loved most profoundly. The man I resembled by accident and gift of birth. The person with whom until now I had most closely identified. And I felt complicit.

I was ashamed and frightened of the father I loved. I felt wretched for Nana. I hated my mother for suffering so, and for not fighting back, and I pitied her too. I felt guilty because I didn't know how to stop it or ease anybody's pain. So I sat there silently night after night with every muscle in my back knotted and the sinews of my neck taut until I could find an excuse to leave.

I would buy trinkets to try to please Mama and goad Daddy into buying her nice gifts—a new set of china one year, a mink stole another. When I was twenty, I went with friends to Mexico, where I spent an outlandish amount on a long blue leather coat for her. But her sadness was immutable.

We had no language to bridge these abysses, and gestures did not help. Now and then, I caught my mother brushing away tears, but never Nana. They went about the business of making our home work—doing those practical tasks that are by definition endless, and doing them well—and playing this deadly game that would drag itself out for more than a decade.

In turn, I kept doing the only things I knew would bring them surcease of pain, albeit temporarily: making A's and winning prizes. The chasm between who I was and who I seemed to be grew ever so slowly wider and deeper. And from the time I was fifteen until a few months before he died twenty-seven years later, an unholy war would erupt periodically between Daddy and me. I brought to it all the qualities we shared, both good and bad, and for the most part, it played itself out through politics. On the issue of race, our knives would be drawn and sharpened.

Nor would the battle lines ever change. No more than a few years before he died, I happened to see that network television would broadcast the Texas A&M/University of Texas Thanksgiving football game—an annual ritual that had always been a high point in Daddy's year. Out of a nostalgia that took me wholly by surprise, I sat in Manhattan watching A&M slaughter Texas in a game as brilliant as any I'd ever seen. And when it was over, and I called Daddy from New York to congratulate him on his alma mater's stunning victory, he said flatly, "They're just a bunch of niggers."

I was so stricken I managed only to gasp, "Oh Daddy!" though I drew it out for several syllables. So he said, "I guess that's pretty awful," and when I tremulously replied, "Oh yes!" he went on: "You have to remember that when I went to A&M, we had only the Corps; it was the Army. There were no women and no niggers." And I knew that if football couldn't do it for Daddy, nothing ever could. Perhaps it was then that I finally gave up.

For a pleasant-looking girl with an agile brain, however, Lamar in the early 1950s made turning your back on the bad things easy. America had won the war and was benevolently helping the world master the challenge of democracy. Optimism was our state credo, for modern Texas had grown out of the frontier, where strong men and women had triumphed over unspeakable perils. (Nobody worried about the Native Americans, much less the slaves, and we learned such a skewed version of Texas history that I didn't know until I was past forty that Sam Houston had opposed secession, much less why.)

Within a few months of starting Lamar, I was part of a core group of maybe twenty boys and girls who went around together, dating each other and going out for one or another sport or extracurricular activity. The girls had slumber parties where we acted silly, our most daring adventure being a skinny-dip in someone's pool and our most scandalous, a torrid game of spin the bottle. A dark-haired, blue-eyed girl named Madeline Moore, who had a husky laugh and smiled like Debbie Reynolds, usually came up with the best pranks. None of us drank or smoked, much less took drugs, though the boys showed up occasionally with beer.

Apart from an occasional titillating story, nobody I knew talked about sex. I hid a couple of "dirty" books under a floorboard in the attic and, in keeping with a perilous sense of guilt, masturbated in a way that was suitably unpleasant, so that I could give it up for long stretches to feel virtuous, however temporarily. Most of the girls were flirts, but Madeline was the most shameless. She could tilt her head and bat her long brown eyelashes and stand just so—with her right hip thrust up and a little forward—and you thought the boys were going to fall to their knees and pant.

Among one another, the girls I ran with were modest and secretive; when we went skinny-dipping, we did it at midnight. Now and again a girl would disappear from school, but never anyone I knew. When an ungainly girl turned up one day wearing an attractive football player's letter sweater and a sly expression, I suspected she'd done something I wouldn't but did not pursue the speculation. For formal occasions, we hooked ourselves into Merry Widows—tight corsets with whalebone stays. On the average school day, we wore girdles with tight skirts, though they did nothing for a girl who was really fat and the rest of us didn't need them for anything other than psychic protection.

We walked down the halls between classes swishing our bottoms, greeting our friends with big grins and a glee that was more or less genuine. The group style was hearty, known in the jargon as "gung-ho," the mood and gestures expansive. We didn't do high-fives, but the tone was the same: "Hi, there!" "How're you doin'?" "Whaddaya know?" The possible variations were scarcely unlimited, but the point was that we were on our way to inheriting the world and loved every second.

From time to time, one of the clubs—our high school equivalents of fraternities and sororities—would have sock-hops in the gym, the admission fees going to the kitty for the annual country club gala. Whoever was sponsoring the night's event would drape crepe paper streamers along the walls, hang balloons from the ceiling, and bring a stack of records. Bing Crosby, Perry Como, Doris Day, Frank Sinatra, Tony Bennett, Rosemary Clooney, and sometimes Nat "King" Cole, who toyed so seductively with our repressed emotions:

> *They tried to tell us we're too young,*
> *Too young to really be in love.*
> *They say that love's a word,*
> *A word we've only heard,*
> *But can't begin to know the meaning of . . .*
>
> *And yet we're not too young to know*
> *This love will last though years may go,*
> *And then some day they may recall,*
> *We were not too young at all . . .*

It was a chaste tease, and my style. I'd put one hand on a boy's back—if we were really a hot item just then, maybe I'd actually touch the skin at the base of his neck—and we'd put our cheeks together and go to it. Decades later I read an article by a man in his mid-twenties who had just discovered that dancing is fun and was looking back enviously on our way of doing it—moving our feet together, each the mirror image of the other, with the girl occasionally twirling under the boy's arm. "These people were actually touching each other," he wrote, "and moving within a certain structure. And it looked cool."

Boys would cut in every few minutes, and changing partners over and over kept the steam from building. But as the evening wound down, the songs would get slower and more provocative: "When we are dancing and you're dangerously near me, I get ideas, I get ideas . . ."

And most of us thought that surely our partners must have gotten ideas too.

After all this erotic stimulation, we would pet in the backseats of cars, but the waist was the limit, and one night I slapped a cadet from Texas A&M who ran his hand up my leg. Slapped him hard. Boyfriends lasted about six months with me, until our fondness dissolved in incomprehension. I had wonderful friends who were boys, but romance was something else altogether.

Once a year, the clubs would have formal program-dances with proper bands at the River Oaks or Houston Country Clubs. The boys wore tuxedos with cummerbunds and sent corsages, and unless you were badly out of favor, the flowers would be gardenias, camellias, or orchids. The girls wore hoop skirts or layered petticoats at the very least, and I remember beautiful dresses Nana made—one with a dark blue velvet top and cascades of light blue tulle, another of pleated yellow organdy with little puffs over the arms, still another of bright red satin.

On these special occasions, each of us would have a little white program with fourteen dance slots, the first, seventh, and last dances being reserved for the couple with a date. A committee would fill the rest of the slots with whatever mixture of names struck them as suitable—or sometimes funny. (Needless to say, committee members were supremely popular, if only for a week or two.) Then, if a club had one hundred members attending the dance, they would invite, say, twenty-five more boys to come as stags.

If you liked your date, as I usually did, the dance was at least fun and often exhilarating. It would begin with the bandleader announcing the first dance, and we'd swoop about the floor with our dates. And then he would announce an encore, when stags could cut in, and the great shuffle began, with partners changing every few minutes. After two, three, or even four encores, the bandleader would announce the second dance. Out with the program, check the designated partner, find the partner in the melee—and the whole thing started over. The seventh dance marked an intermission, when they served cookies or cakes and fruit punch. The last dance was always to the tune of "Good Night, Sweetheart."

At one end of the River Oaks Country Club ballroom a huge plate glass window looked out on a giant oak tree with Spanish moss dangling voluptuously from its branches, and when the lights dimmed for the last dance, the spotlights would turn it into an image of the Old South risen, the gracious life reborn. We could easily have been at Tara in the years before the War, and under the sway of the music and the gentle rocking motions, the idea that anyone might resist this allure was flatly preposterous.

During the Christmas season, on the evenings when no one was giving a dance, there were open houses, sometimes three or four a night. The girls wore cocktail dresses, the boys wore suits, and we all mastered the art of chatter. Three minutes here, two there, but more often just a passing smile, a wave or a nod, and a phrase or two. Once you got the hang of it, nothing could be simpler.

In my last year of high school, the Christmas festivities seemed to extend till June, as graduating seniors were feted with lunches, teas, cocktail parties, dinners, and even an occasional party on a yacht in Galveston Bay. One month in the spring I counted twenty-four consecutive nights when I wouldn't be home for dinner, and then, after a blank evening or two, the whirl started over.

In short, not much time or energy was left over for what people call school. By my senior year, I'd taken all but four courses I needed to graduate, so each semester of that year I had only two "solid" subjects. I could work on my sewing or flit around with my friends and get into whatever mischief caught our fancy. (Given that we had no civics textbook—the one proposed having been rejected for including a reference to "one world"—the notion that I missed out on an intellectual feast may well be illusory.)

My biggest academic triumph came when, on a lark, I asked my teacher on the spur of the moment to give me the solid geometry final. She did, and though I hadn't studied, Daddy had made sure I understood the concepts, and I made a perfect 100.

Far more important in the long run was an English class taught by a very upright lady named Miss McCarthy. In that course Madeline and I began to get the glimmer of a notion that books might be something more than the vehicle for a good grade. That Nancy Drew, Cherry Ames, the Hardy Boys, and all the rest of their hard-charging soul mates might not be the last word in literature. It isn't that we discovered *War and Peace* or even *A Tale of Two Cities*, and I, for one, found *Julius Caesar* a bore. Perhaps it was a poem of Emily Dickinson's or a Hemingway story, but from time to time I paused for a moment or two, spiritually speaking, and felt the power that can come from the shape and resonance of words.

The book that touched me most profoundly was Anne Frank's *Diary of a Young Girl,* which came out in 1952 with an introduction by Eleanor Roosevelt. There I found a lovely, dark-haired girl just my age, with a father she adored and a mother with whom she couldn't communicate. ("I have to be my own mother," she wrote. "I am my own skipper and later on I shall see where I come to land.") She flirted as I did and also enjoyed the fact that boys fell for her and sometimes behaved foolishly. When she felt acutely alone, she turned to books, as I did, and tried to be cheerful. But she was forced to live in terror and isolation, and, before she was sixteen, ended like the girls in those hideous pictures I'd seen from Buchenwald and Bergen-Belsen, where in fact she died.

My father admired the Jews, for to his mind they were smart and hard-working. When his aunt had brought back a family tree from Germany in the 1930s and gloated as she spread it on the table, saying, "Look at all that fine Aryan blood," he'd tapped his finger on one branch and asked: "How do you explain that Rachel?"

There were a handful of Jews at Lamar, as there were in West University Place, but since they were kept out of River Oaks by restrictive covenants, most of my Jewish contemporaries lived on the other side of BuValo Bayou and went to San Jacinto High School. Because of the discrimination they faced in Houston and the emotional trauma that wracked my family, I knew Mrs. Roosevelt was right when she wrote, "I felt how close we all are to Anne's experience, how very much involved we are in her short life and in the entire world."

The rancor and bitterness at home had left an indelible mark: I believed in Evil and knew it could live at the heart of what seemed beautiful and fine, and I was quite sure that something not unlike the Holocaust could happen where we lived. I sensed obscurely that I needed to be among people who felt an obligation to try to curb that evil, but how to do that was another question altogether and one I had no qualms putting off for the time being. But because of Anne Frank and the Holocaust, I wanted in time to meet Jews and to come to know them well.

CHAPTER FIVE

I never thought seriously about going to college anywhere other than the University of Texas in Austin. Daddy offered me a car to go to Rice, which was part of our neighborhood, really, and more important, perhaps the best college in Texas, but home was the place I most wanted to flee. The swimming coach at Texas A&M had promised to have the school coed by the time I was ready, but given my clash with Daddy, the University of Texas' long-standing rivalry with A&M was a big mark in its favor. A counselor suggested Radcliffe, but the East was too alien. (Once, when I tried to shame a sadistic dentist, I asked, "Are you from the North?" It was the worst insult I could think of, and to my young mind, East and North were interchangeable.)

My decision came long before anybody had heard of Willie Nelson, and the armadillo that would symbolize the 1970s music scene was still nothing but a tiny plated dome with four feet, a long skinny tail, and a pea-sized brain that often delivered it to the middle of a road when the Schlitz truck was barreling past. But Austin, with its wonderful old red granite capitol, felt like the freest, juiciest, most authentic place in Texas.

In the spring of my junior year of high school, I had gone to Austin with Susan Black for Roundup, the University of Texas' annual fiesta with round-the-clock parties, a gala parade with papier-mâché floats almost as stunning as the Rose Bowl's, and a grand ceremony in Gregory Gymnasium where the new Sweetheart of the University was crowned. Susan's brother had arranged for us to stay in Littlefield, the freshman dorm, a spacious old Spanish-style building with sand-colored stucco walls, dark wood beams, burnished tile floors, and, on either side of the entrance, two glorious magnolias.

The room belonged to Ann Chipman, a slow-talking beauty from a little town in East Texas who had just been named one of the university's five Bluebonnet Belles, and that Saturday night, with us looking on, Ann's friend Ellie Luckett was crowned Sweetheart. Ellie was a small, blue-eyed blonde with dimples, and when Susan and I got the chance to meet her the next day, she seemed gentle beyond anything I'd ever imagined. Sick of the nameless rot inside, I wondered if the beauty and sweetness she radiated might rub off if I could somehow get close to her.

Roundup weekend had introduced me to the hale-and-hearty world of sororities and fraternities, and when a swimming friend from College Station said in passing that she didn't need a sorority, I found her comment odd. My Lamar friends' parents talked about sororities and fraternities as though real life started there. All the engaging young women I'd met had belonged to something or other—Ann and Ellie were both Kappa Alpha Thetas—and this social world seemed yet another adventure you jumped into if you had the chance.

And evidently I did. Mother took me to Forney to see Aunt Kate, whose daughter had been president of Pi Beta Phi at Texas some ten years earlier. Mama hoped to contribute to my career as a sorority girl by letting Emily look me over, and although the meeting was stiff, Emily wrote the recommendation. But according to Mama, word came back that the Pi Phis had been seriously interested in me already.

If graduation had meant an avalanche of parties, summer rush was even more frenetic, for girls like Madeline and I went to two or three a . day for weeks at a time, meeting young women we'd spend the next few years with and learning what to expect of life at the university. There were teas, lunches, and swimming parties—one of them at Jim West's, who scattered silver dollars on the lawn for trick-or-treaters at Halloween and who once, during an overnight party, had all his guests' cars painted baby blue. We played bridge, at which I was hopeless, and canasta, where I was not much better—my main consolation being that Madeline was marginally worse. We wore hats and gloves and clapped at skits. It was exhausting.

As for my studies, there was no contest; I had gotten a letter from the university's Plan II office, Plan II being a liberal arts program that enrolled about one hundred freshmen and promised a core curriculum of rigorous courses taught by the best professors. It was heralded as the university's Yale College, and being asked to consider it seemed a very great honor. Mama thought I should take physical education or home economics, which she imagined more likely to prepare me for a job if I should need one, but instead of taking this advice as a mark of her common sense, it struck me as yet another sign of how little she knew her daughter's questing soul. So she and Daddy took me to Austin for the interview, where we met with the director, Willis Pratt, a Byron scholar who looked rather like Mephistopheles and spoke with an ironic tone I'd never heard before. That a man so singularly fine would accept me into a classy academic program was a challenge I intended to rise to.

Gradually I narrowed the number of sororities I cared about from twelve or so to five and signed up to share a room at Littlefield with a girl from Wharton with huge blue-gray eyes whom I met at a summer rush party. And finally, in early September, we took the backseat out of the car and filled it with the new clothes Nana had made. I blubbered over leaving Nana, waved goodbye to Glenn, and then Daddy, Mama, and I piled in front for an oppressively silent three-hour drive.

Pulling up at Littlefield was like being let out of a submarine that had been cruising for months on the ocean bottom. Girls were careening up and down the wide stairs ferrying piles of clothes, sheets, towels, radios, and all the paraphernalia of freshmen. Now and again somebody would collide with an immense clatter and howls of dismay as the debris settled and the lines backed up. But the day was too fine to end in a snit, and by late afternoon the dorm was full and the heavy lifting done. With ill-concealed relief, I told my parents goodbye—my father carrying stiff-upper-lip about as far as it can go, while Mama looked faintly confused.

And so began one of my great adventures—in mind, soul, and spirit. For the very air was crisper in Austin and the sky seemed a more pristine blue. The hills dotted with cedar outcroppings, along with the striated cliffs streaked ochre, rust colored, lavender, and gray that framed Lake Austin to the west gave the city a gentler tone than Houston in all its flat monotony. My spirits always rose with the land when we left the humid coast behind, and as we crested the hill at Bastrop thirty miles to the southeast, I would strain for a glimpse of the university tower and the capitol dome. In the 1950s, they were the town's only tall buildings, for Austin in those days had a manageable feel; it was drawn to human scale.

Our room was on the third floor in the center, just above the entrance, so that we looked down on plate-sized, waxy white magnolia blossoms while checking out the latest couples; it was an ideal spot, in fact, for gossip. (Madeline provided more than her share. Some days she'd have four dates, and we'd take bets on whether the boys would run into each other coming and going. She giggled through the close calls, and I won some money.) There were two small bureaus and a plain pine desk, and our beds folded into the closets. With the bathroom as well as the phone down the hall, there was an almost constant to-ing and fro-ing past our door.

Across the hall lived a short, dark-haired girl from Highland Park High School in Dallas whose toes pointed out like Daisy Duck's when she walked. Her name was Jayne Upton, and her nose had allegedly been pushed off-center in a neighborhood touch football game when she collided with a guy who went on to be named All Southwest Conference running back. The first thing I ever heard Jayne say was "Shit!" I was dumbfounded. Grinning mischievously, she then gave the finger with both hands. Now I was flabbergasted. She would stand in the hall singing off-color songs at the top of her voice or giving orders like a little Napoleon. She was even more outrageous than Madeline, and I loved her instantly.

My swimming friends from College Station lived on the ground floor, and scattered throughout the building were girls from all over the state, including places like Buffalo or Mount Pleasant or Falfurrias that I'd never even heard of, as well as places I'd never been, like Amarillo and Big Spring. In fact, in 1953, I hadn't been to El Paso, Brownsville, or Corpus Christi either, so walking the halls at Littlefield was a way of getting a belated education on the subject of Texas.

The one thing I found I *couldn't* do was eat dinner there, and the problem wasn't crummy food, though it was bad enough. The problem was that whenever I sat down at table, the muscles in my back would knot and my stomach turn with the memory of dinner at home on Buffalo Speedway. So for four years, I went out almost every night for a hamburger or ate raisins in my room, the ordeal of family dinner having left psychic scars that did not begin to heal for more than a decade.

The relentless round of parties that constitutes Rush Week started in another day or two, with girls racing in and out of Littlefield, changing clothes from casual to fancy and back again, drowning in lemonade and iced tea and almost foundering in cookies and cake. We jabbered and sang, smiled for hours on end, and posed for snapshots until even outgoing Texas girls began to think there might be such a category as "too-much-of-a-good-thing."

Choosing a sorority meant hurting someone's feelings, so deciding was hard. But Jayne and Madeline and I colluded to pledge the same sorority, and finally it was done. We handed in the cards marking our first, second, and third choices, and when we got the notices back, the three of us had gotten our first choice, Kappa Alpha Theta.

In the midst of our hooplas, however, and just as we were leaving for the Theta house and the celebration we knew was waiting, my roommate burst into our room in tears; she'd been turned down by her first and second choices. I told Jayne to go on and stayed as my roommate sobbed. Knowing it might happen hadn't prepared me for her desolation, and as I sat there helplessly with my arm around her shoulder, I knew that nothing was worth that kind of pain.

By the time I got to the Theta house and Ellie drew me into her arms and chided me for being late, I had turned against sororities in my heart. I didn't withdraw, though I did consider it, but I spent the next four years in acts of mild rebellion against a system I saw belatedly to be cruel and unnecessary. Lifelong friendships were made in the Theta house, and my "big sister," a dark-haired whirlwind named Pat Hinds, was the first woman I met who was studying for a profession. (Not only was she the law school's "Portia," its version of the university sweetheart, but she got the 1953 Dad's Club award as Most Outstanding Girl. On the latter occasion, the student newspaper ran an interview that ended with Pat saying, "I don't necessarily expect to do court room work. I'd be satisfied just sitting in a corner briefing cases." When I rediscovered that statement years later while scanning back issues of the *Daily Texan,* I teased her unmercifully.) But though I played the sorority game, I thought the price too high, and my energies went in other directions.

The most important outlet was Plan II. I was taking freshman English with Dr. Pratt, who introduced us to world literature, the life of the mind, and the precise use of language. "Miss Buchan," he would say, "it is not 'more or less.' It is either 'more' or 'less.'" Once he caught me spelling "basically" two different ways in the same paper and wryly called my laziness to the class's attention. I left his courses tiresomely insistent on the difference between "anxious" and "eager."

We started with Confucius and swept on to the Greeks—a bit of Homer, *Agamemnon, Oedipus Rex,* some poems by Sappho—and then to Vergil and the world-weary Aeneas. By the time we got to Chaucer, I was not only thrilled to find that I could recite the first twenty-two lines of the prologue as well as my father could, but I was also hooked for life on the study of what Matthew Arnold had called "the best that has been thought and written."

I discovered words for pain and the revolutionary notion that finding them mattered. I discovered words for anger and outrage and people to admire who expressed them. I found out that people had ideas that shaped the way they lived and that some ideas were more compelling than others. I got excited about the turn of a phrase and the shape of a sentence.

And though English was the most captivating, I liked my other classes too: world history, pure math, biology—all of them taught by men adept at engaging the curiosity of young minds. So challenging, in fact, were these courses that five of us decided to study together: Sally Sparks and Carol Hamilton, pledge sisters from Amarillo; Shirley Nelson, who'd been at school with Sally since the third grade and now roomed with her at a boardinghouse a block off the Drag, the university area's main street; and Pat Tracy from San Antonio.

Well into our second year, we all took these sessions seriously enough to come prepared to teach as well as to learn. We would sit cross-legged on Shirley's and Sally's beds devouring Ritz crackers and handfuls of raisins in a room with high ceilings and windows open wide, and we'd throw out questions, take turns analyzing problems, and endlessly drill one another.

Sally, who had a disgustingly good memory, once came up with a mnemonic device in which each first letter of a series we needed to know for a quiz spelled out "Silly Old Celia Buchan." (We all remember the device, though nobody has the slightest memory of what it stood for.) We learned the thirteen uses of the olive and the seven reasons for the fall of Rome, though on the exam I forgot to note the barbarian invasions. By the end of our first year we could multiply in Roman numerals and by the end of the second, describe in reasonably accurate detail four buildings on the Acropolis and the layout of the Roman Forum. We thought we were well on our way to mastering the essentials of Western culture.

At night I would walk around the campus alone, entranced by the play of light and shadow thrown by leaves undulating in the breeze and alive to the beams pouring from high library windows where hundreds of thousands of books waited. Not that any particular writer or period grabbed me by the scruff of the neck and dragged me to an intellectual feast; I was far too raw and undeveloped, and the competing forces still too potent. But illumination was the theme, and I was Grandma's child, giddy with the promise and romance of learning.

On top of our formal courses, Carol and I got involved in a study group that wrestled with the big existential issues. With a motley assortment of about fifteen people—one from the law school, a couple of divinity students, another from business, several from Plan II—we read Dietrich Bonhoeffer, Niebuhr's *The Nature and Destiny of Man,* and a little Marx; we thrashed over Camus's *The Rebel* and Sartre's *No Exit.* We went en masse to a heavy-handed production of Beckett's *Waiting for Godot,* where the tree in the background looked like the Cross, and another of Arthur Miller's *The Crucible,* which we took to be a clever knock at Wisconsin senator Joe McCarthy in a state where he was celebrated.

My psychic security, such as it was, came from playing by the rules, fitting in, and winning prizes, but anger and rebellion still pummeled my soul. I distrusted the hard-playing Texas world I'd been such a part of, and though I certainly couldn't have said so then, I was somehow going to have to connect these apparent irreconcilables. Thus my years of floundering, which were only beginning.

In my freshman year, Ellie was president of the University Y, a gathering place for dissidents calmly plotting against the pieties of the day. (She reminded me of Melanie in *Gone with the Wind,* and those who find Melanie namby-pamby don't bother to learn the language of southern culture, for it was she, after all, who got the husband and respect she wanted and was ready to kill the Yankee soldier.) Ellie's heir-apparent, Peggy Rowland, who hailed from Tulsa, Oklahoma, and had an almost bawdy laugh, would come to have an even bigger impact on my life.

Ellie and Peggy were gregarious in the southwestern style of the 1950s, but though their charm came from the welling-up of generous spirits, it was not an end in itself. There was principle behind it—there were convictions—and pity the naïf who mistook their good manners for complacency. In retrospect I'd hazard a guess that Ellie was by nature a reformer, while Peggy was a revolutionary.

On a campus like the University of Texas in the 1950s, the language of moral and political commitment—at least the language that could be heard—was primarily Christian. In the 1960s, the language and style changed, and students very like Ellie and Peggy would be in the front lines on the civil rights marches and demonstrating against Vietnam in a style that would be instantly recognizable. I can picture Ellie, for instance, putting a flower in the barrel of a guardsman's rifle, while Peggy might have been all-purpose organizer and camp cook in an antiwar protest. But if the "enemy" in the 1950s was harder to name and the pressure against overt criticism far more overwhelming in a conservative state like Texas, there were people who knew not only that we didn't live in the best possible world, but that we could do something to make ours better—and I was drawn to them.

So eventually I made my way over to the square yellow brick building on the Drag that housed the University Y and met a man named Block Smith who had presided there for decades. "Presided" is surely the wrong word, for although he was the Y's heart, soul, and brain, he was by no means regal or imperious. Quite the contrary: he was a plain, rather slight man with penetrating hazel eyes who spoke softly in a time and place where the preferred cultural styles were loud and autocratic and disciples flocked to men with "charisma."

Block Smith and the Y made a deep impression on me and many of my friends.[*] In those years when the spirit of Senator Joe McCarthy ruled Texas, Block would invite people to speak at the Y who were anathema to the official university, and he did it in so quiet a voice that if you didn't know it already, you'd have had no idea that he was being downright subversive. Although the words "Ye shall know the truth, and the truth shall make you free" were inscribed above the entrance to the university's administration building, the people who ran the place seemed to think they knew all about the truth already. The faculty commonly acquiesced to dictates from on high curtailing dissent, and once Block

---

[*] As it turned out, we were part of an embryonic movement that would quicken a decade later. In 1998, historian Doug Rossinow published *The Politics of Authenticity,* in which he traces a major segment of the civil rights movement and the protest politics of the 1960s to the University of Texas Y, calling it the most radical not only in the South but possibly also in the nation.

left a meeting with a prominent member of the journalism faculty saying, "Next time we go to one of those, I'm gonna give you a liver pill so you'll stand up for something." Block had been standing up for things all his life, and he wasn't always thanked for it.

By then in his late sixties, he was the first man I ever met who named racism and opposed it. "Have you heard Marian Anderson sing?" Block would ask, and then he would play her records for his listener. George Washington Carver, Benjamin Mays, and Langston Hughes had visited the Y in earlier years, and Block was always organizing interracial student gatherings with people from historically black Texas colleges such as Prairie View A&M, Bishop College in Marshall, and Huston Tillotson in Austin. He was good at unsettling people because he did it without putting them down. He had an abiding faith in human possibility—or perhaps he simply believed in divine grace—and you knew that he would wait for you patiently.

He would also ask, "Do you know Gawd?"—that really is the way it sounded when Block said it—and when you had to tell him, as I did, that alas, I did *not* know God, he honored the struggle. A sixty-eight-year-old man of faith who takes a doubting eighteen-year-old girl seriously and offers what feels like real respect is what I call a primitive Christian, which is altogether different from what you're likely to find in the mainstream churches or wherever proper people gather.

That year, a group called the Sons of the Republic, spearheaded by my hometown multimillionaire, Hugh Roy Cullen, invited Senator Joseph McCarthy to speak on liberty, of all things, at the San Jacinto battleground. Since this was where Sam Houston won independence for the Republic of Texas from the Mexican general Santa Anna, Block pronounced the invitation an appalling travesty, and Peggy helped organize a campus demonstration against it. Some five thousand people showed up to object to honoring McCarthy along with a bunch of Texas heroes, and after petitions were circulated, a delegation that included former *Daily Texan* editor Ronnie Dugger took a forty-foot list of names to Cullen, who declared the invitation sacrosanct.

This episode occurred less than a decade after the university's president, Homer Rainey, had been fired for allowing three economics professors to subvert the free enterprise system by teaching books such as John Dos Passos's *U.S.A.* Only a few months earlier, the state legislature, which controlled the university's budget, had voted almost unanimously to praise McCarthy. (The handful of men, including Maury Maverick, Jr., who ducked the vote by hiding in the men's room were subsequently labeled "shit-house liberals" by Maury, Sr., the flamboyant former New Deal congressman from San Antonio.) For weeks the capitol dome seemed like Mount St. Helens on the verge of the century's most spectacular eruption, but the university's president, Logan Wilson, said nothing official. And since Peggy, after all, was just a girl and Block's bunker was off campus, the rumbling finally subsided.

Late in the spring, a group of outraged Arab students protested the election of Shirley Strum, a Jew from Tyler, to be editor of the *Daily Texan*. Peggy, who ran the election committee as well as Orange Jackets, a campus service organization for women, sat down with the outraged students and eventually sweet reason prevailed. On campus in significant numbers, the Arab students were never reconciled to Shirley's eminence, however, and the first I heard about the state of Israel came from a Lebanese student who spent an outlandish amount of time trying to convince me that Jews were subhuman people with no business living there.

It was the best year of my life to date: in the midst of a huge university campus with almost twenty-five thousand students I made enduring friendships with both men and women and fell hopelessly in love with learning. I found dissidents with whom I knew my lot would be cast—though I had no idea where my rebellion came from, psychologically speaking, and the form and language of dissent remained uncertain. Whenever I wanted a date I had one, and I went to more parties than a sane woman should stomach.

The young men I liked—Jerry Wilson, Sam Perry, Speed Carroll, Jack Ratliff, Ray Farabee, Don Stone—were headed for campus organizations like the Cowboys or Silver Spurs. (The comparable women's groups were Orange Jackets and Mortar Board.) With all their individual differences, these men remind me of two well-known contemporaries, Jim Lehrer and Bill Moyers: serious but ready to laugh, keen to know and to do, understated and wry, ambitious to rise in their professions, and fine company.

The campus organizations that young women such as Jayne, Madeline, and I joined were busy with various causes that shall remain nameless because they were local and eminently forgettable. But our membership in them signaled, I think, the belief we shared that there *was* such a thing as the common good and that we wanted to work for it. With our Ship-and-Shore blouses and long, full skirts, our thick white socks and loafers or dainty Capezios and the men with close-cropped hair and baggy trousers, we were earnest, hard-driving, and, it would seem, terminally straight.

Mark Russell, who is about our age, has inimitably mocked our generation for its lack of flamboyance: "You see those tee-shirts with Martin Luther King's picture on them, or 'Up the Establishment!'? You know what we had on our tee-shirts? Nothing! *Nothing!*" And he does that word as though it has five syllables in it.

Perhaps the most irritating note that first year came from a law student in his late twenties who was a member of the state legislature from the tiny South Texas town of Tilden. His name was Bob Wheeler, and he would trail me into the library while nattering endlessly. "You're just going to marry a rich doctor or lawyer and live in River Oaks," Wheeler would complain with his face squinched up like he'd flushed a polecat. Or he'd trot out a list of my shortcomings: "What do you mean you don't read *The Nation?* . . . Christ, you don't even read the *New York Times!*" Within an embarrassingly short time he established the fact that I could seldom answer a single question on the *Times's* current events quiz, and so he gave me Arthur Schlesinger, Jr.'s first volume on Franklin Roosevelt as a way of cutting into my political ignorance.

Though I didn't placate Wheeler, I was still so absurdly busy that Anna Hiss (Alger's sister), who was head of the women's physical education department, made a chart to help me organize my time. She divided it into half-hour segments, and that chart made me cry—though not in front of Miss Hiss. I didn't know how to slow down, for the dark was menacing, so I did the only thing I knew: I worked and played harder.

After my grades for the first semester were posted, I ran to a phone and called home to announce that I'd made all A's. Then, to prove to myself that it wasn't a fluke, I did it again the second semester. I slept no more than five hours a night, often setting my alarm for four in the morning and then reading with my elbows propped on the desk facing the great tower that chimed every quarter hour. Years later a man I loved gave me a volume of Wallace Stevens and inscribed it with the last lines of a poem, "The House Was Quiet and the World Was Calm," that described those hours most magically and ended: "The truth in a calm world, / In which there is no other meaning, itself / Is calm, itself is summer and night, itself / Is the reader leaning late and reading there."

I believed in truth and thought I could find it there if only I leaned long and read enough.

CHAPTER SIX

*T*he summer between my freshman and sophomore years marked the virtual end of one path and the start of another. For the ax that would ultimately shatter the complacency of the late 1940s and '50s fell in May, 1954, when the United States Supreme Court handed down its unanimous decision in *Brown vs. Topeka Board of Education*. Most people I had known at Lamar, and the majority of my sorority sisters, would either take a pass on the struggle for racial equality or slip into a rear-guard action. Most of my close friends at the university would side with integration, and for many of us it became *the* defining issue.

My grandmother had somehow transmitted whole to me her interest in all people, whatever their color or background. A black woman, Cecil, had inspired me in childhood to believe I could do anything, and the emotional devastation in my home had disabused me of the notion that white people had a superior purchase on virtue. That summer, I read the more than one thousand pages of Gunnar Myrdal's *An American Dilemma,* which had so profoundly influenced the Court's decision. Though what I would actually *do* remained unclear, the weight of my life fell irrevocably on the side of equality for Negroes.

This stance meant cultural revolution in Texas. While I was growing up in Houston, for instance, another woman exactly my age named Barbara Jordan lived across town, but it was *unthinkable* that we should know one another. We lived in self-contained worlds, hers black, mine white, that shut out anyone different, and we went to schools that had no contact with one another.

The notion that Barbara Jordan might have anything to teach me was so heretical that nobody I knew before I got to the university would have dreamed of entertaining it. Had some improbable situation thrown us together, I might have stooped to notice her without sacrificing my standing in the community, but the idea that we might enjoy each other's company or actually be friends was as absurd as the idea that Texas mosquitoes were created for our happiness.

For me personally, the civil rights revolution meant a very nearly violent revolt against my father, and a vehicle for rebellion that made me feel so righteous was no inconsiderable blessing. For in some confused way, I knew I had to fight him for what he was doing to my mother and grandmother, and a man whose familiar refrain was "I'm doing the best I can!" does not respond to the usual arguments.

The summer of the *Brown* decision, I worked as an occupational therapist at a polio hospital called Hedgecroft. Nell Schwartz, an old friend of my parents, had started the hospital several years earlier. Her obsession with it was said to have broken up her marriage, and none of her own children wanted to touch it, so she fixed on me; if I'd take a degree in business administration, she'd think about making me her successor. As it was time to begin thinking about what I would do with my life, and with whom I'd pass it, I spent the summer of 1954 in regulation white—uniform, stockings, and shoes—learning about Hedgecroft while working with people whose lives had been mangled by a killer disease.

My favorite patient was a man named Barry Bishop, who lived in an iron lung. Only a few years older than I, he had been a Plan II student at the university when he was stricken two years earlier. Barry could spend an hour or two in a portable lung, but otherwise he lived encased in a giant cylinder and could move nothing but his neck and eyes. We would talk or I'd read to him, and we came to love each other in a quiet, hopeless way.

While spending my days with the maimed and humiliated, I was also seeing sorority rush from the other side. Mama told me about the Theta alumna who confided that by the time they invited me to join, they even knew where our family shopped—a comment no doubt intended to suggest that Thetas were discriminating and thorough, but one I found loathsome. In fact, I thought the woman was a schmuck, though that was a word I didn't learn to use until much later.

As the months went by and I watched alumnae with little better to do than blackball young women they considered their social inferiors, my heart hardened against them. It was the first time I'd seen women wielding power and, in the name of principle, deliberately wounding those who'd done them no harm. They rejected the daughter of a teacher I loved, and the girl was hurt so badly she dropped out of school. They rejected another who subsequently married a young man from one of Houston's first families, and I hoped maliciously that her dazzling marriage gave them stomach cramps.

Then too, my friends began marrying—the first of them Frances Sharp, who became engaged to the boy across the street. Since the street was River Oaks Boulevard and her fiancé's house a mansion whose lofty white columns were wrapped with ribbon at Christmas to look like giant candy canes, the wedding promised to be the social event of the season.

On my way to a late afternoon tea for Frances, I had my second pagan mystical experience, or moment of truth. As I recall, I was still wearing my white uniform when I walked up the circular drive in front of a great stone mansion. A long, black Cadillac was pulled up to the entrance, and a chauffeur was holding the door for an elderly lady dressed in lace, when I suddenly thought "No!" My revulsion was that emphatic and quite irrevocable.

My worlds had collided, and at eighteen I knew that, for me, being rich wasn't worth the price; the narrowness and constraints of a privileged life far outweighed the glamour. I didn't *want* to behave decorously and hold my tongue. I didn't *want* to spend my days in hats and gloves and girdles or go to an endless round of luncheons and teas. I didn't *want* to make polite conversation with people who thought sororities and fraternities really mattered.

Grandma's world had triumphed over the one so many others longed for—the one grounded in the belief an aspiring Texas politician would later put succinctly: "Money is the way you keep the score." And though my respect for money and its uses has grown considerably and I love a handful of very rich people, I have never had a second's regret.

In 1947, the University of Texas had been the locus of a key Supreme Court decision on race when Heman Sweatt of Houston successfully sued to be admitted to the law school. By the time I got back to Austin for my sophomore year, loud voices all over the state had begun reminding everybody what had become of Sweatt, academically speaking. His days at the law school had been unhappy; he'd been assigned a study area isolated from the white students and, needless to say, had not been invited to eat alongside them. More important, he had flunked out after only a few semesters, and his failure was thought to presage the failure of any Negroes who got "out of their place" and presumed to infiltrate "our" institutions.

Daily Texan editor Shirley Strum, however, who had grown up in the part of Texas most like the Deep South, hailed the *Brown* decision while predicting that "Negro children . . . will be unacknowledged martyrs for the future equality of their race." All through my years at the university, the *Texan* would periodically report on places where Negroes would be welcome on campus. Undaunted by dire warnings that their efforts would be misguided, the Y and several campus ministries began organizing to picket movie theaters on the Drag.

As acts of defiance, however, these were piddling compared to the inflammatory proposal that Tina Bowie, a Negro woman from Houston, should be allowed to live at the Christian Faith and Life Community. This was an interfaith group of men and women who'd taken over a seedy mansion a few blocks from the campus where most of the women lived. Jayne and Madeline stayed there during our sophomore year, along with Ann Chipman, my hostess from that first Roundup, and Pat Tracy, from our original study group. So although I never lived at the Community, I was close to people who did—people who were now on the verge of doing something our culture branded as truly radical: treating a black woman in all respects like a human being.

The issue divided friends, and I knew one girl whose parents flatly forbade her to live with a Negro. Without suffering much more than the occasional insult or obscene gesture, however, Tina lived at the Community until she left the university, while others on campus took smaller steps—very slowly. The most highly publicized incident came in my senior year, when a Negro woman named Barbara Smith was cast to sing Dido in Purcell's *Dido and Aeneas* and the Board of Regents forced the head of the music department to withdraw her from the production. (In the 1980s, Barbara Smith made her debut at the Metropolitan Opera.) Leading the faculty charge against the regents' disgraceful action was a thirty-year-old philosophy professor whom Arts and Sciences dean Harry Ransom had recently recruited from Yale. His name was John Silber. His influence on my life would be extraordinary, though impossible to quantify, but that is getting ahead of myself.

I had been chosen to live at Littlefield a second year as an adviser—a mistake on the part of the selection committee since I was inept at "hanging out" and felt unnatural advising anybody about much of anything. But I had a wonderful roommate, a freshman named Sydney Fielder who had an angry keloid scar that ran all the way from her left ear down her shoulder and midway to the elbow from a third-degree burn she got at six from a pot of boiling water. Despite that trauma, she was mischievous and playful, and it was Sydney who introduced me to a Yogi Berra maxim we would both follow to our peril: "When you come to a fork in the road, take it!"

In the spring, along with Jayne, Madeline, and a handful of others, I was tapped for Orange Jackets, the campus service group that Peggy had used for serious political organizing. Then, after walking across the stage at Gregory Gym in a skin-tight, shiny red dress with a Chinese collar and slits halfway up my thighs, I was elected Cowboy Sweetheart. (The occasion was the Cowboy Minstrels, an annual entertainment on campus, and it never occurred to me that there was anything wrong with white men playing the buffoon in blackface. Later, John Silber would challenge a Cowboy I was dating on that subject, and I responded by "forgetting" all about my participation in it until somebody reminded me forty years later. So much for the clarity of my fight against racism.) A few weeks after the Minstrels, I turned up as one of the five finalists for University Sweetheart, a special honor for a sophomore.

The great thrill of the spring, though, was the possibility that Carol Hamilton and I might spend the summer in Europe—three weeks at an ecumenical work camp called Agape in the Waldensian Valley west of Turin and two months simply wandering around. Peggy had gone to Agape the summer before and come back with tales of hiking in the Alps and riding on Vespas, and she made a special trip to Houston to persuade my parents that I should try it out.

Agape was a conference center run by a Protestant pastor named Tullio Vinay who'd fought in the Resistance. Students came from all over the world to dig ditches or cisterns and build walls together, and Daddy said if I was keen for manual labor, he could find some for me without my leaving Houston. Since he nonetheless agreed to foot my bill, however, Carol and I wrote off to Agape.

And that spring, at a touch football game between the Cowboys and Silver Spurs, I met a young man named Willie Morris. He was a lanky, loose-jointed guy from Mississippi with a thatch of light brown hair and a face that belonged behind a tall ice cream soda. I'd read his column in the *Daily Texan,* and I not only liked the wry way he ridiculed our pieties but thought the rhythms of his prose now and again sensational. "Uncool" in a way that seemed to guarantee a lively mind, he took me out for coffee and promised, after being elected *Daily Texan* editor, to send his first issues to us at Agape.

Willie had an infectious gaiety when he was young, and when "gay" didn't mean what it does now. He drew people to him whose spirits were heightened in his company, so our lives often felt more charged and delicious when he was around. Decades later, my friend Speed Carroll would remember Willie as the only person he knew at the University of Texas who seemed larger than life. A West Point Rhodes scholar who met him in 1956 on the boat their group took to Southampton found him "the most fascinating guy in the whole bunch," amidst competition as tough as it gets. He was outrageous in an era when outrageousness was in short supply.

He was always telling wildly improbable tales I took to be scripture, like the one about a guy who got a bad grade in some course and hired a crew to paint the professor's house olive drab when he went out of town. Or the baseball players who figured out how to get into the tunnels under the university where they found the master mechanism for the clock in the tower and programmed it to strike twenty or twenty-five on the hour. Eventually he would tell me that he could have come back from England on a submarine when his father was ill but couldn't afford the time, and I, whose gullibility seemed inviolable, passed that story along to the august Harry Ransom, who took it for granted that I was telling the truth. One of the few times I ever saw Willie abashed was when Dr. Ransom referred to that submarine when the two of us were seeing him for one reason or other, and I realized suddenly that Tom Sawyer had been at it again.

As a mere freshman, he had been given a front-page column in the *Daily Texan,* which was unprecedented, and so by the time I got to the university he was already an institution. The column was almost always funny—Willie never seemed to have to work at being merry; like the thatch of brown hair, humor came with the territory—and in those days it always seemed a friendly kind of humor. He would tease his more straight-laced contemporaries who might be proposing the merger of, say, the Panhellenic Council with the Advisory Committee to the Deans of Women by asking, "And do you think we should give all the Hottentots a quart of milk a day?" When a hard-pressed roommate tried to wake him up for a class he'd insisted the night before that he *had* to make, a sodden Willie rolled over and said, "I wouldn't get up now to see Mamie Eisenhower mud-wrestle the Queen of England." If time is not particularly kind to quips like these, neither is it to most humor from twenty-year-olds.

He seemed so much less parochial than the rest of us. His job at the *Texan* required him to read campus newspapers from all over the country, so he knew what was going on at institutions like Yale and the University of North Carolina at Chapel Hill. And because he also looked over the big city newspapers, he could talk knowledgeably about the blight of Senator Joe McCarthy or the mess the British were getting into at Suez. He could make politics come alive in spicy anecdotes, and if you add to all that the fact that he had a passion for books and spoke of certain authors as though they were related, if distantly, you have a truly interesting person. He was biding his time in the boondocks, but nobody I knew doubted that he would end up in the very midst of the action.

Carol Hamilton was a dark-haired twenty-year-old about my size with a happy disposition and zest for adventure. Two people could scarcely have been better suited to spend a summer wandering through Europe together. We even walked at the same pace, which was a good deal faster than that of most people, and it turned out we could cover eight miles a day and a major art gallery without a whimper. I'd once crossed the state line to Oklahoma, just to say I'd been there, and had spent a few days in New Orleans with my parents. But in June, 1955, with backpacks and a contraption for fixing a meal over a canister of dry heat, Carol and I set out for what would prove to be the most momentous summer of my life.

We first stopped in Washington, D.C., to visit Barry Bishop, whose parents had had him flown up from Houston in a specially equipped plane and had installed him and his iron lung in their home in nearby Virginia. In his room I was overcome, as ever, by his ineffable sweetness. He would lie there smiling at our reflections in the angled mirror a few inches above his head, gasping for breath now and then as he gave us the latest news or told us a story. No one else I know has had a fate so terrible, but never once did I hear him complain.

And so it happened that the first great art museum I ever saw was the National Gallery, just down the hill from the United States Capitol. Dumb with amazement at the treasures around us, Carol and I stood in a high-ceilinged room full of Rembrandts, including one of his young wife Saskia, plain but luminous, and another of a rather finer young lady with an ostrich-feather fan. We then made our way through one room after another hung with paintings by Vermeer, Duccio, Velázquez, Van Gogh, Degas, Picasso. The list seemed endless and the rush of pleasure totally unexpected.

In those rooms I discovered an affinity for painting for which nothing had prepared me. The only person I knew who took art seriously was my Aunt Bernice, who had married my mother's brother Avery and so was not even blood kin. Whether or not one can inherit such an affinity, I had no reason to believe the genes had been available. But as I stood there in the National Gallery, I felt as though I'd found a piece of myself that had been missing. The part of me that responded to language, it seemed, had a kindred spirit that thrilled to color, form, and line.

In a less exalted mood, we rambled around the army medical museum, where the most memorable exhibit was a row of jars displaying penises in various states of decay from syphilis. And then we went to the Capitol and sat in the visitors' gallery listening to the entire U.S. Senate, most notably a Massachusetts charmer named John F. Kennedy, apologize to Senator Herbert Lehman of New York, whose telephone, it seemed, had unaccountably been tapped.

A few days later in New York, we sat at a counter in Schraft's while a waiter giggled at my saucer-eyed shock as it dawned on me that the man sitting next to me wearing a dark gray business suit with a snappy tie and light gray fedora was in fact a woman. Dazed by the sheer excitement of walking the streets of mid-Manhattan, we saw Orson Welles play Captain Ahab in a bare-stage production of *Moby Dick;* Jason Robards doing Eugene O'Neill's *The Iceman Cometh* at the legendary Circle in the Square; and most moving of all, Susan Strasberg as Anne

Frank in a Pulitzer Prize–winning play that ended with the horrible pounding on the door and a stage that went suddenly black. Then, very nearly sated, we climbed late one evening onto an overnight train at Grand Central Station that would take us under a full moon to Montreal, where we would board a lumpy student ship called the *Arosa Kulm* for Southampton.

In the mid-1950s the Atlantic crossing took eleven days in that kind of ship, which was time enough for me to have a minor shipboard romance with a skinny, world-weary guy who went to Dartmouth. We cuddled under lifeboats and he asked me to meet him at various places in Europe and even to come up for Winter Carnival, but I turned my back on all these lovely invitations. Since high school, whenever it seemed that cuddling might move into territory more serious, I would freeze in something very like terror. I felt stupid and found it impossible to talk about, even to Carol. For that matter, I didn't even know how to think about it. So I fell silent and turned strange, to myself surely as much as to him, and we parted in a state of mutual incomprehension.

So it happened that the first great churches I ever saw were Westminster Abbey and Canterbury Cathedral. The first castle we saw was Windsor and the next was Chillon in Switzerland, which Byron had made famous. My first mountains were the Alps, which Carol and I got to know while hitchhiking over the Simplon Pass into Italy. My first deep valley was the one about which Milton had written the awesome sonnet that begins, "Avenge, O Lord, thy slaughtered saints. . . . "

We heard Shakespeare at lunchtime in the crypt of St. Martin in the Fields and worked our way through the National Portrait Gallery absorbing what we could of British history. We wandered the lanes of Oxford in a magic trance that for me would have lifelong repercussions. We spent an afternoon at a town called Camogli on the Italian Riviera with a burly rugby player named Gustavo Giampiccoli whom we met at Agape. We saw the Leaning Tower of Pisa at three in the morning under a full moon with four Italian men trailing us, along with a fifteen-year-old boy who had promised on the train to lead us to the Tower and whose hand Carol refused to let go, however improbable he may have seemed as a protector. We learned the layout of Florence so well that forty years later I could find my way blindfolded, we saw *Aida* in the Baths of Caracalla in Rome, and lay on our backs in the Sistine Chapel and contemplated Michelangelo's God.

We slept in youth hostels, on benches, in crowded trains, and once in Munich, we suspected, in a whorehouse, and on our first night in Paris, we unrolled our sleeping bags on the floor of the first-class waiting room at La Gare du Nord. (An attendant trying to win Carol's favor let us into the first-class accommodations despite our third-class tickets.) Though the air was strained once for a couple of hours, we never even had a spat and enjoyed the same things almost equally.

We made friends in likely places and unlikely ones as well—one of them a Pakistani woman who taught us how to wear a sari. We fought off bedbugs with only partial success, made do with basin baths and cold showers for almost two months, and laughed to the brink of hysteria when Carol came out of a continental toilet with a giggle and said: "I'm suffering from culture shock!" The cap on my front tooth broke, starting a series of adventures that in the end gave us a way to jettison tiresome Italian men: I had only to ease out the temporary cap and grin to send them flying.

From our parents' generation, Cornelia Otis Skinner had written *Our Hearts Were Young and Gay* about going to Europe with Emily Kimbrough, and that's the way it was for Carol and me too. We loved each other and Europe and life in approximately equal measure, and I'd never been happier. Here was friendship at its best—and adventure and laughter. All around us were monuments to the human spirit and its creative powers that I could spend a lifetime knowing. Matthew Arnold's "the best that has been thought and written" had been infinitely expanded to include music and art. In my most reverent moods, the future loomed as one long homage to the treasures of Western civilization.

Three weeks after I got home, Grandma had a heart attack and died at seventy-six. Daddy consoled himself with her relief that I had returned safely, but he refused to let me go to the funeral on the grounds that it would be morbid. In fact, his siblings squabbled about selling back the coffin since she'd been cremated, and then they fought over her meager possessions. (Grandma had passed along many valuable qualities, but emotional wisdom, it seemed, was not transferable.)

Her stamp on me had been indelible, but the world I lived in was wholly different from hers—as she'd hoped it would be. In the years to come, the towering question for me would be how to use the values and qualities she had given me for purposes she would have honored.

CHAPTER SEVEN

$\mathcal{W}$hen I got back to the university, I wrote a painful letter and resigned my small elected position at the Y. Agape had been a fine experience in international living, and I had been awed when Pastor Vinay talked about his days in the Resistance against Mussolini and Hitler. But I had also faced the fact that I was not a Christian; it was really that simple.

Most people I loved and honored *did* call themselves Christians, and because of them, I had tried, to the point of desperation, to believe. But many friends were no more hidebound about definitions than Sydney, who could say matter-of-factly years later, "I never bought into sin, or hell fire and damnation. I took what I wanted, then played around a little with Zen Buddhism, but I'd always circle back to Christianity." I found that I simply *could not* do that; in their agnosticism, Daddy and Grandma had marked me, and I couldn't fake it.

I *hated* not being able either to believe, on the one hand, or to refuse to take the articles of faith seriously, on the other. I felt pig-headed, wretched, and *lonely*, for since I was a kid, I'd always been part of a gang, and there was no community of disbelief here to join—no comrades in this struggle. For the people I found the kindest and most understanding, but also the best fighters for justice, were those like Thelma Hamrick, Block Smith, and Peggy Rowland, whom I called primitive Christians.

My isolation in unbelief left me with a practical problem I had no way to get my mind around, much less to measure: if I couldn't work against racism through the Christian community, how *could* I work against it? I could picket alongside them, of course, and did. But being a tag-along felt very little better than standing on a street corner preaching to myself, and somehow I would have to find another way.

Ironically, Christianity still played a potent role in my imaginative life, as I signed up for a year-long course in Italian Renaissance art. The professor was Marian Davis, whom the art students griped about because she was so demanding. She expected us to know some five hundred paintings, sculptures, and buildings well enough to identify them by artist, date within a quarter of a century, and location. And then, of course, we had to be able to describe what we were looking at and make connections.

Shirley Nelson and I took the course together, and we'd walk around the campus testing our memory of Cimabue, Giotto, the Pisanos, Titian—whomever—while absorbing the eloquence of stone, wood, and paint and learning about color, line, and space. We interpreted a figurative language that told the hard Biblical story in strange, compelling images that had shaped and haunted the Western imagination for more than five centuries and now slipped into ours: God creating Adam and Eve; the Serpent; the Expulsion from the Garden; the Virgin and Child; Gethsemane; the Crucifixion, the Resurrection, and finally Christ Triumphant. This was heady stuff, and more; until now we'd had only one female professor, a woman who had been more than a little scatter-brained, but Miss Davis taught us that women could be fine teachers at the same time she was helping us learn to see.

During this, our third year, Jayne, Carol, and I were living at the Theta house, Madeline having deserted after our sophomore year to marry Peggy's co-president at the Y, and Jayne and I were engaged in a guerrilla war with the chair of our alumnae board—a woman I'll call Mrs. Tobin—who'd have considered it a Class A sin to appear in public without heels and a pearl choker. After I'd started using my laundry bag as a suitcase, for instance, Mrs. Tobin decreed publicly that "ladies do *not* take their laundry out the front door of the Theta house." So I'd rudely sling my bag over my shoulder and walk right past her on my way to the bus station. Pushing her even harder by keeping a bottle of sherry in my closet, though it was against university regulations, I was daring her to report the Thetas' Sweetheart finalist.

Meanwhile, the parties didn't stop, and the rest was a mishmash. Our Orange Jackets meetings dissolved into puddles of trivia, but I was getting to know a number of Jewish students. Now and again I would go out with Willie Morris, who was putting out a lively *Daily Texan,* writing not only the editorials but his column and a sheaf of news stories as well. And he really caught my attention in his quarrel with the university powers-that-be over press censorship, which he touched off by running an article from the *St. Louis Post-Dispatch* attacking the oil-depletion allowance.

Daddy may have been agnostic, but he genuflected to Big Oil, and so I found Willie's defiance thrilling. A young man calling his elders parochial was using a language forbidden to women, though we could cheer from the sidelines. But on a campus built and supported largely by oil money, Willie was taken to be looking our gift horse in the mouth, and the Board of Regents told President Logan Wilson to hold him down to a college cheer.

Such a patronizing taunt was insulting to a young guy's manhood, so Willie launched what would prove to be a celebrated career of thumbing his nose at powerful men with money. He ran blank spaces where editorials should be and wrote with mock ponderousness that students should take pains *not* to sit on the grass. The battle ended in a standoff, which, given the disparities of raw power on their respective sides, was unheard of in Texas.

The brouhaha won Willie a good deal of national attention, spiced by a letter from the venerable J. Frank Dobie saying the regents were "as much concerned with free intellectual enterprise as a razorback sow would be with Keats's 'Ode on a Grecian Urn.'" Furthermore, he parlayed his eminence into a Rhodes scholarship to Oxford, the university with the ancient stone walls and lichen I had fallen irretrievably in love with a few months earlier.

Here was a guy who fought with flair and fought to win. Who sidestepped tangled questions of faith. Who laughed and moved on. And now he would actually *study* at Oxford rather than peering through the gates as Carol and I had done. Siding always with the little guy in the David-and-Goliath battles, and a secular pilgrim ready to prostrate myself before the icons of Western civilization, I began to look at Willie a little more attentively.

A few months later, Roundup came again, and once more I was one of the five Sweetheart finalists riding in a parade down the Drag perched on the backs of open convertibles amidst a pageant of lavish floats and marching bands. After the usual folderol that night at Gregory Gym, with my friend Bob Armstrong as master of ceremonies, the Bluebonnet Belles were presented and took their places on platforms at the back of the stage. Then Bob announced, one by one, the six women representing the other Southwest Conference schools, each of whom slowly paced the horseshoe runway and waved while the university band played her alma mater's song. After they found their places, he then announced the five of us who, in turn, made the circuit, and finally the current Sweetheart of the University of Texas.

And when the stage was filled with young women dressed in ball gowns of every color and hue, the hall went dark and Bob teased the audience as he said very slowly, "And now, the Sweetheart of the University of Texas for 1956–57." The band struck up "The Eyes of Texas," and he finally announced "Miss Celia Buchan." So when the lights flashed on, the cheers erupted, and the spotlight beamed on center stage, I was the one who was standing there.

It isn't easy to be blasé when several thousand people are applauding and singing "The Eyes of Texas" to you. I *did* think fleetingly, "So much for you, Mrs. Tobin!" before I went down for another turn on the horseshoe, but it was no time for spite. My parents and Glenn were jumping up and down and waving from the fifth row, and so I gave myself over to having a wonderful time. At the end of the ceremony, a mob poured onto the stage, and in the melee, I was pushed this way and that until I tripped over my hoop skirt and fell into a great mound of pink and white satin.

As soon as I got back to the Theta house, I called Barry Bishop, though it was a ghastly hour in Washington, and Carol and I took turns talking to him until almost two in the morning. He was as thrilled as I had expected, and that was the best of it for me.

The next day, the *Texan* had a wildly alliterative banner headline— "Charming Celia Captures Campus Crown"—that suggested maybe somebody had had too much booze when he wrote it, and my picture was on the front page of the *Houston Chronicle*. Willie sent a dozen and a half long-stemmed yellow roses and several others sent red, and for a few days my room was a florist's annex.

But I felt like an impostor. My mental image of a "sweetheart" as being lighthearted and gay—or certifiably *good,* like Ellie—exacerbated the split between the person I was and the one I seemed to be—a split I had no idea how to describe, much less to heal. I couldn't go around scowling; that would be silly and ungrateful. I couldn't even face it in solitude, for I had no words other than those of Niebuhr and Tillich, which was not my language. So a few weeks later, when I was tapped for Mortar Board and then elected its president, I gave a teary thanks, saying how much more this meant to me than the other honor I did not name. And since being president of Mortar Board was suitably earnest, I resolved simply to keep my chin up and put my hope and energy there.

In the summer of 1956, I drove with friends to New York City to spend the summer, stopping overnight at Willie's home in Yazoo City, where his mother treated me like Queen Elizabeth—or Princess Margaret at the very least—and Willie tantalized us with his upcoming departure for England. Subsequently we stayed with the Bishops in Washington, and there, for the very first time, Barry allowed his picture to be taken in the iron lung, looking up at me with such delight that, forty years later, that photograph is still one of my treasures. It was published in the *Houston Post,* and when Barry died of pneumonia a year later, I was grateful in the midst of my wretchedness for the exquisite moments of pleasure we had shared.

On the way home we stopped in Amarillo for Carol Hamilton's wedding. She was my closest friend among those who'd already married, and I knew that in the next year the numbers and the rate would accelerate. An era in our lives was drawing to an end, and if it seemed tacky and ungrateful to be sad, I couldn't help it, though I would learn to hide it better.

The phenomenon of my senior year was the brash young philosophy professor, John Silber, who had begun making a name for himself as soon as he hit campus the year before. Jayne had taken his introductory class, and the stories she brought home were tantalizing. For Jayne could be not only mischievous but cocky—and such an accomplished flirt that she usually got away with everything. But when she came into Silber's class thirty minutes late and went up afterward to bat her eyes and wriggle out of it, he said "You're not late, Miss Upton, you're absent!"—cutting through her wiles with such dispatch that even Jayne cackled with relish. I'd been putting off my Plan II philosophy requirement because everyone said it was boring, but now I signed up happily.

John Silber was a very handsome man at thirty—only ten years older than we—lean and wiry, with thick blond hair, a fine square jaw, fierce blue eyes, a wicked grin, and a presence that was electrifying. His right arm ended just below the elbow in a vestigial stump he used with great dexterity, and when he stood before that class, or stalked back and forth in a transport of intellectual glee, I forgot not so much that he had one hand but that most people have two.

A native of San Antonio, he spoke our language, though he'd gotten a Ph.D. from Yale. There was nothing arcane or esoteric about him, for philosophy to Silber was about how you know and what you do about it. The word "charisma" could have been invented for him, and if he ever had a down time, he certainly didn't show it to us.

On returning our first set of papers, he read mine aloud word for word, tearing it ever so slowly to pieces and holding it up as an example of an A student doing F work. (It was an English paper, he declared flatly, not a philosophy paper.) He didn't identify the essay as mine, but now and then in the midst of this ritual blood bath, our eyes would meet and battle was joined. Whatever it took to win this man's respect, I was determined to do.

He was immensely patient, we discovered, with a student who was trying hard but didn't quite get it, and cutting only to those who hadn't done the work or were grandstanding. That year I *never* saw him mistake the one kind of student for the other, and he invested the life of the mind with such urgency that every class was an adventure. We jousted with him. We explored. We dissected. We found.

I would also climb the stairs to his third-floor office, where he'd sit with his feet propped on his desk, his tie loosened, and his sleeve rolled up, and we'd talk about whatever outrageous thing was happening then on campus. The most memorable that fall was a motion from the faculty itself that they refrain from getting involved in campaigns for governor or lieutenant governor. The resolution was supported by the distinguished economist Clarence Ayres, a principal target for the legislature in the Rainey years but a rebel, it seemed, no longer. So in the faculty senate, after Ayres suggested that they draw a little circle around a small area of political activity, Silber jumped up to point out that this little circle happened to enclose 98 percent of his political interest.

I had *never* met anyone more defiant or persuasive—even when you were convinced he was wrongheaded, if not perverse—and he would sit in his office actually savoring the risk. With three small children and no tenure, he was taking on a lot more than any riverboat gambler did, and as far as an outsider could see, if he was convinced his cause was just, he wouldn't pull back even if nobody else supported him. On a campus in the 1950s where "working within the system" was the credo, John Silber by himself was an education in dissent.

I finally squeaked out an A in the introductory course and then signed up for his class in ethics, along with several friends as keen to take him on as I was. This was the class Silber would often refer to as the best he ever taught, and when a superb teacher is at the top of his form, the experience is breathtaking. He was a wizard with the Socratic method, and the tension could be mesmerizing as he sliced away at the intellectual ground under a student's feet until he or she was backed into a corner and saw no exit. Sometimes he was like a conductor—pointing to an urgent hand in the back, calling in a comment from the side, sketching connections, slowing us down, leaping forward, orchestrating harmonies, pulling things together.

He plucked analogies from the realms of music, sculpture, architecture, history, literature, psychology; he simply *knew* more than most people and could *use* what he knew more deftly. Once when I cited a dream to illustrate some point or other about perception, he grinned roguishly—I think he even blushed—and said, "I hope nobody here knows Freud." But we kept coming back for more.

Long afterward it dawned on me that several women in that class, including me, had been half in love with John Silber, who had probably never before been the object of so much concentrated female attention. Since Yale was still a men's college, his earlier teaching experience had not prepared him for Texas coeds, and more worldly men have had their heads turned by less. Though sex itself was out of the question, it is little wonder that he put in one scintillating performance after another, for the air had a sexual charge we were all too innocent to recognize, much less to acknowledge.

Not long after registration, Willis Pratt, arbiter of Plan II, called me in to say that in signing up for the ethics class I was taking a sophomore course when I needed senior credit to graduate. But if I read an extra book and wrote an extra paper, he said, all would be well. This was fine with Silber and fine with me, but as it was a busy semester, I didn't get around to the extra assignment. Then, as we parted for the summer, Silber said, "Why don't you read *The Brothers Karamazov* and write a Kierkegaardian interpretation of Ivan?" So I said "Sure!"

That summer I read Dostoevsky and came back asking plaintively, "What have you done to me?" Silber grinned. So I read it again, and then read the "Pro and Contra" section over and over. Seven months late, I handed in a twenty-seven-page paper when I'd only been expected to turn in seven pages. I was auditing one of his courses when he gave it back with "A+ Excellent—You're on your way!" scrawled across the title page and "This was well worth waiting for. Thank you very much!" at the end.

Writing that paper was my most substantial intellectual adventure until well into graduate school and his response, the most gratifying. He had helped me know I could do good work, academically speaking, and that I loved the challenge.

Silber's endorsement mattered because I was facing the question of what to do with my life. Until then, everything had proceeded by obvious stages in arenas I'd had little trouble seeming to master, for after graduation, I'd gotten a reprieve from ultimate seriousness by going to work for Harry Ransom, a vice-president on his way to becoming one of the university's most creative administrators. Silber would tell Ronnie Dugger, who quotes him in *Our Invaded Universities,* that Ransom "could not tell the difference between the actual, the possible, and the totally inconceivable. He was, therefore, a man who could imagine new possibilities." Suggesting the swirl of daring and excitement Ransom generated, he said provocatively, "He's not the kind of guy who walks out on the limb. He climbs out on the twig and jumps up and down on the leaf!"

During my junior year, Ransom had begun bringing in outstanding young scholars—Silber in philosophy, Roger Shattuck in French, William Arrowsmith in classics—his vision of a truly first-class institution inspiring them to forsake the obvious places like Harvard and Yale to come to what was then, intellectually speaking, the boondocks. Known colloquially as "Harry's boys," they were all fine teachers as well as among the most promising scholars in their fields, and they exuded the confidence that some of the most exciting things in American higher education were about to happen at the University of Texas. Students stampeded their courses, for they were young, vital, and sexy, and they seemed ready to consign our university's second- or third-rate status to the dustbins of history.

Ransom had taught a senior Plan II seminar I had taken and asked me to stay on "interpreting him to students and students to him." Since I had very little idea what he was talking about a good deal of the time, I was reluctant but intrigued. The invitation was flattering and his powers of persuasion so highly developed that people would soon talk about being "Ransomized." To be one of "Harry's girls" at a highly charged moment in the life of an institution I loved was a chance I ultimately couldn't resist.

The year after I graduated Jayne and Carol Querolo and I rented a house on Bridle Path in west Austin, where we had a string of adventures deriving largely from our ignorance of all things domestic. We *were* resourceful, however, and when the health department threatened dire consequences if we didn't cut our grass, we called in the chits. Silber came with his lawnmower in return for the times I had kept his enchanting son David and two lively daughters, while Bill Arnold, one of the rowdies I'd refused to desert in the eighth grade, cooked a huge pot of spaghetti for a milling bunch of kibitzers. Traffic stopped at the sight of a one-armed man mowing the lawn while seven or eight able-bodied guys sat on the porch laughing and telling outrageous stories, and Sam Perry and Jerry Wilson hid a bottle of bourbon in the garage so Bill couldn't find it.

All of which was great fun but, alas, beside the point; the world was closing in, and the words and ideas at my disposal were not helping. For to an imagination so recently inflamed by Kafka and Dostoevsky, the gung-ho Texas style now seemed thin, and the prospect of spending my life among people for whom literature, art, and ideas were not urgent matters chilled my anxious soul.

Instead of working directly for Ransom, who typically didn't get my part of his act together that year, I ended up mainly teaching freshman English and found it so satisfying that I began to think about getting a doctorate so I could teach in college. Literature would then be my profession—the material with which I would build my intellectual and spiritual life. But that idea was only beginning to germinate, and a different decision felt more urgent.

For to heterosexual women who came of age in Texas in the 1950s, the notion of not marrying was unthinkable. To be sure, the strong women at the university who'd had such a powerful influence on me—Anna Hiss, Marian Davis, and those in the Dean of Women's office—were almost all unmarried, but if my friends and I allowed ourselves an opinion, we thought their singleness a shame. They couldn't *really* be role models for us because, for whatever reason, they had forfeited the chance to fulfill what the very air taught us was our destiny. So we felt sorry for them, though we managed not to say so.

By the time I graduated, three of the five women in our original study group—Sally, Carol, and Pat—had married, and Shirley was engaged. I had already been in five or six weddings, and more were imminent. So accepting Harry Ransom's offer to "interpret him to students and students to him" had been a delaying action in an inevitable process that was leaving me acutely anxious.

For not only did you marry if you had the chance, you did it sooner, rather than later—the only questions centering on the man and the kind of life you wanted. Anna Karenina and Emma Bovary had graphically illustrated the perils of marrying a respectable bore, and I think it was Emma's gruesome death by arsenic that stilettoed that message into my spirit, though Anna's pitching herself under the train also made the point clearly enough.

Though I'd told myself I would be a volunteer in whatever community I lived in—I even imagined running for the school board, where red-baiting and the fights over race in the 1950s had, figuratively speaking, bloodied the streets—I actually imagined women's collective lives in any one of the big Texas cities to be an extended version of Kappa Alpha Theta. And this gave me what Huck Finn called the "fantods"; there was nothing I wanted less than to be stuck with a group of women who thought bridge fun and fussed over the moral character of girls who wore ankle bracelets or colored socks.

Furthermore, the role of community activist assumed that I'd marry a man who'd most likely expect my help in making his way up "the ladder of success" in whatever profession or business he chose. This presented a problem, for when an "up-and-coming" young man wrote me about how important a wife was to her husband's career, his letter so upset me that I refused to go out with him again.

Though a superb professional, my father had disdained careerism and people who brown-nosed; he'd have looked with soul-withering contempt at anyone who implied that my mother should help him win prizes his own commitment to his work and skill at doing it couldn't win for him. So I could *never* have married a man who expected me to compensate for some deficiency in himself or failure of nerve.

It wasn't that I minded helping—in fact, I took helping for granted. The question was: what *purpose* would I be advancing? The interests of Shell over Humble, or vice versa? The First National Bank over Texas Commerce? Houston over Dallas? People I loved *cared* about such matters, but I didn't. If, as Bob Wheeler predicted, I married a doctor or lawyer and settled in River Oaks or its equivalent anywhere in Texas, I knew I would be expected to keep my mouth shut about race—and about the Joe McCarthys of the world, and everything else controversial. Alternatively, I would have to learn some convoluted way of speaking that went against my natural grain and spend my life being patronized for caring passionately about things that conservatives who dominated such enclaves considered irrelevant or insignificant in the "real" world. (If I'd said I wanted to make war on capitalism, I'd have sounded so ridiculous that even *I* would have laughed. Still, I wanted to cheer when Block Smith responded to the question of whether a rich man could be bribed: "No, because he's already been bribed.")

At the same time, sex had become a problem: I couldn't say no indefinitely, and by now, slapping a man's face seemed at best inept, if not unkind. Though I didn't look forward to what we called "going all the way," I assumed the experience would be okay but resented pressure that seemed unrelenting.

That fall, a mentally unstable law student began pursuing me, and I grew frightened enough to call a law professor I knew slightly, who interceded with Dean Page Keeton, who told the man in turn to stay away from me. (He broke his promise to do so about six weeks later and Keeton got him into a psychiatric hospital.) A married theology student fantasized a deep attraction between us, and my will seemed paralyzed in his presence; I didn't want to be involved but somehow couldn't help it. I alternated between shame and bewilderment and hadn't the slightest idea how to talk about it or who could help me.

So when John Silber asked, "What's wrong with you? Aren't you ever going to fall in love?" I could scarcely have been more vulnerable.

The air itself said it was time, and in his most languorous, insinuating voice, Louis Armstrong was singing, "Let's Do It":

The birds do it; the bees do it;
Even educated fleas do it.
Let's do it: let's fall in love. . . .

Some Argentines without means do it;
People say in Boston even beans do it!
Let's do it. Let's fall in love. . . ."

The whole of creation seemed to be there in his song—sponges, oysters, jellyfish, electric eels ("though it shocks them, I know"), English soles, Cape Cod clams, goldfish (who did it "in the privacy of bowls"), ladybugs, moths, dragonflies, giraffes, hippopotami, Pekingeses in the Ritz—they all do it, and so "Mama, let's fall in love!" Those of us who'd been clinging to the illusion of "purity" didn't have a chance.

Six weeks later, Willie Morris came back from England. He gave me a ring I kept in a box for a couple of weeks, confused in ways that thinking could not begin to address, and by the end of the Christmas holidays we were engaged.

After two years in Oxford as a Rhodes scholar, Willie proposed to take me there for a third that we would pay for ourselves. Outsiders saw only a fairy-tale life, but of all writers, Franz Kafka was the one with whom I then most identified. Blinded by the inner sense of suffocation and panic Kafka so brilliantly evoked, I would solve my problems as I understood them by bolting from Texas.

CHAPTER EIGHT

*O*n paper Willie and I were a real match. The *Houston Chronicle,* in fact, did a feature on our upcoming marriage that breathlessly listed our respective awards and achievements. He beat me out by making junior Phi Beta Kappa, but then he had taken easier courses. While I got the Dad's Club award as Most Outstanding Girl, he was too controversial for the male equivalent. He was a Rhodes scholar, but in the 1950s women were not eligible.

Since I wanted to live "on the front lines," somehow engaging the big issues of my time, and the world I lived in reserved its levers of power for men, the only way I knew how to be "where the action is" was to marry a man who might hold one of those levers. Until I was fifteen, my father's love had been the most potent force in my life. And this truth had made me so sure that a man I loved would love me in return that, when conflict estranged us, I understood only that I needed to find a different kind of man to be my partner. Since Willie was very nearly Daddy's polar opposite, and by now I was very nearly my mother's, with stupefying innocence I assumed I had thought of everything.

So Willie and I seemed roughly equal, and Harry Ransom, with tongue only slightly in cheek, asked me to promise our letters to his proposed new manuscript collection. For days Willie laughed at the minister who told us to decide who'd be "president of the corporation" in three areas: the outside world, the household, and the bedroom. Willie thought it hilarious that anyone should imagine me deferring and claimed to have been afraid I'd throw the minister out the window.

And he was not only ambitious in ways I admired, and dedicated to the same ends, but superb at what he did. Even now people tell me how much his 1967 classic *North Toward Home* meant to them: it touched the hope-springs of our generation, and it is the Texas section of that lovely book that has always been the most evocative for me. In a typical passage, he describes his response to an evening we spent with a young graduate school couple:

> Stirred by the conversation and by all the books I had seen, I went to the library, promising myself to read every important book that had ever been written. I was at a loss, because I did not have the faintest notion where to start. I picked out the most imposing volumes I could find—Lord Bryce on the American Commonwealth, which put me to sleep for ten nights in a row. . . . [I kept reading] in a great undigested fury: Hemingway, Faulkner, Wolfe, Dreiser, anything in the American literature and American history shelves that looked promising. I started buying Modern Library books with the money I made writing for the newspaper, and I pledged to myself, as Marilyn Monroe had, that I would read them all, and in alphabetical order.

There you have it, I think: the zest, the hope, the ambition, the delicious self-mockery. I'm not sure I'd ever known someone who could be serious and funny at the same time, and Willie was clearly an apprentice of sorts to the writers he read with such undigested fury and taught me to admire.

As a Mississippian, he took race at least as seriously as I and felt as fundamentally at odds with the place he came from. In fact, while Texas governor Alan Shivers was preaching "interposition," which meant rejecting the Supreme Court's *Brown* decision, Willie had written in the *Daily Texan* that "no insurmountable barriers to the social integration of Negro students exist on the University campus." At a party in Yazoo City, when his friends insisted on talking about race, he said he'd met black men at Oxford who were smarter and more sensitive than he. And we had a lively discussion that ended with a young planter saying, "Well, I don't want my children going to school with niggers because how would they know they're better?" This pretty much said it all, as far as I could see.

Of course, marrying Willie gave me a precious chance to defy my father in ways he could not object to openly. A man who thought drive and brains mattered could hardly complain about a Rhodes scholar who had captured national press attention. And the prospect of living in Oxford amongst the most promising men of our generation was way beyond anything I had ever hoped for.

So Willie was escape, defiance, and adventure. And I expected us to go through life as crusaders together—he as a journalist, I as a college professor—and complementing each other; while he was actively fighting the most important social and political battles of our day, I would make sure we lived always in the presence of the "best that had been thought and written."

By the time we got to Oxford, some six weeks after our wedding, I had clues enough to predict how that marriage would end if I had known how to read them, but I didn't. Quite the contrary, I was so committed to the idea of marriage as a freely chosen partnership that it was unthinkable to me that our marriage could fail.

For one thing, today's twelve-year-old girls probably know more about sex than I or any of my close friends did when we left college. I did not take the pain and disappointment of sex with Willie seriously because I didn't know that one should take sex seriously. Though I read *The Joy of Sex* and some pornography Willie gave me, they didn't make the sex better—they only left me more frustrated.

In time, Willie would write about our passionate honeymoon, but the passion was his. When I said I felt too raw for a repeat performance, he sulked and turned his back. And though I hadn't heard of it then, I acted implicitly on the advice a formidable British queen gave her daughters: I simply lay back and thought about England.

Beyond that, Willie was a loner. His father had died a few days after our wedding, and on the ship over to England, he spent a lot of time lying in his bunk with his face to the wall. I took this to be grieving, but it turned out that whenever he was troubled, confused, or just out of sorts, he would take to his bed and throw up an impenetrable barricade of silence. The tall tales and high spirits he saved for the most part for company and the pub.

Our everyday exchanges were usually pleasant enough, but neither of us had the slightest idea how a man and woman went about loving one another or managing intimacy. Since his parents, like mine, had lived in a state of barely contained hostility that nobody talked about, we had nothing, really, to go by; and for whatever deep psychological reasons, Willie wasn't about to risk trying.

Still, the command to make the best of things was lodged deep in my psyche, and amidst thirty or so Rhodes scholars nothing could have been more gratifying than suppressing my fears. We crossed the Atlantic on the *Queen Mary* with the 1958 Rhodes class, and since a friend from Lamar who'd come to the pier had told one of them I was a red-blooded egghead's dream girl, I began that trip with a certain aura. Nothing, in fact, could have been more exhilaratingly safe: I was desirable and off limits. As a senior member of the Rhodes community, Willie was the source of precious knowledge about Oxford, so our table was always crowded. And since all these gifted men were showing off for each other, they were at the top of their form: funny, hopeful, sly.

The ship's management had the gall to show a movie about people traveling first class on the *Queen Mary,* and we practically rioted over our grungy accommodations. Somebody ran a pair of trousers up a flagstaff, and Bob Childres, a sexy former football player from Ole Miss with a hard-edged laugh, drank everybody else—even Willie—under the table. We stood on deck in crisp fall weather watching whales on the horizon and fell into long disputes about the respective merits of Faulkner and Hemingway. With a slew of partners, I danced until two and three in the morning. And once, when I got up before dawn to see the sun rise over the ocean, I was bathed in such radiance that only the most unyielding heart could have been ungrateful.

Oxford itself was even better. For two years, Willie had been weaving tales about members of his own Rhodes class, and the first of them I actually met was a man from Amherst called Van Doorn Ooms, whose ancestors were Dutch and who had a wonderfully low, resonant voice. He had just got back from two weeks in Perpignan listening to Pablo Casals play Bach and Beethoven, and we ran into him just outside New College, where Willie was reading history and Van was doing graduate work in English. He had a high, domed forehead, green eyes, a tennis player's wiry build, and after an hour or so in the nearest pub, a nearly incandescent smile.

We were joined that day at the Turf by David Palmer, an Englishman with red hair and freckles, buck teeth, and an air of sublime amusement.

He might have played Puck in *A Midsummer Night's Dream*—he seemed always up to something—and he liked nothing better than telling stories about eccentric Oxford dons, like the one who used bread crusts for bookmarks, or the president of Magdalen who, on being told that a Fellow of the College had killed himself, said, "Pray don't tell me who. Allow me to guess."

As I was soon to discover, when David was really inspired, his glasses would fall down his nose as he rose grandly to the balls of his feet and conducted Beethoven's Ninth with sweeping flourishes, whether or not to music from the phonograph. A scholarship student from Kettering in the Midlands who doted on Americans innocent of British class snobbery, he could quote long passages from Chaucer and do a wonderful imitation of his tutor, John Bayley, who was married to the philosopher/novelist Iris Murdoch and was so otherworldly that he once managed to run over himself with his car and break his own leg. There David would be—sprawled on the floor—here came the phantom car, rolling backward down the hill, and then he'd get this frantic grimace on his face.

A few days later, Willie and I climbed the steep stairs to a nondescript flat on Beaumont Street shared by Neil Rudenstine and John D'Arms from Princeton and Mike Hammond, who'd been head of Boys' Nation and had ridden in the presidential limousine with Harry Truman. John played a pretty good barroom piano and Mike sang barbershop while Neil smiled beatifically. My first night on Beaumont Street I also met Angelica Zander, a Brit who looked rather like Ellie Luckett and seemed fond of Neil, and not long afterward, Theresa Waugh, Evelyn's oldest daughter whom Johnny was on the verge of pursuing. The standard Beaumont Street fare, I would discover, was peanut butter and jelly on limp white bread, though their conversation was a good deal more varied and spirited.

By the end of my first month, I had also met Jean Herskovits, a tiny woman from Evanston, Illinois, and Swarthmore College whose father Melville, a famous anthropologist, had worked with Gunnar Myrdal. And I'd begun to know Dick Sylvester, a West Point Rhodes scholar whose father had been a general and whose life Oxford had turned upside down. Jean was getting a D.Phil. in African history while, to the army's dismay, Dick was reading English at Worcester College. With an occasional Englishman or Englishwoman, an Indian, African, or Australian thrown in, these people would come to mean Oxford to me. I became part of a new gang of men and women who clearly wanted to matter in the life of their times.*

Willie had found us an airy flat called South Lane House, which took up one end of a stucco home built by a German don at the turn of the century. It was adjacent to the Dragon School, a sort of prep school for Eton, and from the bedroom upstairs, all you could see were gardens and playing fields with a spire or two in the distance. Downstairs was a little kitchen adjoining a light-filled parlor with an overstuffed sofa and chairs and a round oak dining table set in an alcove framed by a big bay window.

At the other end, in North Lane House, lived two elderly sisters who edited something or other, and in the middle lived the don's daughter, Herma Fiedler, who had divided her house and rented out the two ends so she could bring in enough money to go on living there. Miss Fiedler and the sisters were women who most likely would have married had so many of their male peers not been killed in World War I—that is to say, they were women of my grandmother's generation. They played the cello, violin, and viola, respectively, and once a week brought in someone else to play either the violin or the piano, and so the music of quartets would drift in on the evening air. The garden was filled with flowering trees and roses that blossomed late into the year, and two feet from our door was a fine English magnolia.

From almost the beginning, I spent an hour or two nearly every day with either Van or David, and often both. Sometimes Willie joined us and sometimes he didn't. We would stroll along the banks of the Cherwell down into the Christ Church meadows or through the Oxford Parks in the most glorious fall I had ever seen—Texas weather not lending itself to brilliant displays of color—and they would grin at my open-mouthed astonishment. We'd stop to watch a late game of cricket, or wander down-

---

* And they *have* mattered. When I began this book, Neil was president of Harvard, Angelica had published extensively in art history and curated several landmark exhibits, John had served as provost and graduate dean at the University of Michigan and would soon become president of the American Council of Learned Societies, Mike was dean of the Shepherd School of Music at Rice University, Van was vice-president of the Committee for Economic Development, Dick chaired the Slavic Languages Department at Colgate, and Jean was a professor of history at the State University of New York at Purchase, where she had been chair of the faculty senate. As for our British friends, David Palmer had been professor of English at the University of Manchester; Margaret Forster, one of the most versatile and prolific writers of her time; Julian Mitchell, an unusually gifted writer for television and motion pictures; and Dennis Potter, the creator of such landmark BBC series as "The Singing Detective."

town to have lunch at George's Café in the old covered market, where butchers' stalls, fishmongers, flower sellers, and greengrocers were jumbled together. They cajoled me into eating haggis, which was awful, and treacle, which was worse.

They took me through the colleges, pointing out their choicest features: Sir Joseph Epstein's *Lazarus,* for instance, and the bawdy carvings under the chapel seats at New College, or the epitaph for an organist that reads, "Here Lies one blown out of breath, Who lived a merry life and dy'd a merry death." Sometimes they'd take turns parading their erudition: here King Charles I took refuge during the Civil War, there Lewis Carroll, a.k.a. Charles Lutwidge Dodgson, wrote *Alice in Wonderland,* and way over there was the college that banished the poet Shelley for atheism. In the Duke Humfrey Library at the Bodleian, we saw huge leather-bound volumes chained to the wall, as they had been since the sixteenth century, and peered into long cases filled with ravishing illuminated manuscripts—Celtic, French, Italian, German. We pored over the sale tables at Blackwell's and sat up till all hours reading Tennyson, Hopkins, or Yeats aloud:

> *The woods decay, the woods decay and fall,*
> *The vapors weep their burthen to the ground,*
> *Man comes and tills the field and lies beneath,*
> *And after many a summer dies the swan. . . .*

David, in fact, could weep with "Tithonus" or wax stentorian over the mighty British fallen:

> *Bury the Great Duke*
> *With an empire's lamentation;*
> *Let us bury the Great Duke*
> *To the noise of the mourning of a mighty nation. . . .*

And Van liked intoning the fate of Helen and Troy:

> *A shudder in the loins engenders there*
> *The broken wall, the burning roof and tower*
> *And Agamemnon dead. . . .*

On drizzly evenings we scarfed Cadbury's chocolate in a smelly, smoke-filled theater while watching an unsettling new film of Ingmar Bergman's—*Wild Strawberries,* perhaps, or *The Virgin Spring,* or *The Seventh Seal*—and then there was the early Fellini and the depressing Polish masterpiece *Ashes and Diamonds.*

By mid-fall, South Lane House had become a gathering place for Rhodes scholars and the handful of English men and women they were drawn to. A bunch of them gave us a Wedgwood tea set, so I learned how to do a proper English tea with "digestive" biscuits, though I never mastered the cucumber sandwich. We would sit around trying to explain America to the English, and vice versa, and once, when I told David I found British advertising dreary, he said, "That's because our best minds don't go into it." I felt I had fallen into a state of extreme blessedness, and almost any day could find me defending all things English, including the weather.

We had a little phonograph and a few records, my favorite being one Van gave us of Casals playing Bach, and one evening as I sat alone downstairs, curled in a chair half-reading, half-listening, I began to grow uneasy. Strange sounds seemed to be coming from the garden, but the night was black and I could see nothing beyond the windows. Then suddenly I realized: Casals was groaning as he played.

That low, involuntary cry of pleasure mingled with pain was the groundnote of my first year at Oxford. Many years later, Mike Hammond remembered the way I struck him then: "You had this side to you, which was southern-belle charm, and yet there was something very firm in there too that doesn't always go with the first: a kind of ambition, in the best sense. Spiritual more than worldly. You were determined to transform deserts you saw in yourself—we didn't see it that way—you wanted to water them, to make them bloom, because they disturbed you deeply."

For the English men and women I met seemed to know more when they got to Oxford than I had when I left the University of Texas, while the Americans were only marginally less sophisticated and erudite. In comparison, I felt so ignorant that the deserts to which Mike referred were the source of what seemed an unslakeable thirst.

David had arranged for me to do tutorials with a New College don, and I'd decided to study Greek tragedy. My tutor was a man of little more than forty who'd had polio and was in a wheelchair, and once a week his wife, who'd been his nurse, would open the door for me to their cramped North Oxford flat. I was terribly diffident at the notion that I could satisfy an Oxford don, but it seems I did. And so began a lifelong struggle with these strange, often barbarous plays that have formed and haunted the Western imagination. Men who sacrifice their daughters or nieces for what they call demands of state. Women who kill their husbands for revenge or justice. Children who slaughter their mothers, they say, because the divine powers insist. Men who marry their mothers, mothers who murder their children, young people who murder each other and themselves. Greek tragedy is not for sissies, nor does it mesh with the chest-thumping optimism of the place I came from. Imaginatively speaking, I was in profound rebellion against my native culture for willing itself blind to pain and suffering, and at the same time, I was haunted by the specter of Justice.

And then there was Shakespeare. For my twenty-third birthday, Willie took me to Stratford-on-Avon to see director Peter Brook's *Twelfth Night*. I had no idea then who Peter Brook was, but the production was so magical I discovered years later that it had convinced Lynn Redgrave at fifteen to become an actress. Here too I heard the note of anguish amidst the laughter: while Malvolio writhes, Sir Toby Belch bellows, "Dost think because thou art virtuous / There shall be no more cakes and ale?"

Already steeped in Shakespeare, David Palmer was to become director of the summer school at Stratford, and he or Van, who had gotten a first-class degree in English and could quote from the Bard almost as flamboyantly, would often go up to Stratford with us. That season and the next, we saw Charles Laughton do Lear, Michael Redgrave do Hamlet, and Paul Robeson as Othello. We saw an actor nobody had heard of named Peter O'Toole play Shylock in *The Merchant of Venice,* and Vanessa Redgrave and another newcomer, Albert Finney, as lovers in *A Midsummer Night's Dream.*

All this was breathtaking—no milder word will do—and I was profoundly grateful to Willie Morris, without whom none of it would have been possible. And my gratitude worked to muffle my deep unease with Willie, for when you live intimately with someone who isn't really there, I soon discovered, it is much harder than living alone. That year I saw quite a lot of Willie's back, and nothing I could think to say or do bridged the distances between us. He wasn't interested in what I worked on, and when I asked about his own reading in British history, he said he didn't want to talk about it until he got it down on paper. But somehow the right time never came. At the pubs—the King's Arms, the George, the Bear—and in company anywhere, he told good stories, but after a while I knew the repertory.

Still, I was living among people I came soon to love who were training their minds and cultivating their spirits to be the leaders of our generation. I was working in one of the world's great libraries, the Bodleian, and once, while climbing the great, worn stone steps, I passed a window like an arrow-slit and caught a glimpse of the vice-chancellor in his academic gown preceded by the man with the mace that signified his office. Every day I came across little vignettes like this, evoking ancient rituals and time-honored faiths that promised dignity, wisdom, and authority to those who played by the rules. And I believed them implicitly.

All this time I was learning to cook, with only an occasional outright disaster, and so at the end of November, I invited Van, David, Mike, Neil, Bob Childres, and John D'Arms for dinner to celebrate Willie's birthday. For two days I struggled over a menu that featured beef stroganoff and Dutch apple pie, the first day being taken up by a recipe for vichyssoise that required pushing half-baked potatoes through a fine-mesh sieve.

Then, since Miss Fiedler had given me a box of apples from our garden, I decided I ought to make her a pie too. And when it came out nicely, I thought I'd make the sisters one as well. Which meant running the five blocks to our little row of shops on South Parade to get another pie pan and pick up more spices at the greengrocer's. This meant that at five o'clock the afternoon of the party every single dish was dirty and there was scarcely a place left to stand in the kitchen. And this meant that when Van came by to see if he could help, we pushed all the dishes into the hall where he stood passing them to me while I washed.

So by the time everybody arrived, I was mildly hysterical, we all drank quite a lot of bourbon and then wine and brandy, told many stories, laughed uproariously, and had a splendid time. In the wee hours of the morning, just as I was falling asleep, I saw the moon clearing the apple trees and realized how much I'd come to love each of those men, and thought how hard it would be to find a world more nearly perfect.

A few weeks later, at the onset of the Christmas season, Willie and I went to a midnight carol service at New College, where the boys' choir wore scarlet robes with wide white lace collars and one chunky boy with a thick blond crew cut showed up with an enormous shiner. Not long after, we piled into Miss Fiedler's Bentley and drove to Cambridge, where she took us to tea with F. L. Lucas and his wife, who was her cousin. Lucas was a famous literary critic who'd written, among other things, a book on Greek tragedy—one of those landmark works whose limpid prose makes erudition seem easy. No doubt accustomed to intimidated students, he held forth dryly and at length from the depths of his easy chair, expecting neither his wife nor her cousin to contribute to the conversation, much less two awestruck Americans. They were gods, those Oxbridge dons—their subjects docile, and their realms remarkably comfortable. So when I realized that nothing was expected of me, I sat back and enjoyed the virtuoso performance—as fine in its own way, surely, as Casals playing Bach—while indulging in two new cheeses and a very large portion of German chocolate cake.

The next day Willie and I strolled around Cambridge, sparkling just then in a dusting of snow with great swaths of fir and holly on the storefronts and bells in the steeples playing carols. And as the sun began to set, we lined up for the famous Christmas Eve service at King's College Chapel. In later years it was televised, but nothing had prepared me for the stately procession with smoking censers or the sun shooting prisms of rich color through ancient stained glass windows or the grand music echoing in the high, vaulted chamber. We found seats not far off-center and about twenty rows back from the great gold cross, and while the organ sounded and the boys sang with heartbreaking sweetness, I sat thinking about my mother and grandmothers. Chastened and exhilarated by how much richer my life had already been than theirs, I gave solemn thanks, despite my pagan soul, for my immense good fortune.

The following March I found out I was pregnant. Van was with me at South Lane House when I called the doctor to confirm the test, and I threw my arms around him and squeezed with delight. Though I hadn't intended to be pregnant, I felt no ambivalence. By nightfall, Willie had heard the news with equanimity. We had called our parents, who sounded as thrilled as the script called for them to be. And then, somewhat to my surprise, we went back to life as usual.

Willie was beginning to study for "schools," the three-day written exams that largely determined whether one got a first-, second-, or third-class degree. He was aiming for a first, though he had not taken Oxford quite seriously and one of his peers said if he got one, it would make a mockery of the entire Oxford system. Daring the fates, then, we sat with Van at South Lane House cooking up a trip to the continent, for a friend had left us his car while he went home on family business and we could look forward to driving to Dover in unwonted luxury.

After landing at Calais, we headed southeast, stopping for a leisurely walk around the great cathedral at Beauvais, and then going on down to revel in April in Paris, where I played guide to the treasures Carol and I had found almost four years earlier. We drove to Chartres, where Van introduced me to snails, which I was mildly dubious about but willing to try, and then to Amsterdam, where we asked for Cokes in a house of ill repute and made fools of ourselves once more, if less absurdly, by eating mounds of *nasi goreng*. When accommodations were tight, we shared a room—three single beds in a row—and the only problem seemed to be that I was beginning to have trouble buttoning my pajamas.

For the most part, the trip was a lark, though the instant we landed in England, the car was impounded, a permit having expired a day or so earlier. The last train was leaving in about four minutes, so we made a run for it with smuggled balls of Gouda bouncing in the hoods of our thick British car coats and got back to Oxford in the midst of one of those famously impenetrable fogs at two in the morning. The taxis had vanished, which was probably just as well, and we walked home feeling our way by inches.

In a place so rich with romance and friendship, making the best of things seemed easy, though one day Willie and I passed on opposite sides of the street while making believe we didn't see one another. And as the spring came on, I understood why the English talk and write so much about the weather. When the days stop ending at three in the afternoon and the apple trees bloom and gardens erupt in color, your heart not only lifts, but you feel reborn, and May and June become months of instinctive celebration.

We had a ball at Rhodes House so spirited that fifteen years later a man just back from Oxford told me a scout at one of the colleges had complained that nobody had fun anymore the way they had when Mr. and Mrs. Morris were there. The Warden of New College gave a reception in the fifteenth-century cloisters where the popping of champagne corks punctuated the sounds of a string quartet and couples in formal dress stood chatting idly next to eroded stone effigies of long-dead bishops.

Van gave a reception in our garden, for which we spent two days soaking a ham. Dick Sylvester brought gin from the PX, and since it turned out to be 100 proof, guests began falling into the rosebushes and Iris Murdoch and John Bayley looked on with unmistakable chagrin while I pulled thorns from a crestfallen Englishman who couldn't stand any longer.

But the most sensational event was the New College commemorative ball, a traditional gala held every three years. I borrowed Miss Fiedler's treadle sewing machine and made a bright blue silk dress with a huge bow in back and Willie rented a tuxedo. On a glorious night in June, when the sun doesn't ever quite set in England, two giant tents loomed in the gardens, each with its own orchestra. The dark portraits of the college's distinguished alumni hanging in the fine oak dining hall looked down on tables piled with roasted turkeys and hams, mounds of fresh asparagus, and fat strawberries standing in whipped cream. And men who had eaten three meager meals a day there made up for years of frugality by a night of sheer gluttony. I gave out at about four, but the champagne didn't stop until long after dawn, and everyone else stayed on for a sunrise breakfast.

The question hanging over us was what would happen next, for many friends were packing their books and sending off their trunks, and the money was running out. The Rhodes Trust, however, had just broken Cecil Rhodes's will to allow third-year scholars to be married, so Willie applied for a financial third year which in fact would be his fourth at Oxford. When the news came that he had gotten it, and after he'd satisfied himself that even if our child were born abroad he could still be president of the United States, Willie accepted.

Since I'm not sure I ever wanted to leave Oxford, which had ministered so lavishly to my sense of wonder, the year's reprieve was a delight. David Palmer would still be there, as would several others. And so when Willie finished schools, we headed for Paris, rented a car, and drove to Madrid. Being pregnant in Franco's Spain at the height of summer, however, turned out to be an experience even I could truncate, and Willie didn't thrill as I did to the romance of travel. So he went back to Oxford to cram for his oral exams while I stayed in Paris.

The real world intruded when I had to say goodbye to Van, who had gone with John and Theresa to Greece and was now on his way back to England and then home. The four of us sat late one evening at a little restaurant on the Place St. Michel next to two women smoking long black cigars, one of whom leaned over and asked, *sotto voce,* "Are you from Harvard, Princeton, or Yale?" John and Van blushed, Theresa looked startled, and I giggled uncontrollably.

But Van was the closest friend I had ever had—with each other we found a deep rapport and soul's ease—and Oxford without him seemed very nearly unthinkable. We both sighed a lot that evening in the interstices of laughter, and the next day left each other in tears.

CHAPTER NINE

*W*illie arrived in Paris with the news that he had gotten a second, which didn't dent his *amour propre* appreciably, and after a few weeks in Italy, we went back to England to await our baby, who was due in November. The nicer places to live had already been snapped up, so we found a rather dismal flat, with neither phone nor fridge, on the top floor of a large brick Victorian house on Norham Road, just three blocks from Lane House. To heat water for a bath, you took a match to the pilot light of a small tank above the tub that looked like a prop in a Buster Keaton movie. And then you held your breath— or prayed if you were so inclined.

Our new landlady was an eighty-year-old eccentric named Mary Sturge Gretton, whom we would soon discover was the only woman that Sir Basil Blackwell, the founder of Oxford's most amazing bookstore, had ever called a bitch. But our downstairs neighbors were a delightful couple from Gettysburg, Pennsylvania, named Norman and Nancy Richardson. Norm was a philosopher on sabbatical; three of their four children, the youngest being six, were with them for the semester, and since they lived directly above Mrs. Gretton, they bore the brunt of her ill temper.

We got a forecast of the tirades to come when she kicked a hapless Hungarian refugee out of her tiny basement flat for hanging underwear on the line outside the kitchen. "Ladies," Mrs. Gretton pronounced, with her bony nose in the air, "do not show their underwear in public." Later she chastised me for putting our milk bottles on the stoop: "Ladies do not display their bottles. . . . " I was spared her rages, though, my condition no doubt appealing to her sympathy.

Every day at five she would ring a bell at the bottom of the stairs and call in her quavery voice, "Mrs. Morris, your tea is ready!" and I would lumber down to fetch it. I'd say, "Oh, Mrs. Gretton, you really shouldn't," or, "Surely this is too much trouble for you." But since I couldn't seem to discourage her from making the tea, I began baking banana bread or cookies in return and inadvertently won her affection.

And I couldn't help liking her a little—not only because she was kind to me, but because she was spunky and interesting. She'd been a justice of the peace during the Second World War and talked with real feeling about the damage the war had done to children who were evacuated from the cities to the countryside. Furthermore, she was like a personal link to British literary history; her friends had included the poet and novelist George Meredith as well as the enigmatic May Morris—daughter of William, the noted Pre-Raphaelite poet, designer, and founder of the Kelmscott Press.

Once, over tea, Mrs. Gretton told me rather wistfully about the morning her husband had left her for another woman, and she had long since outlived her subsequent companion, whose ashes she kept in an urn on the mantel. Yet she went gamely on, and in her periodic fits of imperiousness or just plain dottiness, she would sign her letters and even her laundry slips, "Mary Sturge Gretton, J.P., B.Lit., Oxon, widow, etc., etc.," the spidery list curving sideways along the margins and sometimes ending upside down on top.

As my middle expanded, the new presence grew more insistent, with pokes and kicks that rippled my taut skin and woke me at night, and it is just as well I had no idea how profoundly my life was about to change. I ate vegetables I had never heard of, gave up sherry, took long walks, reveled in my good health, and read a book on natural childbirth. Rubbed my belly, talked to the baby, reminded myself that the women in my family and, for that matter, everyone else's had done this before me. Wondered. Stared at the ceiling. Looked out the window. Repeated the cycle. Waited.

I wasn't frightened—merely suspended. For I suspect I had "forgotten" my diaphragm because despite the fine company, my soul had been lonely, and both nature and tradition had given my subconscious an answer. And now that I had to turn sideways to wash the dishes and remove my wedding ring lest a hospital attendant have to cut it off, it was too late to back out. But I didn't want to.

In the midst of fantasizing a dramatic scene—swathed in yards of bright orange fabric, I would sail into a Halloween party as a giant pumpkin—my water broke and I ended up instead at the Nuffield Infirmary in a ward with about ten other women in the last hours of pregnancy. These patients were not the Oxford students I was used to but, for the most part, lower-middle-class women who spoke rather like Eliza Doolittle when Henry Higgins ran across her in Covent Garden. One of them came around with a bottle of gin to make the Orange Squash tolerable, but in a fit of misplaced puritanism, I turned down her offer and went to sleep.

Contractions woke me up around midnight, and eventually I was wheeled up to a labor room where I could squeeze Willie's hand to distract myself. In the early morning, he left to report on our progress to friends holding a vigil, and when Jean Herskovits asked him, "Are you going to stay for the delivery?" he said, "I don't know, Jean; I never was one of those boys who wanted to be a doctor."

The midwife had told me they discouraged fathers from coming into the delivery room because they had a tendency to faint. But Willie put on the hospital gown, and as the contractions got faster and harder just after noon, I was holding his hand so tightly he probably would have had to break mine to get free. A group of student nurses huddled against the wall watching the midwife as she talked me through the last few minutes while saying brightly over her shoulder: "This woman's come all the way from Texas to show you how to do it!" Everybody gasped when she commanded, "Now: push hard one last time!" and out came a squalling, blood-smeared baby. All I could do was grin until I managed finally to ask, "Is the baby all right?" and then "What is it?" And she replied, "Can't you see? It's a great big Texas man!" Willie was much too exultant to faint, and so was I—even when he said the baby looked like an eight-and-a-half-pound fish.

That evening Jean, Bob Childres, and Dick Sylvester came to my room with Willie—I was quarantined now because of a cold they didn't want the babies to catch—and since I was the first of our contemporaries to go through childbirth, they were almost as giddy as I. Dick had brought a can of Fritos from the PX, and they stood looking sappy while I ate all the Fritos without offering them any.

Later, two student nurses came into my room, and as they were leaving, I heard one say to the other, "That's the one I was telling you about." So when the one who'd whispered came back, I asked, "Does watching a baby being born make you more or less eager to have one yourself?" And she replied, "We have to see ten deliveries, yours was my second, and the first woman screamed so awful! She just yelled and yelled and we were all terrified. Absolutely terrified! The friend who was just here hadn't seen yours, and we'd all been telling her about it, saying it seemed like it didn't have to be so horrible." And I told her oh my, it wasn't horrible at all, it really, really wasn't. . . .

For days I would lie propped in bed with my baby at my breast, caressing, whispering, wheedling—doing all the tender, silly things new mothers do the world over. Taking in this new reality. Redirecting my soul to a beautiful, helpless boy who would be at its center for at least the next seventeen years. I can't say how it works, but it did with me. And I would learn that not only did I have his life in my keeping, but he had mine—and saved it, eventually.

We named our son David, after those I already loved—McComb, Palmer, Silber—and the Biblical harpist/singer/poet who fought against great odds, adding Rae for a middle name in tribute to Willie's father. The baby was so strong and ravenous I soon had a cracked nipple, which was excruciating, and then I dressed him so warmly he got a heat rash. The doctor who came to see us chided me by saying, "Don't you see these English babies outside in their prams in all kinds of weather?" And when I teared up and nodded, he told me in that inimitable nononsense British way: "You know it's time to bring them in when icicles form on their eyelashes."

Nancy Richardson, having raised four healthy children, was a source of advice and reassurance, but otherwise the circumstances were not propitious. I had to boil the water to wash David's nappies—British diapers with the texture of loosely woven towels that usually took a couple of winter days to dry. Ladies being forbidden to hang nappies outside, David's room soon looked like an oversubscribed laundry. Since we didn't have either a phone or a fridge, I had to shop every day and in no time weighed less than I had since I married. And it wasn't long before I began to appreciate American machines and to miss them.

When David was about two months old, Mike Hammond came back to Oxford from a prolonged trip to the United States, and I invited him to live with us. For several months, then, he slept on the sofa and talked to me while I was washing or cooking, and I was so grateful for the good conversation, I even washed and ironed his shirts as well as Willie's. The two of them would stay up for hours after I fell into bed, talking in front of the heater and flicking ashes on the floor, and though I tried to persuade them to use the ashtray, it took too much energy to insist. So for months I lost myself in work, and whether or not genes played a role in it, I was following the example of all the women in my family. Though I had found my own mother painfully limited, in this new role I was very like her. The work was there, and I felt good doing it.

Still, every few days I would go off to Blackwell's and bring back yet another English classic that I had never read—*Winnie the Pooh, The Wind in the Willows,* most of Beatrix Potter—so that while David nursed, I would be turning the pages, talking to him about Mrs. Tiggy Winkle, Jemima Puddleduck, Toad of Toad Hall, and so on. *Alice in Wonderland* and *Alice through the Looking Glass* charmed us for weeks, and anyone who looked in on us—and many people did—would have said we were having a wonderful time.

Mike invited his Indian friend Dr. Bughat to cook us fabulous meals. Jean brought the Crown Prince of Basutoland, who was the blackest man I had ever seen and, for obvious reasons, exquisitely courtly. The Richardsons were in and out; David Palmer came once a week for my tutorials in Shakespeare and many other times for fun. No two weeks went by without our seeing the usual suspects.

But if the days were lively and my baby a blessing, the emotional blank I had expected marriage to fill was still vacant. Many years later, a woman I scarcely knew and had not seen since 1959 told me that after a party of ours that spring, Willie had walked her home and then grabbed and kissed her. When I brought David to lunch a few weeks later, she said, I had looked unspeakably sad. Before this, she had thought that I had everything, and when I asked why she hadn't told me about Willie's pass, she said I wouldn't have believed her.

Since our illusions depended so much on the truth's not being spoken, it is hard to know what I would have done, if anything. I remember telling Van that I assumed Willie would have affairs and I wouldn't, though my reasoning escapes me. For somehow I believed that that was just the way it was in "enlightened" society.

And if I came from people who made the best of things, I couldn't have had finer material for carrying on the tradition: I had a big, healthy, energetic baby to love, and the focus of my life had shifted. Nursing him gave me a peace I had never known; I doted on his firm little body, his smiles, his every sign of growing mastery. I even loved the way he smelled. The language we spoke, which needed no words, was a language others did not share.

The practical problems of caring for David in a third-floor walk-up with no conveniences, however, persuaded me that it was finally time to leave Oxford. At six months he was beginning to crawl, and the old oak floor was full of splinters. And not long after the hot water heater blew out the bathroom window, Willie decided that we would go back to Austin, where he would take over the *Texas Observer* from Ronnie Dugger.

Apart from Oxford, Austin was the place I loved most in the world; Sally and Jayne were there, with babies now whom David could play with; the *Observer* was a magnet for some of the most interesting people in Texas; and we would go back to the fight to make the world better. It was called growing up, and I was ready.

Telling David Palmer goodbye was the hardest part of leaving that beautiful city where, as somebody put it, too many bells are always ringing in the rain. The Americans we would see again soon—Van and a handful of others, in fact, would be in New York when we landed—but David Palmer would be far away. Until midway across the Atlantic I felt very nearly inconsolable. But babies, as I learned through the hard years ahead, keep you grounded, and David's letters turned out to be minor masterpieces.

CHAPTER TEN

*L*ike millions before us, we sailed into New York harbor as teary as ten-year-olds, standing on the aft deck of the *Île de France* while the Statue of Liberty welcomed us to our native land. When the ship's monstrous horns blew to salute her, David peed through three disposable diapers and drenched my skirt—a hint, it turned out, of how the next few years would go.

Van met the ship and orchestrated a two-day welcoming party in Greenwich Village with Oxford friends who'd scattered to eastern graduate schools. But Willie had spent the last year immersed in American history and wanted to plunge his hands into the political muck. Since 1954, Ronnie Dugger had put out a weekly newspaper in Texas that people all over the country read, and now Willie had the chance to fashion a *Texas Observer* that bore his own mark.

He was casting about for both inspiration and fortitude, and on the way to Texas, we made a circuit of the great landmarks within easy reach— Hyde Park, Gettysburg, Monticello—reminders at once of the best and most terrible in the American past. In one of Jefferson's magnificent quads at the University of Virginia, David threw up in front of a plaque that said "Kappa Sigma was founded here," and I fancied this to be a sign our son had gotten his values straight a long time before we had.

We arrived in Austin just as the Democrats were coming together in Los Angeles to choose John F. Kennedy as their presidential nominee.

To the horror of most Texas liberals, Kennedy then picked Lyndon Johnson as his running mate, and since Ronnie had led a principled charge against Johnson for six years, he felt betrayed. So commenced my introduction to American political pragmatism.

Willie had a different angle from Ronnie's; he expected LBJ to be more progressive when cut loose from his state constituency, and so his *Observer* would give LBJ a new chance. As Ronnie's protégé and successor, Willie was doing something that was both daring and provocative. And though I was learning about American politics from scratch, as an onlooker at a couple of removes, my seat was roughly third row center. For the *Observer* was the Plan II of Texas politics, its pages devoted to the basic issues of democratic government.

For the first time in my life, however, my men and women friends were living different lives; the women were raising children, while the men were holding down jobs or getting professional degrees. Jayne, for instance, was living in barracks-style student housing left over from World War II while her husband Mark Howell finished law school. When I walked in for the first time, a tiny blonde girl with one blue eye and one brown was chucking bread pellets from her highchair onto the floor, and I was instantly smitten. Her name was Madeline, and she would come to feel almost like my own daughter.

I found Sally, in turn, with two tow-headed sons, the youngest just two months older than David, and she took me to see a house a few blocks away from the one she and her husband Tom Leach were renting between the campus and Lake Austin. It was on Bridle Path, not far from where I'd lived two years earlier, and I took it with the keenest relish for the good times we would have there.

Now those years in Oxford began paying off for Willie, who had always been a gutsy, trenchant writer but, in 1960, had far more to say. His weekly tutorials had taught him something about the way politics works and what it takes to shift power from one group to another. The year he'd steeped himself in American history had given him a context for what was and was not happening in Texas. And the hundreds of essays he'd read had tuned his ear to English prose at its best, with fine results for his own writing.

So Willie was a young man coming into his own, and it was thrilling to watch—and, to some degree, to share. He might not be able to confide the way I had assumed he would, but from midsummer on, he was publishing a weekly newspaper. Since he wrote at least half of every issue, I no longer had to wonder what he was thinking.

And he was turning out wonderful stuff. Week after week—whether he was writing about Hurricane Carla, or Frankie Randolph, the great lady who owned most of an East Texas county and bankrolled the *Observer,* or the pastor of the biggest Baptist church in the world, his perceptions were acute, his wit keen, his prose rich and supple. Each time he came back from a new place in Texas, he made it live freshly on the page. And when the legislature went into session and he began analyzing the play and the players, he was at the top of his form. After reading Willie's description of a state legislature at work, in fact, Norman Mailer would say that neither he nor anybody else need bother with the subject further, and Mailer was not a man to shun competition.

Not only was Willie's writing good in itself, and a contribution to Texas, the *Observer* crowd was nearly as interesting as the Rhodes community had been, with the added sense of working for a common purpose. Progressives in Texas read the paper and a good many contributed to it, and everyone who came to Austin on the weekends was likely to gather together—whether at Scholz's Beer Garten or one of our houses. I had a new gang.

Our gatherings typically included a yeasty mix of lawyers, teachers, writers, politicians, activists, ministers, academics, and no doubt more than a few beggars and thieves. Peggy Rowland had married Ralph Person, an aspiring minister now advising the Presbyterian student organization. The men Harry Ransom had brought to the university—Silber in philosophy, Arrowsmith in classics, Shattuck in Romance languages—were stirring up the campus while igniting their own disciplines, and they would often join us, along with close friends from university days. For the most part, then, we were young, idealistic, sassy, and sure we could help make Texas and our country a fairer place.

So Willie and I had the traditional deal: I made our lives work while he went out to slay the dragons. Theoretically speaking, this did not seem a bad arrangement, for I was wrapped up in David, who was a handful. Given my German peasant background, I couldn't be a person others waited on. I believed in what Willie was doing, I believed in what I was doing. And neither could have done both at once.

It had been so hot when we arrived that Sally was walking around in shorts and bra, and our main relief was going to Barton Springs or Deep

Eddy, sparkling pools fed by cold spring water. Jeanie Dugger often showed up with Celia, my namesake, who had just turned two. Other young mothers flocked to the pools or parks, and I began trying simply to hang out. But I was no good at it.

I marveled at women who slipped into their children's rhythms and routines, fixing picnic lunches, playing cards, and chatting as though life were a big Theta house party, and one clique celebrated for witty put-downs struck me as simply a bunch of idle, malicious women. But most important: never had I been in an atmosphere so saturated with erotic energy. Nobody in my repressed generation can have been more repressed than I, but now something so powerful was in the air that even I could feel it. Something those women seemed to know.

My interpreter to this new world became a man named Bill Brammer, who'd been Ronnie's first associate editor on the *Observer*. I'd met him several years before, when he was a special assistant to Lyndon Johnson, but now he was finishing a book he called *The Gay Place*, set in Austin at a time when "gay" meant something very different from what it came to mean in the 1970s. The title, in fact, came from a poem by Scott Fitzgerald, the novelist whose sensibility most shaped Bill's and whose tone of romantic disillusion permeates the book:

> *In the fall of sixteen*
> *In the cool of the afternoon*
> *I saw Helena*
> *Under a white moon—*
> *I heard Helena*
> *In a haunted doze*
> *Say: "I know a gay place*
> *Nobody knows."*

Bill was a small, dark-haired man with a wiry build and the languorous air of someone who didn't believe in moving quickly or, for that matter, much at all. He could be stiller than anybody I'd ever known, and I trusted him because I felt that he was genuinely curious about who I was. Where other men seemed out to prove something—to win an argument, perhaps, or score points, or feel their own sexual magnetism—Bill simply liked women, and they liked him.

When he was in town, he would come over and talk while I was washing dishes or doing chores. Or we'd sit in back under a big live oak while David attacked the sand pile as though it were a battle zone. Bill had a slow, ironic chuckle, and I liked to *watch* him tell about who had slept with whom and who did what to get even because the stories gave him such a kick. Gradually I saw these new people through Bill's eyes, for like his newspaper editor in *The Gay Place,* he felt "he had been plucked from the one dull world and set down in the other, infinitely more gorgeous sphere of politics and rebellion," and he was enthralled by it.

Although he did not seem personally driven by sex, he had an abiding sense of the havoc it wreaked with our best intentions, and perhaps he was the first person I really cared for who had something close to the tragic sense. The "gay place" was now the world I lived in, and though, as Larry McMurtry would observe, Bill made it seem "more charming and less destructive than it really was," I would not understand that until much later.

I read parts of the book in manuscript—in 1961 Houghton Mifflin gave it their annual literary prize—and it was unsettling. It didn't mock the purposeful sort of life Willie and I were trying for; it just seemed to sit back and watch us all muck up. And it didn't help to dissociate myself from his exotic women in cotton underpants who drifted from one man to another and in between trysts painted their children's toenails. Bill had captured something I sensed was true but didn't understand, and for a long time I just read those lyric passages over and over.

Labor Day sparked the hottest political season in more than a decade, and we felt more passionate about the outcome than at any time before or since. The Democrats had nominated a vital, sexy guy to be president and a Texan from the Hill Country to run alongside him. We connected with Jack Kennedy in a visceral way; with his sailor's tan and the grin of heaven's favorite, he got everybody's juices flowing, and we not only believed the federal government could move us closer to a just society but that these men were as likely as any to lead us there.

I took David to a rally at the state capitol, where Kennedy and two of his sisters lifted our spirits with their clean good looks and the vigor and edge of people who play touch football to win. We drove down to Blanco when LBJ threw a barbecue to kick off his campaign, and I, who was seeing him for the first time in person, was astounded by the bald audacity of a guy who'd stand before hundreds of people and say he hadn't wanted to take the vice-presidential nomination and ride in all those back cars and such. I had *never* heard so much unabashed, unvarnished ego. And when Nadine Brammer, Bill's estranged wife, said, "My, Lyndon was mild tonight," I thought she must have overdone the peyote.

Since the Democrats had to carry Texas to win in November, the campaign had the feel of a crusade. For the first time since Harry Truman, they had a chance at the White House, and even parts of the liberal community that had gone underground through the McCarthy years giddily resurfaced. When Kennedy performed gracefully before the Baptist ministers in Houston and the question of his fealty to the pope seemed laid to rest, we set off firecrackers, figuratively speaking, for an entire weekend. For a month before the election, the phone rang almost every quarter hour, our comings and goings at Scholz's were wild with shouts and laughter, and Bob Wheeler and I bet good money on whether Kennedy would carry oil-rich Houston and Harris County.

Election night was the proverbial cliff-hanger, as the Democrats' early lead began dwindling around 11 P.M., and a night of party-hopping turned into a vigil on Bridle Path in front of the television set. A handful of us were sitting around tallying votes on long legal pads when the milkman climbed the steps, but not until dawn did the votes come in that signaled a Democratic victory. Willie left for the television station to watch LBJ accept the vice-presidency while I sat wondering how I would slog through the day with my lively one-year-old.

From then on, Austin was a mecca for reporters and anybody else alive to politics. Willie would bring home somebody new for dinner every night or so, or we'd all go out to eat Mexican food or barbecue. The style was relaxed and free-flowing, and I twitted Wheeler about the days he thought I'd end up in Houston or Dallas with a husband who put on a suit and tie every day and expected to see me in cocktail clothes in the evenings.

If our knives and forks matched, so much the better, but most of them didn't and nobody noticed. Everybody drank gallons of beer, and sometimes whiskey, and in the course of that first year I discovered margaritas. The parties were raucous, and at one of ours a big state representative pushed the refrigerator about four feet from its moorings. At one of Tom and Sally's, Willie went outside to pee and pushed his arm through the window of their little Triumph which, being plastic, suffered no lasting damage. But people spilled so much beer on the floor that it took off the finish, and the smell of cigarettes, onions, and alcohol the next day was so revolting they left the house and didn't come back until midafternoon to face the clean-up.

From time to time, guys from the other side showed up, like once when Lieutenant Governor Ben Barnes crashed one of our parties, to the amazement of two state legislators who immediately caught him up in a heated discussion on the gas tax. Larry Goodwyn, long before he began thinking about his seminal work on American populism, would launch into fierce arguments with a state senator about political strategy, and he'd get so carried away that once Ronnie compared him to a guy in a light factory turning off all the switches.

The professors could be as feisty as the pols. Silber was so combative he was once asked to leave, though not from our house. Arrowsmith might be raging against a new Shell station down the hill from his house, spoiling a view that reminded him of the hills around Florence. Shattuck, who was much gentler than either, might be off in a corner comparing the *Observer* to the *Village Voice*. Two women who spent most evenings vamping somebody or other got into a running contest to see who could screw the most visiting dignitaries, and their competition was so ferocious that one of them ended up breaking into a lake house with a noted author to steal some steaks and wound up walking down the Drag a few days later with two black eyes he'd given her, along with a passel of bruises.

Some of our best times were when the men from the national press came flooding into Austin and sat around our living room telling wild tales about their travels or the politicians they followed. One night a big blond guy from the *New York Times* named Tom Wicker walked in the door with Douglas Cater from *The Reporter,* and when I met Tom, I felt an extra charge of energy I hadn't yet learned to identify. Years later I would find out that he had said to himself at precisely that moment, "Someday I'm gonna know that woman," and sure enough one day he did.

But that was long after my life began to inch up from the abyss into which it now began to slide. For two problems were beginning to come into focus: motherhood and work. As an engineer's daughter, I had no trouble making our lives function in a practical sense. But my son was a different matter altogether.

David was slow to talk but a blur of energy, and it wasn't long before he started going places he shouldn't—out a window, over a fence, through barred gates. Like Willie, he hated going to bed, and Willie refused to let him cry himself to sleep; no matter what I said, he would pick him up after a few howls and bring him into our bed. I sensed that my beloved child was in pain but didn't know what to do about it and thought it must be my fault.

So I turned to Jayne, who had a superb way with children—her native gift having survived her degree in education—and she introduced me to A. S. Neill's *Summerhill*, a manifesto for permissive child-rearing. Neill ran a school in England where children thrived on a minimum of discipline. I wanted David to be full of joy and curiosity, for so often I myself had felt like Pip when Miss Havisham commanded him to play, and I wanted something different for my son. So I resolved to let him do whatever he wanted short of injuring himself, and when the chaos began to invade my psyche, I just lectured myself on patience.

Then there was my own work, which seemed to exist in a future so remote as to be very possibly a mirage. Always before I had been able to find solace in books, but it was hard to read alongside an energetic, curious boy who was sure to crash over or pull something down on himself just as I got to the best parts.

Jayne and Sally and I tried reading together—books like Edmund Wilson's *To the Finland Station*, Colin Wilson's *The Outsider*, and one of Camus's latest. But the effort felt unreal, as though we were lifting heavy weights just for the hell of it. Unlike my Oxford friends or, for that matter, our gang at the university, nobody around us gave a damn about either Wilson, and the only one interested in Camus was Ronnie, who waxed poetic about him, though Ronnie was not noted for dialogue.

The only women I knew who had paid jobs were teaching school, but having the responsibility for some twenty-odd children seemed to me just twenty times harder than having the one. My house got more disorderly, dishes piled up, I left wet diapers on the floor for hours, toys lay strewn all about. And soon alarm bells began to go off in the night.

My first intimation that our lives as women might be far more perilous and problematic than we had ever dreamed came through Theresa, my oldest friend—the freckle-faced yo-yo champ with bubble gum in her ears. She was living in Austin with a small child when we got there, and one day she came over with bruises on her arms. Her husband was a swaggering guy with a temper, and she blushed and trembled when she told me he had hit her. She was six months pregnant, and since moving in with us was scarcely a real option, I didn't know how to help her.

One night a few weeks later, Theresa's husband got drunk and came after her again. She swept her boy under her arm, ran down the street in her nightgown carrying him, and had the good luck to flag a police car cruising by. The cops arrested her husband and kept him in jail until she could pack up and move back to Houston, where she had the second baby. At least once she tried reconciling, but it did not, and could not, work.

Then the nightmare really began, for Theresa started flaking into bits and pieces. Maybe a year later, I went to Houston, only to discover that she was living alone in an apartment while her children were with her parents. Her mother, Connie, told me the boy had cut his foot and Theresa had just let it bleed, so she and Blake, Theresa's father, had taken in the children. As she spoke, Connie was crying.

No one answered Theresa's door, but it was unlocked and I walked into a squalid room where everything was a scramble—clothes strewn around, remnants of food on dirty plates, shades half drawn over filthy windows, the whole place stinking of urine. Then I heard a muffled noise and made my way out through the kitchen to find Theresa crying on the back stoop with her head on her knees. Her hair was limp and tangled, her dress dingy, her nails bitten deep into the quick. My presence barely registered, and she kept saying she wanted her babies.

I finally persuaded Theresa to come home with me and called Connie to ask if she minded my interfering. She said "Oh no!" and sobbed that in fact she'd be grateful, for she and her husband had simply given up. The next day I went to see Theresa's priest, who blathered. And when I got home, she was doing what she'd been doing by then for two days— walking around aimlessly, mumbling about needing to take care of her babies when she clearly couldn't take care of herself. She had trouble, in fact, deciding to go from one room to the next.

It was the first time I had heard that plaintive, hopeless cry from a friend whose life had spiraled beyond her control, and I was hurt, angry, and frightened. Convinced after three days that Theresa might even try to kill herself, I decided that the best thing we could do was to get her into the psychiatric hospital in Galveston. She had been there before, I now discovered—obviously to no avail—but it seemed our only chance. And she would have to be committed.

Daddy volunteered to leave work early and drive us. Theresa's mother had insisted that Blake, rather than she, go with us to sign the papers, though Theresa told me to my horror that he'd pulled a knife on her once and that he'd made her pull down her panties and beaten her bare bottom with a leather belt. So Daddy told her gently what we were going to do and, knowing he would be her sole protection, promised he would never leave her alone with her father. Luckily, I didn't find out until later that Theresa had already tried to commit suicide, but every time we pulled up at a light, I was afraid she'd open the door and run. When we stopped for something to eat and she went to the restroom, I stood outside in the corridor.

Daddy kept incredibly calm, and since Blake was sitting in the front seat with him, things seemed under control. But the strain was terrific, and when I woke up the next day, every muscle and nerve in my body hurt. Daddy had both driven the car and distracted Blake, and I could hardly imagine how he must feel. But we were proud of one another.

For months I railed against the Catholic church for convincing Theresa that she was in the wrong for not being able to make her marriage work and for making her feel her life was over. I was so angry that I made a cutting remark to a nominal Catholic who took it personally and attacked me for it more than twenty years later.

Theresa was in and out of hospitals, and I saw her now and then until I left Texas. She was invariably sweet and confused. And finally one night some five years after our trip to Galveston, she took enough of the pills she had carefully hoarded to succeed at what she had tried to do repeatedly. Her grandmother wrote that she looked beautiful in her coffin, and in my desolation, I began to wonder for the first time about the way the American Dream worked for women.

CHAPTER ELEVEN

few months after I helped commit Theresa, Orissa Eckhardt
slashed her throat and wrists. Her former husband, Bob
Eckhardt, had been one of the twin heroes of Ronnie's *Observer*—the
other was Senator Ralph Yarborough—and he was fast becoming
Willie's. He was a state representative from Houston whom the liberals
expected to run for Congress, and though many tears were shed for
Orissa, the general sentiment seemed to be that she had been brilliant
but unstable. Bob was now going out with Bill Brammer's estranged
wife Nadine, and the world moved on.

And it wasn't long before I began to wonder if the world might leave
me behind too, if in a less dramatic and horrible way. For the excitement of life around the *Observer* had not been able to obscure the fact
that I could not reach my husband, and I asked Sarah Payne, who managed the paper, "Other people like to talk to me. Why doesn't Willie?"
He whizzed in and out of town, absorbed in what he was learning about
Texas, and dismissed my worries about David as though they were the
detritus of an idle brain.

Then late one Friday night at the Scholz Garten in the summer of
1961, a few days after I'd had a routine D&C, I began hemorrhaging.
Willie took me to the hospital, where I got violently sick while being
stuffed with gauze like some Thanksgiving turkey, and the doctor told
him to leave me there. I begged him to pick me up early the next morning, for a woman was dying of cancer in the next bed and the air in the
room was rancid with misery.

When he hadn't come by nine, I called home but no one answered. I phoned my parents in Houston to ask if they'd keep David for a week so I could rest, and they said they were on their way. Then I dialed home every fifteen or twenty minutes until noon, when Willie finally answered. He got to the hospital an hour later with David in a soggy diaper full of excrement and said virtually nothing while I checked out, or on the way home, or indeed for the rest of the day. After Mama and Daddy whisked David away, he spent the afternoon watching football while I lay stricken in the bedroom.

It was so hot—maybe 95 degrees indoors—that a thin sheet felt like a Navajo blanket. A rusty fan shoved dank air from one end of the bed to another in a monotonous clickety clack. Big flies sat on the dresser and the windowsills, and you could have killed scores if you'd had the energy, which I didn't. The smell of urine had soaked into the floor, and plate-sized black patches marked the places where I had dropped wet diapers and left them. I was weak and profoundly alone; Jayne and Mark had just moved to El Paso, Peggy and Ralph had gone to Ceylon, and Sally and I had not yet broken through the code of silence behind which we hid our anxieties.

Had I been the strong, healthy woman I passed for, that would have been it, I think—the moment I admitted that, for whatever reason, the marriage was impossible. Willie and I did not speak the same language, and though I'm loath to be sentimental, perhaps being unable to reach out and be kind hurt him as much as it did me. He was still breaking free from a mother whose needs were overwhelming and who counted on him to fill them, and his father had been no model at all. But that day marked a breach we would never heal.

Such was the power of the past, however—with its layers of inherited patterns that went back for generations, along with its images of men's and women's roles and the ties Willie and I had forged from our respective blends of strength and frailty—and so radical and deep, if unacknowledged, were my own self-doubts—that whatever thoughts I had about leaving him have left no residue. I had chosen Willie freely, he was David's father, and I summoned my courage to find another source of strength.

By the time night fell and crickets shattered the silence, I had resolved to begin graduate school and work toward my doctorate. I needed a profession and colleagues who spoke the same language, and then, once more, books would be my guide and solace.

But not the only one. For sometime that fall, Willie and I were with friends I'll call Jack and Jill. A person they loved had died, and Jill was weeping on the sofa. Willie had his arm around her shoulder, and suddenly, a voice suggested that we switch partners.

I don't remember having any feelings whatever. I simply suggested that Jack take me home and told him, on the way, that I had never slept with anyone but Willie and couldn't begin this way. I said goodnight and then, like generations of women before me, went on automatic pilot. I shut my eyes against my soul's pain, said nothing the next day to Willie, and brushed aside Jill's apology as unnecessary.

But a few weeks later, the rage I didn't even know how to recognize, much less acknowledge, erupted when I fell into bed with a beautiful man, and then found myself truly, bewilderingly in love. When he said, in effect, "Let's do life!" I heard an oddly familiar voice saying, "Let's do . . ."

He was an Englishman with a bawdy laugh named John Sullivan who looked like Alan Bates in his prime. His thick brown hair was so dark it seemed black in a certain light, and it was always falling alluringly over his forehead. He had merry brown eyes with fine lines that fanned out at the sides and crinkled when he was happy and an easygoing disposition that made the crinkles permanent.

A working-class kid from Liverpool who had gone to Cambridge on scholarship, he had won a starred double first in classics, a distinction seldom conferred even twice in a decade. Bill Arrowsmith had brought him to the University of Texas to edit the new journal *Arion,* which was declaring war on fustiness and limp prose in a vibrant, sinewy language that the antiquarian approach to classics had nearly smothered. As novelist Frederick Rafael, who'd been with him in Cambridge, would write, John was an iconoclast who "did not accept received opinions nor did he confuse an academic with a quiet life."

Arrowsmith had discovered John, in fact, because they had both done racy new translations of Petronius, an author and courtier in Nero's court who'd been described as a man "with a certain air of nonchalance [that] charmed people all the more by seeming so unstudied." *And that was John as well.* Like the Beatles, fellow Liverpudlians with his gusto and whimsy, John had learned to work hard, celebrate both love and lust, and relish absurdity in whatever forms he found it. (An odd outfit could send him into peals of laughter.) Wonderfully generous to people he cared for, he was as nonjudgmental as Bill Brammer, who became his friend in a handshake.

Our connections had come through Oxford; he had called, and I had invited him over and then volunteered to take him shopping and teach him to drive. He, in turn, had offered to teach me enough Latin to pass the reading exams for a graduate degree in English.

And over the next couple of months, in the interstices of these worthy projects, he had told me about his domestic life, which was complicated. Just out of college, he had married a woman ten years his senior—a marriage that was an overnight disaster. After several years, he had left her and moved to Oxford to be a fellow at Jesus College, but his wife had refused to divorce him even when he began living with another woman. Finally he had come to the United States, in part so he could get a divorce and marry again.

Not long after Christmas, his fiancée broke an engagement she said had dragged on too long, and it cannot have been more than ten minutes after we became lovers that I learned at last what all the fuss was about—what all those songs and plays and books down through the ages had been talking of. For in the end, an uptight, lonely, brittle young woman was transformed.

I discovered sex. I discovered passion. I was anguished, guilty, confused, exhilarated. Suddenly I felt glad to inhabit a woman's body, as John and I made love not only in the likely places but also in the woods across the lake, on the top floor of the university tower, in a rare books library with a bust of Vergil looking on, and in a field outside the city, where I had my first "proper" orgasm a few minutes before the police spotted the car and came to ask if anyone needed them.

On top of being a wonderful lover, John took my work seriously before I did. (He would be a founder of the feminist caucus within the American Philological Association.) Through him, I came under the sway of the Cambridge critic F. R. Leavis, who demanded that literature satisfy canons of moral seriousness and psychological depth. You expected something, and if it wasn't there, you said so—a heretical notion in a culture like ours, which operated on the assumption that if you couldn't say something nice, you shouldn't say anything at all.

"It is well to start by distinguishing the few really great," Leavis wrote in *The Great Tradition,* "the major novelists who count in the same way as the major poets, in the sense that they not only change the possibilities of the art for practitioners and readers, but that they are significant in terms of the human awareness they promote; awareness of the possibilities of life." This was thrilling stuff, and when John, by way of Leavis, introduced me to novelists like Henry James and George Eliot, they had a lasting impact.

The key question was what "moral" meant, however, for I was violating everything I had believed in; though I'd always found a tiny fib so hard-going that an astute seven-year-old could have seen right through me, now I lied brazenly about where I was going and where I'd been, and one night I even hid in a gully from a prying neighbor. (It helped to know that Willie was sleeping around, but somehow I never thought that what he did "justified" my own betrayal.)

While the electricity John and I generated was so strong it could have ignited a dry bush in the next county, I defied the gossips—John was simply a delightful friend who was teaching me Latin—and helped Willie believe the line he clearly wanted to. My guard slipped once, when Bob Childres was visiting and I got drunk enough to tell him. But Brammer was the only person in Austin in whom John and I confided.

As one magical month followed another, we discovered chorizos together, and he introduced me to cannelloni and to Auden:

> *Lay your sleeping head, my love,*
> *Human on my faithless arm;*
> *Time and fevers burn away*
> *Individual beauty from*
> *Thoughtful children, and the grave*
> *Proves the child ephemeral:*
> *But in my arms till break of day*
> *Let the living creature lie,*
> *Mortal, guilty, but to me*
> *The entirely beautiful. . . .*

He taught me to appreciate good wine and read Yeats. And he made me laugh, for he wrote doggerel with many delicious verses, my favorite being as follows:

Of all pornographers
None was coarser
Than that randy old pilgrim
Geoffrey Chaucer.
His Wife of Bath
Was lewd and merry:
No wonder they never got
To Canterbury.

Sometimes he even wrote a poem for me, so that in no very long time I learned why people die for love. And in the next few years I would come perilously close.

Everything about that year seemed magnified: beer came by the pitcher, whiskey by quart; balance tipped and proportion vanished. The pain was more acute, the joy more intense, the parties rowdier, the laughter crazier, the politics more preposterous. Many years later, when someone wondered what had brought Tom Wicker and me together, I asked Tom if he hadn't been in Austin trailing the vice-president, and he guffawed: "How could you forget? I came because seventy-one people were running for the U.S. Senate!"

The legislature took up a bill requiring everyone who worked for the state to swear to the *existence* of a Supreme Being—not to their *belief* in one—and virtually the only people who could testify against it were ministers, who were certifiably "good." When a Presbyterian student of Ralph Person's named Stonewall Jackson McMurry III read to the committee from Mill's *On Liberty,* a representative rared back in his big chair and asked huffily, "Who the hell's this John Stuart Mill?" Willie would write about his associate editor, Bob Sherrill, that he came to laugh and stayed because there was so much to laugh at.

With David in nursery school half the day, I threw myself into teaching freshman English, where, for the first time, I read Alan Paton's *Cry, the Beloved Country,* though only a few days ahead of my students. Talking about apartheid in South Africa gave us a screen behind which to think about American racism, for I doubt that many students had given much thought to what it meant to be black in Texas, much less had imagined a black man as a moral hero. And the challenge was all the greater because I had a black woman student who sat all alone in the seat closest to the windows at the end of the front row with an arc of empty seats around her until gradually, over the three months we met, the rest of the students moved in to fill them.

Graduate school was harder on my moral and aesthetic certainties; I found *Paradise Lost* so compelling that I managed to swallow even the infamous lines, "He for God, She for God in him," which put women decidedly in "their place." Though I knew Milton had been a tyrant to his daughters, I wrote of him so admiringly the professor called my paper a labor of love. And then I fell in thrall to the Victorians, who seemed full of grit and despair in equal measure.

Nor could I think of a better or more appropriate combination, for if there was a center, it wasn't holding. Daddy had retired and bought a house in the Hill Country, where his war against Nana went nuclear while Mama drank herself numb. And once, when Willie's mother was visiting and began nagging him about something or other, he threw a ham across the kitchen and disappeared for several hours.

David jammed his head through the bars in a nursery school gate—a feat unprecedented in the school's twenty-five-year history—and it took a crowbar to get him out. Then he climbed out a baby sitter's window, ran down a steep hill through a barbed-wire fence, and skidded out onto a busy street where cars swerved to miss him. More than one friend said I should beat him within an inch of his life; others said it was a phase he would grow out of. Neither convinced me, but I had *no* idea what to do, and muddling through seemed the only option.

Then I realized that John was sleeping with other women, but when I confronted him, he was philosophical about it—otherwise, he said, people would catch on to *us*. And though the words made sense, the emotion did not. His house became known as "Liberty Hall," and at one of his increasingly famous parties, I was so miserable that a woman I scarcely knew told him that, bizarrely enough, I had seemed jealous. And though before that year I hadn't had the slightest idea what jealousy was, I knew she was right.

Two years of the *Observer* was all Willie wanted, and so, facing the grim prospect of leaving John and Austin, I applied for a Woodrow Wilson Fellowship and admission to several graduate schools. After the acceptances came, I decided it would be only fair to let Willie choose between Columbia and Stanford since, after all, he would have to find work wherever we went. Of course I assumed he would pick New York, with so many Oxford friends in close proximity, and when he chose Stanford instead, I was aghast, for I literally could *not* imagine how I would cope.

At the prospect of parting, John sat in my living room and told me solemnly that he wanted to marry me and father my children, and I replied that I needed time to think. We both knew these things already but had to speak for the record. He managed to smile, though I did not.

At the big farewell party he gave me, I got so drunk by midnight I had to be carried home. And the next morning, as I lay in his bed, I felt for the first—and, as it would prove, the last—time that I wanted to stay *forever* exactly where I was. But finally the stoic genes kicked in, and I got up and left.

Willie and David and I drove out of Austin at sundown that evening and then across the desert to El Paso through a moonscape that looked as bleak as my spirit. And after a day or two at Jayne's and Mark's with Madeline and her baby sister Celia, Willie went back to Austin, where he intended to put out the *Observer* through the election, and I took David by the hand and climbed onto a plane for San Francisco.

The snug bungalow where it all began for me

Our gang, my first

Daddy and his little girl running toward him on Galveston beach

Wrapped in a towel after a dip in Galveston Bay and huddling on the running board next to my favorite uncle, Mickey, with Grandma looking on

*With Mama,
before the hard
times came*

*The big house on Buffalo Speedway, where we moved when I was
thirteen*

*Mama holding Glenn in 1945 with me sitting next to them,
hoping for the best*

E. A. Snapp, Jr., with his girls' swimming team

A typical moment in the elegant life of River Oaks

With Madeline, Jayne, and others acting silly at a fraternity costume party

With Willie at the Theta house

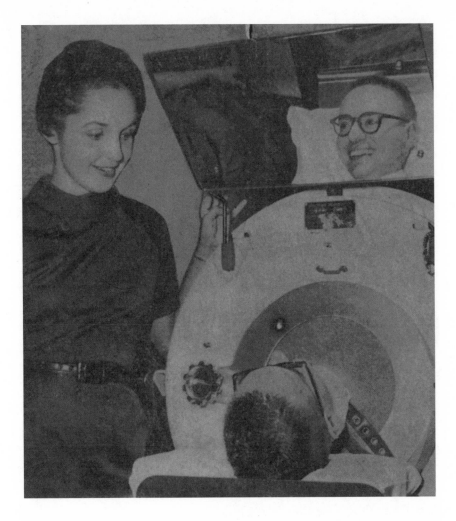

With Barry Bishop in the only picture he allowed taken after polio confined him to an iron lung

Receiving an armful of roses as Sweetheart of the University,
while the audience sang "The Eyes of Texas"

With Willie after he received his degree in the Sheldonian Theatre at Oxford

John Sullivan in my New York apartment, with David and Ichabod in the mid-70s

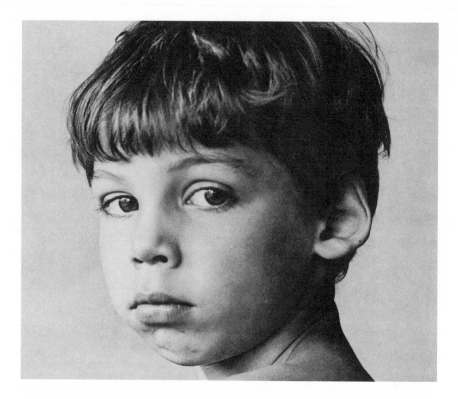

David at seven, captured by Hans Namuth in a petulant moment in Mississippi

Mother and adolescent son cutting up on winter holiday in Minnesota

With Bob Eckhardt, enjoying one of our favorite pastimes

Daddy in our living room, reading my Christmas promise of a lavish dinner of his choosing only a few months before he died

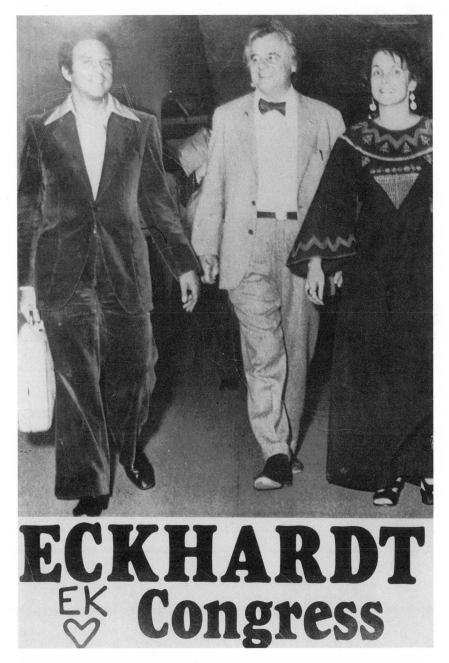

ECKHARDT
E K
♡
Congress

With Bob and Andy Young at the Houston International Airport

With Shirley Garner and Sally Leach at a Plan II reunion

Friends for more than forty years. Seated from left to right:
Sam Perry, me, Sally Leach, Peggy Person. Kneeling behind: Bill
Arnold and Ray Farabee

CHAPTER TWELVE

*T*he most important thing Stanford taught me was that good things *can* come from cruel times, but in 1962 that idea seemed little more than a piece of idle, well-meaning rhetoric. I spent most of my time there grinding my teeth, the beauty of northern California filtered through a haze of pain, and my hands began to tremble. I took hard courses from fine professors, worked doggedly, now and again knew inspiration, and ended with as good a master's degree as I could have gotten anywhere in the country. But it is the experience I am happiest never to have to repeat.

After two years in the midst of a flamboyant crowd engaged in political fights over serious issues where lives might be at stake, I felt like I'd been remanded to junior high. Palo Alto seemed a small town where nothing happened, and Stanford, a place where uneasy young professors in tight collars spent their energy shining up to old guys in tight collars whose energy had faded decades earlier.

As you walked past buildings a friend labeled "late Southern Pacific," you got no hint of the protests that would erupt a few years later, and anyone who suggested that the campus might be a dormant volcano would surely have been written off as a true, if harmless, eccentric. During the ten months I spent in Palo Alto, the nation edged through the Cuban missile crisis, Medgar Evers was killed, and Martin Luther King, Jr., gave his mesmerizing speech at the Lincoln Memorial—while Stanford students threw Frisbees in the quad and roped surfboards to the tops of Porsches.

Much later I would realize that I'd just missed the birth of a cultural revolution in the area. Joan Baez, who had gone to high school in Palo Alto, gave a concert at Stanford that Shirley and I attended. As I recall, we thought she had a beautiful voice but wondered why she sang barefoot and found her running political commentary tedious. Unbeknownst to me, Jerry Garcia and others who would become the Grateful Dead, along with a remarkable number of other musicians on the verge of colossal success, were learning their trade and finding their voices in bars on the fringes of Palo Alto and the towns just around it.

But Shirley was there, and the friendship that began ten years earlier, when we drilled each other on why Rome fell and the thirteen uses of the olive, now began to develop into something durable. She had gone to Stanford when Willie and I left for England, so by the time I got there, she had made a place for herself. After helping me find a nursery school for David, she guided me through a first-rate syllabus and faculty. And with her husband away for months on geology field trips, we began spending our spare time together. David now had an aunt and I, a sister.

He was a baffling child, rude and winsome by turns. Though lithe and full of energy, he found it hard to connect with people he didn't know. He would freeze at a direct question, often turning sullen or using a kind of sign language, letting his eyes talk for him. When I left him at school, he would cry as he had in Austin, and then settle down to play, more often than not by himself. Alone with me, he seemed happy, though so anxious and clinging at bedtime that our pediatrician eventually prescribed sleeping pills.

One night Shirley and I put a latch on his door and I said he had to stay in his bedroom and go to sleep, but he shrieked with such abandon that we could not bear it and finally let him out. Years later she told the story to a psychiatrist who scolded her for backing down, and she said, "But you should have heard him wail!"

Sometimes I was sure that David was troubled because I was—a conviction that could do nothing but intensify my own misery. But he seemed so unlike me that I felt at a loss to think how to reach him. I could explain only so many times that being rude or sullen was bad and, furthermore, that if he were rude and sullen to other children, they wouldn't play with him and he would be lonely. Still, common sense did not take us far. So I sought out friends and took David along, hoping that the pleasure the adults took in each other's company would spill over and make him more secure.

So it happened that often, on weekends, I would take David to the San Francisco zoo or to watch planes take off at the airport, and then head to Chinatown to see Jerry Wilson, my friend with the antic spirit who'd seemed a brother since I met him as a freshman at the University of Texas and who loved David like a nephew. Or Jerry would come to Palo Alto, where once, as he walked in to find David captivated by a puzzle of the world, he was startled to hear a three-year-old cry, "I've lost Afghanistan!"

Now and again we would go to my sophomore roommate Sydney's Marin County mansion, which had a walk-in fireplace and an Otis elevator with a telephone where she used to hide to get away from her children. It had pantries, closets, nooks, and crannies where David and Sydney's three kids could play hide-and-seek indefinitely while Sydney and I fixed meals that seemed to run into one another.

That year these friendships took on more weight than friendships ever had with me, for I was engaged in what felt at times like a life-and-death struggle to decide what to do about John Sullivan. He had freed my body and spirit from a repression I hadn't known existed, and I couldn't imagine a more intense longing than I felt to hold him and be held in turn.

But Willie was David's father, and I thought he needed me, while I knew that John did not. I wasn't convinced that my failures of intimacy with Willie justified breaking a commitment made in good faith. And I was not only grateful—through him I'd had a life more interesting than any I could have expected otherwise—but I thought he would go on fighting the good fight I believed in and wanted to be part of.

My quandary seemed hopeless. I would drive up and down, in and around the hills above Stanford, wondering all the while how people could make lists of pros and cons, for it seemed a bloodless exercise. For hours I would sit staring out a friend's huge picture window at the boats sailing gaily around Alcatraz in San Francisco Bay—tempted to flip a coin since I could argue persuasively for one side or the other. The stone that Sisyphus was condemned to shove eternally up a hill could not have felt heavier, and perhaps it was the weight itself that finally did it.

I decided at last in negatives; I couldn't leave Willie unless I couldn't stay, and I thought I *could* stay. Still, there *was* a trigger. I was taking the exit to Chinatown when it dawned on me that the afternoon before I left, John had slept with a woman he'd just met and had invited on the spur of the moment to my party. She had looked baffled and responded oddly that night when I mentioned what John had said they'd done together that afternoon, and suddenly, months later, I understood why.

I felt so sick I pulled the car over until David threatened to open the door and run, and then I got furious that John hadn't even waited until I left to begin a new relationship. I knew then that he could never be faithful and that I couldn't bear that.

Still, I had never written a letter more painful. A few months later, on a bus crossing the Mojave Desert, I sobbed while reading *The Age of Innocence,* which read like my own story, and I would never be sure I had made the right decision. I only knew that if I had left Willie and married John, my life and David's would have been very different.

It was yet another powerful man who would prove in some measure my salvation. He was a native New Yorker named Irving Howe, a Jewish socialist who had come to Stanford a year earlier after leaving his wife for a woman who then had decided not to leave her husband. He had turned for solace to a pair of graduate students, Bill Wyman and Jane Daley, who were good friends of Shirley's, and by the time I got to Palo Alto, they had a ready-made group and I joined it.

I remember the first time I saw Irving in the quad at Stanford, standing with his hands in his pockets and his head tilted, with a wry expression I found indescribably touching. It was our common misery, really, that brought Irving and me together; his pain made it seem as though we lived in the same universe. Sitting over steins of beer in one of those grungy student bars that fringe every university campus, I actually told Irving my sad story even before I told Shirley, and his mocking eyes grew gentle. And I think that's what bridged the gigantic distances between us. I had let Irving know that I was holding onto a window ledge on the twentieth floor with the tips of my fingers. I knew that after I managed to climb back into the room, I needed to learn all over again how to live. And that's what Irving taught me. He showed me how to transcend my pain by transcending his own through his ravenous appetite for politics, literature, and ideas, and in the candor, outrage, and laughter he brought to speaking and writing of them.

For obvious reasons Irving was in a mood as foul as mine, and he hated Stanford with bracing clarity. He found those surfboarding California students bland and appallingly polite. So here was this mesmerizing, mercurial guy who seemed innocent in many ways, and who was funny, tough, and skittish around dogma, brushing aside the standard lit crit pieties.

Once he asked in class, as he was likely to do as a way of leading into a discussion, "What was the first thing you thought about when you read *Old Times on the Mississippi?*" An excited young man about halfway back started waving his hand, and when Irving called on him he said, after T. S. Eliot, that Twain "had found the perfect objective correlative for his emotions." He sat back looking immensely pleased with himself as Irving abruptly stopped pacing and stared. I gulped as Irving asked, with elaborate politeness, "Is that *really* the first thing you thought of?" The eager young man assured him: "Yes, it certainly was!" And then I let my breath out slowly as Irving said, "I believe it!" and dropped his head, starting to pace again.

When he thought my academic work was good, his glee was infectious. When I was bumbling, he was usually patient and never cruel. At the end of my first paper, on *Huck Finn,* he wrote, "Almost, almost," which in the years that followed I thought might become my epitaph. Fondness didn't make him easy, but from time to time, he would pat me on the shoulder and say, "Come on, baby, stop kvetching and do the footnotes!"

His zest was irresistible, along with his lovely self-mockery. I recall the picture he drew of taking out a nice woman who was a musician and getting stuck schlepping her cello. Irving could always win you to his side by picturing himself as the guy who invariably got stuck schlepping the cello. He had this Woody Allen way of mocking his own gracelessness that made me forget most of the time that for a deeply cultured and sophisticated man, he was the most parochial person I'd ever known.

I'm not convinced that Irving ever took me quite seriously, though he would write in my copy of his best-selling *The World of Our Fathers,* "To my favorite student, my dear friend." The fact that I was a *shiksa* from Texas and had never actually known a communist was a fatal disqualification, I think, in Irving's eyes. In 1964 he ended a letter to Bill and Jane by saying, "Why don't you folks come to the next MLA meeting in New York City . . . and see the big-time?" Then he added: "I was in Texas: sort of a cheap version of Palo Alto." But Irving was *such* a ham you overlooked a lot, for he would get caught up and sometimes even lost in his own fantasizing—he had, as Jane put it, a streak of madness—and it was thrilling to be on the scene when it took him by the throat.

As we read a string of fine books under his tutelage—*Tess of the D'Urbervilles, The Portrait of a Lady, The Sound and the Fury, Middlemarch*—Irving showed us how to be generous without turning our brains to mush by finding the best in Hemingway, for instance, a writer with whom you'd think he would have no affinity. Sometimes he'd say he was giving life lessons rather than teaching literature, but usually I think he was doing both.

Once I remember suppressing a powerful instinct to laugh out loud when Irving, in his best New Yorker's imitation of a southern accent, read from *Old Times on the Mississippi*. It was a little like the Oxford Players when they did Tennessee Williams and one character said, "I think I'll go on down to the laboratory," putting the accent on that second syllable. And I had the chutzpah to disagree with him; once I wrote slightingly of "The Wasteland," and Irving responded by saying, "Celia, you're going to be a crotchety old lady." Which wasn't the half of it.

Willie arrived just before Christmas—relaxed and off duty, good with David, and genial company. Since I was the reason we were at Stanford, I may have had more weight in his eyes, as well as my own, so that we almost recaptured our original equality. And though the "good" Willie exacerbated my guilt, he also made me think I had made the right decision and we could pull this marriage off.

After spending a couple of months sitting in on classes, he applied for a fellowship to get a Ph.D. in history. He was admitted to the graduate school but denied the fellowship, and without it we couldn't afford to stay. So he took off on the bus for New York to talk with John Fischer at *Harper's* magazine. A former Rhodes scholar from Oklahoma, Fischer had written to say that he admired Willie's work and liked the idea of establishing a Rhodes tradition at *Harper's*.

After a few weeks, Willie came back full of New York City, and around the time he decided we were moving there, Irving announced that he too was escaping Stanford to join the faculty of a new graduate school at the City University of New York. So he proposed that I go with him instead of going to Columbia. I wrote two English professors in Austin for their advice, and they both said, "Go with Irving Howe." And so I did.

Committing myself to Irving meant, ultimately, that if I ever had, I would never again see things simply. Irving was a Jew, and I came out of a Protestant ethos. He was a socialist and I, a liberal Democrat. He was an urban sophisticate while my roots were in the Western frontier tradition with an admixture of Olde England. Most important, he was a man and I, a woman—the elemental fact that would ultimately undermine our friendship.

But if Irving was the sign of a bent I already had for complicating things, he may have been the best proof of its value. His mark on me is rich and indelible: he taught me once more to fall on my face and get up again. He confirmed my belief that politics mattered and books were worth a lifetime commitment. And whenever I take on something new, I think about how Irving would have read it.

Most of all, during the hardest years of my life, he was my mentor, my inspiration, and my friend. I treasured him and he knew it. He taught me to work steadily, in my own way, for a world more attractive. And for as long as I live, whenever I find myself in one of the cruel places, I'll feel his hand on my shoulder and hear him saying tenderly, "Come on, baby, stop kvetching and do the footnotes!"

In May, Willie flew David to Austin to stay with my parents while I finished my master's thesis, and he then went on to lay the groundwork for our arrival in New York City. While taking Irving's Henry James seminar, I had decided to write on *The Awkward Age*, according to Leavis one of his most brilliant novels and one in which the relations between men and women were even more tangled and morally complex than usual. I was so lonely without David that I worked fast, and by the end of a month, Irving said, "It's good enough. Get out of here!" So Shirley and Jerry gave me a farewell dinner and put me on a bus for El Paso.

After two days at Jayne's with Madeline and Celia, I flew on to Austin, where no sooner did I get my fill of hugging my blessed little boy and coaxing him into forgiving my desertion than I was blind-sided by Daddy's war on Nana. He had refused to let David go into her room, and the day after I got there, while Mama sat weeping into her tumbler of vodka, I heard him shout at her that she was filthy. When I tried calling the airline to change our tickets, my hands were trembling so badly I could not hit the right numbers.

Too many other people I knew in Austin were miserable, notably John, though he put on a jaunty air. And finally, since I either made things worse or could do nothing to help, I packed up David and escaped on a nonstop jet to LaGuardia Airport.

CHAPTER THIRTEEN

*N*ew York City taught me that I'm at heart an urban peasant, to borrow a phrase of Vivian Gornick's, and if that seems odd for a woman from the suburbs of Houston, Texas, so be it. Perhaps there *is* something to the notion that we are born with affinities we discover only when we're lucky enough to find the settings or circumstances that evoke them, and New York turned out to be my heart's setting. For walking the streets of that great city leaves me in a state of exaltation for which nothing had prepared me. I came near dying there, and it may well be that the sheer energy of Manhattan was my salvation.

Apart from Oxford, I had mostly lived in places where nobody walked, so the physical surge and tumult of the streets, not to mention the crowd's democracy, felt like a constant affirmation. Every day I met anew what was then called "the family of man." The life force is perpetually erupting there, and I found that one could know that a place can be cruel and dangerous and love it shamelessly.

As the years passed, Manhattan would turn into a metaphor for life itself without ever ceasing to be a literal place where the slightest thing could be absorbing—doorknobs, cornices, carvings high up on a building, shoes, hemlines, hairstyles, briefcases, hands, colors, street signs, manhole covers, noses, ears, horns, bells, human laughter. At one time or another I found each of these a source of wonder, not to mention the things for which New York is celebrated—its jazz clubs and museums, Lincoln Center, the ballet and dance, every kind of ethnic restaurant, the theater on Broadway and off, Carnegie Hall, the Battery and Central Park.

David and I had season tickets to the New York City Ballet just after it moved to Lincoln Center, when George Balanchine was in his prime and choreographing one new work after another for the best dancers of their generation—Suzanne Farrell, Peter Martins, Patricia McBride, Jacques d'Amboise, Allegra Kent. We saw Gelsey Kirkland debut in *The Firebird,* Cynthia Gregory in *Giselle,* and Mikhail Barishnikov just a few weeks after he defected.

We heard Pavarotti sing Roberto in *La Bohème,* Robert Merrill and Joan Sutherland in *La Traviata,* Beverly Sills as Lucia. We saw Julie Harris do Ophelia at the Delacorte Theater in Central Park and Nicol Williamson do Hamlet on Broadway. We heard Johnny Cash and Bob Dylan at Madison Square Garden, Alexander Schneider and Peter Serkin in a theater at the Metropolitan Museum, Pete Seeger at Hunter College, and Mahalia Jackson at Carnegie Hall. Had I kept the programs, I would have had to add an extra room to my house. Most of that was in the far, rather than the near future when David and I landed at LaGuardia in the summer of 1963, but it was in the air as a sense of promise.

Willie had taken a railroad flat a few blocks from *Harper's:* a third-floor walk-up on East 28th Street between Park Avenue and Lexington. On the ground floor were the Gibson Girl Bar and the Delmore Cafeteria, which drew the taxis and the cops so we never had to worry either about safety or cabs in a pinch. And though the windows apparently hadn't been washed on the outside for decades, you could make out the Empire State Building from David's. The kitchen was in our bedroom, which you had to go through to get to the toilet, and despite or perhaps because of its obvious shortcomings, it was a sporting place. People who made it up the stairs invariably gaped when they walked into a cheerful, inviting space, and for a while their expressions were worth the price of admission.

We had lived in a succession of furnished places, and now, for the first time, my nesting instincts came into play. After a week of sanding and painting, we discovered the Pottery Barn and a string of funky antique stores, and on weekends we would go with Bob Childres and his new wife Clare to flea markets in Connecticut and upstate New York where you could find Victorian chests, spool beds, or a dry sink with possibilities. I got a carpenter to use tiles I had brought from Amsterdam to make a bewitching coffee table of wormy chestnut that puzzled David, who wanted to see the worms.

Jack and Betty Fischer were not only welcoming but pulled strings to get David an interview at the Bank Street School, one of the best progressive schools in the country. Though Willie ritually brushed aside my anxieties about David, I was convinced that an ordinary nursery school would drive him deeper into isolation. So David needed help, I needed help to find ways to help him, and a lot was riding on this new start.

But on the way to the interview, our taxi had to slow down to ease past a pile-up that had happened no more than fifteen minutes earlier; a body was lying covered with a sheet and sirens were wailing from every direction. And when we got to Bank Street, David couldn't talk to his prospective teacher or put a simple puzzle together that ordinarily he'd have done in seconds. So I sat there with the leaden feeling that had grown so familiar; for although the crash may have jolted him, as it had me, it had *not* caused his troubles. And for them I had no solutions. It is one thing to grit your own teeth, but you cannot grit your child's. Nor could I command him to be light-hearted when I wasn't.

To my astonishment, Bank Street accepted David, and when I later asked the teacher why, she said, "He flirted with me!" Those big brown eyes had been as winsome to her as they were to me, and without her and other teachers like her there, I don't think David would have made it.

As it was, I spent the first couple of months sitting for hours a day in a corner of the roof garden until he trusted the school enough not to tear up when I moved toward the stairs. Once I'd scarcely got home when the phone rang to call me back; David had fallen off a jungle gym smack onto his head. I ran down the stairs, hailed a cab, said "Run the lights!" Once there, I raced up three flights and closed my eyes for a few seconds at his classroom door to calm myself before I burst in and grabbed him. We hugged one another and cried a little, and then his teacher took me aside and said she was puzzled because he hadn't thrown his hands up in the ordinary protective reflex. My face flushed hot and stayed that way, my teeth literally clattered, and after a while I took him home early and we carried on.

Willie was to write in *New York Days* that during this period, "Life pullulated for me." For me, on the other hand, a lot of it was plain hard work, and as sporting as the 28th Street apartment was, life had a tendency to close in there. No more jumping into the car and driving off to see planes land, or to watch seals on the rocks, or the surf breaking. Everything was *much* more of a production.

Several times a day I climbed up and down three flights of stairs, often with heavy bags of groceries and almost always with a four-year-old too big to carry but not quite big enough to find the stairs easy on his own. The laundry was three blocks away, and the wait for the machines tedious. Five days a week I took David down and across town to Bank Street and then picked him up when school was out. And since ours wasn't a neighborhood designed for kids—the nearest green space was Madison Square Park, which had a sand pile with a few pitiful grains of sand but mainly served as a hang-out for tattered, dirty men with pints of rotgut—I spent a lot of time arranging for little boys to come home with David and vice versa. Which meant, in turn, that I spent a good deal of time with their mothers, some of whom I enjoyed and some of whom I didn't.

In Willie's account of our time together in New York, I am also struck by the absence of dailiness. There are various ways to explain this, but the simplest is that his life and mine were very different then. And this was true for most men and women of our generation. Willie was absorbed in his thrilling new job, for which David and I were the backdrop. As he wrote in *New York Days, Harper's* magazine was the heart of his existence. On the other hand, the vast amounts of time David and I spent doing ordinary things together grounded me in the common life that stretches back for millennia and created a bond between us too strong and deep to violate with impunity.

As the City University Graduate Center was still under construction, our classes were held at Hunter College on Park and East 68th Street, a quick ride on the Lexington Avenue subway, which had a stop on our corner. So getting to class was the least of my worries. The problem was fitting everything in.

Apart from Irving, the best thing about CUNY was a medievalist named Helaine Newstead. It was she who had brought Irving to New York, and we liked each other. One of only two women professors I was to have in graduate school, she reminded me of Marian Davis at Texas— droll, tough-minded, superbly professional. In her mid-fifties and never married, she had the air of a woman with a romantic past that verged on the torrid. She got me a series of small stipends to cover tuition while introducing me to Chaucer beyond the prologue to the *Canterbury Tales,* for all of which I developed a passion, and then to Sir Thomas Malory, about whom I would write the initial chapter of my dissertation.

Willie loved bringing people home for lunch or dinner, for in the long history of *Harper's* there may have been another editor who lodged above a bar, but not within living memory. He was tickled the day he brought Jack Fischer and C. Vann Woodward to lunch, for instance, and I had fixed beef stroganoff and crème brulée, which seemed so incongruous in that setting. (It took me a while to learn that lunch was different from dinner—and lighter, usually—so it may have been only the three flights of stairs that saved us.)

I had only *just* discovered that history could be both interesting and beautifully written, and I felt awed at the prospect of meeting the dean of southern history. But Vann Woodward would turn out to be not only an intellectual influence—a southerner who wrote eloquently about the way the South had been corrupted and weakened by racism—but a real friend. We heard what an astronomer I later met would call "the cosmic click"—that instant recognition of affinity—and in that funky place began a process of weaving in and out of each other's lives that would last more than three decades.

Once we had John Silber to dinner along with Roger Baldwin, the colorful cofounder of the American Civil Liberties Union, and Norman Dorsen, by now a good friend, who would soon be the ACLU's president. Just past eighty, Baldwin was at least as vigorous as anybody there and entertained us with stories from his unconventional life.

One story was about being imprisoned as a conscientious objector during World War I and almost being locked out of Leavenworth one evening because he was outside the walls planting tomatoes when the bell rang for curfew. Another was about a sheriff on Martha's Vineyard whom he invited for a drink after assuring him solemnly that whoever had reported nudes frolicking on his beach must have had the DTs. Sitting on his porch, they were reminiscing happily, when they were struck dumb by the sight of a huge naked woman who rose from the ocean and slowly climbed the hundred steps up the cliff, then followed the path to his house and, without a word, walked up the porch stairs, crossed the wide-plank floor between them, and went inside. When the door banged after her, they sighed collectively and recommenced talking.

But I remember the evening best for what happened after we finished eating and I went to read David a bedtime story. I was halfway through one of C. S. Lewis's Narnia fables when I heard a knock at the door and opened it to find Baldwin with the dinner plates. I showed him the kitchen and, after he left with Norman, asked John and Willie, "What in the world were you all doing while an eighty-year-old man cleared the table?" Willie hadn't noticed, but John said he'd decided he had two choices: one was to jump up and help, and the other was to do it himself the next time. I was skeptical.

As always, the good, the lively, the interesting, and the awful mixed unpredictably in our lives. Just before Thanksgiving, David and I were going to the Upper West Side to visit a friend from Oxford with a daughter David's age, and as we climbed onto the cross-town bus at 86th Street, I heard a voice from a woman's transistor radio say, " . . . and Governor Connally was also shot." I froze for a second and then touched the woman's arm and asked, "What was that?" She turned slowly, looked down with a blotched face and unfocused eyes, and told me. And by the time she said, "Doesn't it just make you want to weep?" I was in tears. The president shot in Dallas, damn it, a city full of right-wing kooks and home-grown militia. I stumbled to a seat and pulled David onto my lap, and as I sat there trembling, I had no doubt, generally speaking, who had done it.

As soon as the bus pulled over and stopped on Central Park West, I scooped David up and ran three blocks to my friend's, and when she opened the door, we rushed to the television and then sank to the floor as Walter Cronkite choked up and took off his glasses, wiped his eyes, and announced that our golden prince, John F. Kennedy, was dead. And so began that whole wretched saga.

As Mary McGrory wrote more than thirty years later in the *Washington Post*, Jack Kennedy's "hold on people came from charm, not virtue. He perseveres as a uniquely romantic and charismatic figure in the American presidency. He made a whole generation of Americans into idealists, who then went to strange countries and ate bad food and worked for nothing to show America had a heart. He convinced his contemporaries that government service was glamorous and fine." Even those of us who didn't go into the Peace Corps or public office had nonetheless been inspired by his example to believe that things were possible we hadn't dreamed of earlier, and none of the shameful revelations that eventually came out quite destroyed the heightened sense of life he had awakened.

The next few days were a jumble of hysterical rumors, horrid scenes, stricken faces and deadly silences, sepulchral voices and dull, thudding drums. We had no television set, and when Bob Childres called to say that a nut named Ruby had shot Kennedy's suspected killer, we threw on our coats, ran down the stairs, and grabbed a taxi to the Childreses' place, where we watched that incredible scene played over and over while we drank and argued and wept.

Not long after Dallas, Tom Wicker was with us on 28th Street, wrung out still from having been on the press bus close to Dealey Plaza when the shots rang out, and I remember grilling him about Jackie Kennedy. By then we had heard so many stories about Jack's philandering that her dignity in the midst of this horror had seemed all the more awesome. We had thought her frivolous and vain, but in those few days, she won us forever. And I would realize that people who go through such traumas together have an indelible bond, even if they part.

Over the next year, old friends and new crisscrossed and mingled in that unlikely flat with the grimy windows. One evening we threw a cocktail party for Bill and Rose Styron, whom I was meeting for the first time and whose example would so fatefully shape Willie's idea of what a writer's life should be. Shirley came for Christmas, and over the holidays, Mike Hammond, with his friend Bughat, cooked a five-course Indian meal including the *chapati*s. But a lot of what happened in that apartment remains a blank; people who later became friends—some of them good friends—tell me we met there for the first time, and I don't remember it. I don't even remember their faces.

For my soul was fraying; from time to time, I could feel something slip, and I had no idea how to do things differently. Whenever the murk and confusion lifted, I came back to the same core problem: in some fundamental way Willie remained a stranger, and that failure of intimacy was eating into me like acid on soft tissue. On top of that, chaos was his natural habitat, while for me it was poison.

If I had not thought he needed me, it all would have been much easier. It might, in fact, have been a snap. I could have left with gratitude for the good times we'd had together—for places he had taken me and people he'd brought into my life, with admiration for the distance he'd come from a small town in the Mississippi Delta, with good wishes for what he was trying to do at *Harper's*.

But with a kind of elemental simplicity, Willie was convinced that he needed me, and he convinced me in turn. (Whether or not it was true— perhaps it was simply the romantic in him—this need was an article of faith between us, and so deeply did Willie believe it that he was later to write that his trauma over our separation had lasted longer than the marriage itself.)

Nevertheless, a year after we got to New York, my will cracked with the weight of his need on the one hand and of our failures of intimacy, the demanding work, the mess I was expected to tolerate or clean up, my anxiety about David, and the strains and stresses of a turbulent city on the other. I was thin and haggard, my hands shook. I was drinking so much I had a perpetual hangover and smoking so much I had a hacking cough. The empty space inside was pressing so hard against my vital organs that it was all I could do to breathe. I wrote a plaintive letter to Van Ooms, but he did not answer. I wrote another to John Silber, who wrote back cataloging my shortcomings.

I don't even remember what precipitated the break—perhaps nothing more than the sight of Willie's clothes strewn about, or another of his eighteen-hour wordless retreats to bed. But finally I told him he had to leave and pushed him out the door.

The next few weeks were horrible. I was so nearly paralyzed with grief and the heavy weight of failure that I asked a friend to organize David's birthday party, and though I know I didn't, I have an image of myself lying on the sofa with a towel over my forehead while little boys knocked candy out of *piñata*s.

Willie was so distraught that Bob Childres told him about my affair, arguing that he was taking on too much responsibility for the failures in our marriage. Willie pounded on the door until I had to open it, and when I did, he slugged me. And after the shock passed, I didn't much blame him; in fact, I think the pain was cleansing, like my relief that the lying was over. But when I took David to school, I had a deep gash in my lip and had to tell the teacher that David had seen us fight.

That fall was not only my worst semester at CUNY, but the worst in my academic life. Years later, when I looked over the papers I wrote then, I found them chilling—bleak, graceless, mechanical. I wasn't close to my fellow students, a city university being for the most part a place people zip in and out of. Irving was off writing a book and courting a woman he would subsequently marry. My New York friends were connected with Willie, whom I'd put indefinitely on hold, and I felt more of a burden to David than a blessing. Had I known this would be perhaps the worst period I would go through, I might have met it with more equanimity, but I thought it could foreshadow the rest of my life.

Since money was tight, my parents sent us tickets to fly home for Christmas and I persuaded Shirley to join me in Austin. Late one sodden California evening, I had told her about John Sullivan, but we had both had so much sherry that either she forgot his name or I had failed to mention it. Not long after we left Palo Alto, Shirley had gotten a divorce, and on his way to Vancouver to teach that summer, John had stopped to meet her. On a whim he had asked her to spend the summer with him, and on a whim she had agreed.

So my initial chore in Austin was to tell Shirley again, and my hands were shaking so pitifully that I picked at the food though I was faint with hunger. She was dumbfounded. Later she wailed to John, "But Celia's my best friend!" and he replied, memorably, "Oh, I sleep with all Celia's friends." She felt he had betrayed her trust, and I agreed with her.

When I saw him first that Christmas, he was wearing a burgundy velvet smoking jacket a girlfriend had given him, he had let his hair grow long, and his holiday decorations looked like they had come from a bordello. Though he promised to finagle a leave to spend the next year in New York, a chasm had sprung open between us and the romance, though never the love, was over.

The night before I left Austin, John Silber called. He was just back from New York, where he said he'd confronted Willie with his shortcomings as husband and father. But that being said, he wondered if I could be so misguided as to think John Sullivan smarter. Taken aback, I commented that believing in Willie's intelligence didn't mean that I could live with him. Still, though I had already dismissed the opinion that had reportedly surfaced on the cocktail party circuit that since Willie was a genius and I wasn't, I ought to be more flexible, my ethics professor had not yet lost his power over my imagination, and his blatant disrespect for my lover simply added another weight on my already wilted spirit.

When we returned to New York, Willie met our plane in a flurry of resolution; the "new" Willie had been hatched by way of a therapist to whom he'd gone because I had insisted. No more "That's just the way I am," no more weekend drunks, no more clothes strewn about, no more head turned to the wall, no more, no more, no more. All the way home, David bounced with the joy of seeing his parents not only together but smiling, and that night we treated ourselves to a feast at Luchow's that hinted at the chance of reconciling.

Years later, Mike Hammond told me he had felt that even during this period, "There seemed to be a real marriage there. You had different agendas, but they weren't incompatible; in fact, they were close to each other. You were, in that way, soul mates." My sense of shared purpose and fair play, in fact, had made me promise that if Willie would go to a psychotherapist, I would go as well. I had no doubt, however, that *he* had the problem and the therapist would hand out my customary A.

On the contrary, the consulting psychiatrist said I should go into psychoanalysis, adding that I would probably have to be chained to the couch. I was aghast. And when he said only strong people could handle it, I was not mollified. All I needed was for Willie to behave reasonably. And for us to get a manageable apartment. And maybe a house in the country.

I told the psychiatrist I didn't understand analysis and could not afford it. But he was unrelenting, telling me that a couple of programs offered two years' free analysis to those who satisfied certain criteria. So I applied, wept through more interviews, dragged myself out of psychiatrists' offices, and waited.

Since *doing* something was easier, however, and necessary under the circumstances, I found an apartment on the Upper West Side at 94th Street and West End Avenue, and we moved to what would prove the most congenial part of Manhattan. The Juilliard String Quartet practiced from time to time in our building; any day you might see poets and writers such as Adrienne Rich or Alfred Kazin buying cherries or artichokes at a sidewalk market on Broadway and 93rd; my butcher spoke four languages and sold better beef than you could get even in Texas; at Zabar's, only a ten-minute walk down Broadway, you could buy a salami called "love and garlic"; and Riverside Park was only a block and a half away, with the lordly Hudson River flowing beside it. Now David had a neighborhood with other kids in it and real places to play, and Bank Street was a mere zip on the express subway.

But it was the house in the country that caught my imagination and held it. It was a 150-year-old farmhouse known as the old Baldwin place, seventy miles north up Route 22, and we found it in the winter when you could stand on the porch and look down through the bare branches all the way across the valley to the small town of Pawling. It was built on a slope with a creek on the up side and a fine stone wall on the down that reminded you how hard the land had been to till, for it was built one stone at a time over the course of decades by farmers who had very little in the way of equipment. A hill that rose behind the house was wonderful to climb, and at the top you looked north to the foothills of the Adirondacks.

The massive dogwood tree in front was said to be the tallest in Putnam County, and a giant sugar maple rose maybe seventy-five feet above the stream to tower over the property. The house had two parts, and the family from whom we bought it had torn a hole about ten feet in diameter in the ceiling of a big room above which the farmhands had slept. They intended to make a two-story living room but ran out of money, and when we took the house over, it looked rather like a bomb had exploded. Upstairs you had to be careful not to wander down a hall and drop right through, and the morning after the party we threw to celebrate our new acquisition, Bill Styron looked up with bloodshot eyes and said, "My God, I could have killed myself." A pair of swings hung from the rafters, and a friend later said, "I'm kinda sorry you fixed it up because I liked telling people I knew somebody with a whole pop art room."

We bought a ratty old station wagon and began driving up every weekend, and as the spring came on, I grew sappy with delight. For the house was flanked by remnants of an apple orchard, and from twisted old branches sprang flowers that made the place a fantasy land. From our bedroom windows you looked out at upturned masses of dogwood blossoms, the tree's glory far surpassing its advance publicity. Soon the road below was blocked from sight by hedges of lilac with a fragrance so intoxicating I threw open the windows and left them up all summer. Amidst crabapple and peach trees behind the house appeared an undulating bed of peonies jumbled together in mixtures of white, pink, and fuchsia—one of them with plate-sized flowers so voluptuous I called it Blanche Dubois.

Bob and Clare Childres were building a house on the other side of Route 22 on property with a big pond where we could all go swimming, and as soon as the semester at Bank Street ended, we moved up for the summer. David and I would drive Willie along the back roads through the sweet-smelling, mint-green fields to the morning train at Brewster and pick him up late in the afternoon at Patterson, the town we officially lived in.

That summer was the happiest I ever spent with Willie; he was on his best behavior, I worked fanatically, and both of us were full of hope. I found seventy-nine-year-old twin carpenters, George and Charlie Burton, who lived down the hill and were slow-talking, slower-moving, fine old craftsmen full of rambling stories about the Baldwins and life along the ridge before the highway came through, when they were all young together. I won their hearts, I think, when I spent two days sanding a door, for they began lending me their tools and showing me how to use them.

David roamed the hills with the boys from Baldwin Road while the Burtons and I knocked around indoors amidst piles of paint cans and brushes, sawhorses, door hinges, rolls of tape, nails, screws, latches, tarpaulins, and stacks of brick and old lumber. We learned the elemental value of water when the stream ran dry for the first time in living memory, forcing us to drill a well. Plumbers put in baseboard heat and ran pipes for a downstairs bathroom. And using old brick in subtle shades of red and ochre, a mason built two fireplaces I designed—one of which, being open on four sides, is still called Celia's Folly.

There were six rooms and a long hallway upstairs, and I sanded every vertical wood surface three times—with coarse paper, then medium, and at last fine. I painted the walls white, the floors gray or dark red, and the woodwork with vibrant New England colors—periwinkle blue, deep rose, mustard, dove gray—and spent the summer spattered with tiny multicolored flecks of paint and reeking of turpentine.

By David's birthday on the first of November we had transformed that house. In an antique store outside Brewster I found a lovely French fruit-wood table nine feet long and oval-shaped when all three leaves were in, and it became the center of our social life in that home and every one I've lived in since. The side room with its towering fireplace and twenty-five-foot ceiling had one set of windows on top of another like an irregular Congregational church, with rippling old glass that reflected the play of light, and leaves, or fire in patterns that could be mesmerizing. I refused to hang curtains, so every room was swept with light, and wherever you were, you looked out on trees and clouds and the bounty of nature. Until winter closed the house down, I kept a vase of fresh flowers in every room, and when it didn't smell of lilac or mock orange or chrysanthemums, it smelled of wood smoke. It was a happy, happy home!

The other grand addition to our life was a black Labrador puppy we named Ichabod Crane for the Washington Irving country he came from. With a mournful face and a tail that wagged like a metronome, he looked like a study in ambivalence but had the joyful soul of a wood sprite. He thought he was a lapdog, and even after he topped fifty pounds, he would jump on the sofa and, after a slobbering lick or two, squeeze in as close as whoever was there would tolerate, fold in on himself, and fall asleep. He had a huge voice box, and when he thought David or I might be in danger, he barked so ferociously that the threat, such as it was, invariably vanished.

We would go on long walks up the hill behind the house, with Ichabod bounding along and crisscrossing beside us, or down a nearby country lane where the trees met in the middle. I learned that his feet were webbed when he plunged into the Childreses' pond and, while I stood there dumb with fright, mastered the art of swimming in mere seconds. Once he got into a losing battle with a skunk, and the stench was so vile I nearly threw up while scrubbing him with an old wives' concoction of soap suds and tomato juice. He was like a beloved person to me—happy, infuriating, and free.

By the time the sugar maple had turned an almost incandescent yellow, we had a lively circle of friends who crossed back and forth over the Connecticut state line or up and down along the Hudson to spend leisurely evenings in one home or another and walk in the woods together. The route between the Styrons' home in Roxbury became almost as familiar as the route to the Village Theater had been when I was ten. The freedom of the country had been good for David, who played baseball or bicycled with his buddies along the winding roads and learned to hold his own with some fairly tough customers. Willie and I were relaxed and enjoyed each other's company. Our new life seemed stable and full of promise.

Driving back to the city after a party we threw for David's seventh birthday, I was rummaging in a pile of discarded papers and found a letter I had misplaced a few weeks earlier. It was from a doctor I'll call Stanley Crouse, a psychiatrist with Downstate Medical School, which had accepted me for two years' free analysis. The next day I made an appointment to thank him kindly but to say I no longer needed a doctor's services. His office was on the Upper East Side, which I took to be an enclave of stockbrokers whose wives wore sable, and when a tall, skinny, red-headed guy opened the door, I saw that he was much too young. Gawky, really, and milquetoastish. Would not have been right for me, even if I had still needed analysis.

He listened for an hour as I explained that I had solved my problems without the helping profession. But since he was polite and the powers-that-be had allotted us three visits, I said I wouldn't mind coming again. On the second visit, I grew irked that he did not seem to take my few remaining problems seriously. On the third, I began to weep and decided I might try analysis after all. And so began the long process that did so much to save my life.

On my first day of the analysis proper, he opened the door and nodded slightly as I walked in and sat in the same chair I had used during our interviews. Instead of sitting behind the desk, however, as he had done before, he lowered his bony frame into a deep chair behind a couch with a square paper headrest on a pillow and wordlessly gestured me toward it. "Oh my God!" I thought, "What *have* I got myself into?" I lay down slowly on the couch, stared at the ceiling, and could think of nothing to say. Finally I babbled something and waited for a response, but there was none. My stomach knotted, my eyes filled with tears, and somehow I found myself talking about Theresa.

The psychiatrist who said that my analyst might have to chain me to the couch turned out to have been prophetic, for the process of loosening my grip on my will, albeit only for fifty minutes a day, was so painful that I resisted ferociously. So often would Dr. Crouse ask, "Why are you so hard on yourself?" that it became very like a litany. Years later, when he said that for the first three years we weren't even doing analysis, that he'd just been putting on Band-Aids, I stammered out an apology. But he pointed out that, after all, he was a doctor and healing was his profession, whatever form it might take.

So there he sat listening, day after day for close to an hour—five days a week, eleven months every year—while I was alternately boring, furious, seductive, desperate, hostile, tentative, sure, irritated, miserable, petty, grandiose, confused, hysterical, coy, lost, matter-of-fact, wheedling, defiant. I was as obnoxious as I knew how to be, but he neither withered nor gave up on me. And by increments so minuscule as to be quite invisible to the naked eye or spirit, I grew to trust him. He was the first person I'd known who wanted nothing of me apart from my own well-being; I was neither his dutiful or defiant daughter, his prize student, nor his trophy wife. I didn't have to perform to win his affection or even his attention.

"Didn't have to," however, also meant "couldn't"; the ways I had always used to connect with people were useless with Stanley Crouse. I could not flirt or make A's or scrub his floor or grit my teeth, though he expected me to get up from his couch every day, no matter how acute the pain, and come back the next day for more of the same.

Over the course of the next few years, I begged him now and then to hospitalize me to save me from a sense of overwhelming desperation, but he insisted wordlessly that I save myself. And so, together, we did. Gradually we took my psyche apart and rearranged it in a more sustainable way. And the stronger I got, the worse the marriage became.

I began the analysis in December, 1965, and by the next fall, everybody who was interested in that sort of thing had heard that Willie would succeed Jack Fischer to become the youngest editor-in-chief in the history of *Harper's* magazine. This meant that at thirty-two he took his turn as the proverbial toast of New York. Virtually every writer, editor, publisher, and camp follower within a one-hundred-mile radius wanted to know him, and whoever he wished to see would have been delighted to meet him for lunch, drinks, or dinner. The writer David Halberstam would later say that for a time Willie owned New York, and this was the time.

The period was intoxicating in more ways than one. Joan Didion wrote somewhere that when she left New York, it was like getting up from a six-year hangover, and like so many of the people we saw now, Willie thought of whiskey as a kind of amniotic fluid that enabled creativity. In fact, Jean Stein VandenHeuvel gave him two manuscript pages from her celebrated *Paris Review* interview with William Faulkner, where he said the tools of his trade were "paper, tobacco, food, and a little whiskey." When Jean had asked, "Bourbon, you mean?" he'd answered "Between scotch and nothing, I'll take scotch." The largess of *Harper's* and Willie's days of glory there meant drinks at lunch, drinks in the late afternoon, drinks at dinner and often through the evening.

With gusto and single-mindedness, he began gathering a staff of like-minded writers: Bob Kotlowitz, Larry L. King, Marshall Frady, John Corry, and Halberstam, the *New York Times* reporter who'd won the Pulitzer for his dispatches from Vietnam. Apart for Kotlowitz, Willie's gang could be described as good old boys, a term I think Willie appropriated, in fact, to use for them. Their famous gatherings at Elaine's restaurant began in the seventies, but the pattern was set in the sixties when Willie took over *Harper's;* they'd adjourn after work along with whoever showed up in the late afternoons and go somewhere to drink and carouse. Most prided themselves in putting away vast quantities of booze, and for the next few years, Willie and Larry had celebrated contests as to who would be left standing after one of their many evenings together. Within a year, Willie added Midge Decter, who didn't often drink with them but was so attuned to the "good old boy" note that she would take to feminist-bashing in the seventies with the fervor of a true believer.

As John Corry would put it in his autobiography, Willie "adored being editor of *Harper's* . . . thought [it] the center of the literary world, and in the strength of his conviction everyone around him thought it was, too." To put not too fine a point on it, Willie was blown away by being editor-in-chief of *Harper's.* It isn't that everything else was second best, for there *was* no second.

And though I tried, a group of good old boys was not a group I could really be part of. These were not men like the ones I'd been close to in Oxford who took women seriously, or at least who had seemed to. Women weren't partners so much as part of the scenery or the staff that put and kept things together. And since they found it hard to resist groupies, a lot of women fawned on them, the pull of fame and/or notoriety being apparently irresistible—and not merely to empty-headed floozies. Just after her husband had humiliated her in public, as he often did, one woman we frequently saw who was beautiful, rich, and gifted told me quietly, "I'd do anything rather than be alone."

Some of us tried to resist, however ineptly. One afternoon at the Styrons' in Connecticut, Halberstam's wife Elzbieta, who'd been Poland's most exciting actress, sat on the floor and played with the children after failing to cut through the men's self-absorbed jousting. For me, being around them was rather like living with a cyclone—often dramatic and exciting, but you had to watch out for the funnel and no matter how expertly you dodged, you were stuck with the clean-up.

I felt most at home with Larry L. King, our West Texas compatriot, who was grand company. In fact, his riotous essay "My Hero LBJ" had its origins at our country house while he nursed a hangover and I laughed till I almost literally wet my pants over his various contretemps with Lyndon Johnson. And Larry could also be my champion. Once, when Willie told me irately to get off his back, Larry pointed out that I had been working since the night before while Willie had slept till noon and had had a leisurely brunch and a walk, and all I had asked him to do was help me move something heavy I couldn't manage alone.

But however delightful, Larry was still a good old boy, and in a piece he did for *Harper's,* he listed the guests at one of "Willie Morris's Old Southern Boys" parties as "Robert Penn Warren, Ralph Ellison, William Styron, Tom Wicker, C. Vann Woodward, Marshall Frady, Morris, and a half dozen others." In an essay called "Requiem for a Texas Lady" that I wrote years later, I wondered if that half dozen had included the women there. One, I pointed out, had won a Pulitzer, another was a distinguished translator of Russian poetry, a third was a poet and writer of children's books. And since I had organized the party, cooked, and then cleaned up an extraordinary amount of debris, I thought I deserved more explicit and generous mention than I got. (After both of us had plunged into very different lives, Larry responded generously in print.)

The two years that followed Willie's elevation at *Harper's* were a crazy mixture of misery, confusion, celebration, anxiety, hard work, excitement, terror, and disgust. Fine writers from all over the country wanted to publish in the magazine, and when Willie thought they were good enough, or promising, he wanted to see them. He was publishing stories about virtually everything that mattered in the country; he connected with fine black writers and ran stories on the civil rights movement that was transforming the places we had come from. And as John Corry said, his enthusiasm was infectious; more often than not, he brought the writers home, and when people think they're changing the world together, their company can be inspiring.

In 1967 Willie published *North Toward Home,* an autobiography in three sections: Mississippi, Texas, and New York. On the dust jacket, John Kenneth Galbraith called it "the most sensitive, amusing, and generally enchanting book I have read this year." The Harvard psychiatrist Robert Coles was even more flattering when he said it was "an almost unbelievable achievement," praising it for "plain, unselfconscious teaching" that made the reader into "much more of an American." I agreed with them, for it was Willie at his best, the Willie I had thought I was marrying—moving and playful at once, serious when it counted, often eloquent.

Years later a distinguished Harvard professor who admired the book and taught it told me, "The first thing kids pick up on today is that he doesn't understand women—not even his old grandmother." But I didn't realize this when the book was published, though I had helped to edit it and my care with the manuscript had brought tears to Willie's eyes. Still, it was true: in a book about his life, Willie had written scarcely anything about his wife and child. I knew he didn't know who David and I were—and knew that he didn't know that he didn't know—but this latest evidence of our being taken for granted slipped right by me. I read *North Toward Home* as a triumph, and I read it still with an almost hallucinatory sense of wonder that the person who wrote it is the man to whom I was so unhappily married.

But indeed he was. And not long after David and I went back out of focus for Willie, I too began abusing alcohol even more than I had earlier, both as a solace for my anxieties about my son and as a safety valve for the skyrocketing tensions between Willie and me. Then one treacherous night, after drinking from late afternoon until well after midnight, I ended up in bed with Jack II.

Like their predecessors, Jack and Jill II were gifted, glamorous, and fine company, and we'd spent the evening in their home enjoying a superb meal, spirited conversation, and a movie classic. But when I woke to find myself with Jack, every cell in my body and soul revolted. I remembered nothing of what got me there, but I knew that for me, this *had* to be rock bottom. The next morning we all made believe nothing untoward had happened, and with an abject apology to Willie, and an equally abject, though indirect apology to Jill, I swore off hard liquor and rededicated myself to my Stanley Crouse's couch.

Good times remained; a boy was growing, work was done, the city was a never-ending source of fascination. But when times were bad, Willie and I played out our mutual antagonisms, as often as not, on subjects like the South, and sometimes it was even funny. During one week, for instance, every evening as soon as he got home, he put on a record of the Tara theme from *Gone with the Wind* and then played it over and over. After about five nights of this, I snatched it off the turntable and broke it over my knee, and then he did the same to the first two movements of Beethoven's Seventh.

The more our straightforward personal communications disintegrated, the more we argued by using literature as a code language. Repeatedly Willie cited the story about the time a woman asked Faulkner which of his characters he most identified with and he said "the corncob"—the tool Popeye uses to rape Temple Drake in *Sanctuary*. In turn, I wrote a paper for Irving pointing out that Faulkner never wrote about a white woman of childbearing age who wasn't a bitch. Furthermore, I said, it was hard to find, in all those pages, any marriage worth the having. (For Willie this meant I was insensitive and hostile to the South, and he eventually responded in an essay in *Harper's* by saying I had called Faulkner a second-rater.)

We also fought the subterranean war of writer versus academic. Except for a handful of distinguished historians, most notably Vann Woodward, anything to do with the academic world now became fair game to Willie. He seemed to lose interest even in our Oxford friends, and one Thanksgiving when we joined a handful of the old gang in a flat just off the Harvard campus, he retreated behind the sports page as though he found the conversation dull, and I batted the paper down and said "Talk!"

In turn, I refused to think of writers as the elect. At Norman Mailer's forty-fifth birthday party, when one of his hangers-on told me I'd be a better English teacher for being there, I walked out. Along with Bob and Billie Kotlowitz, I got apoplectic at a dinner *Harper's* gave at an elegant restaurant for a famous writer whose wife got drunk and went on the attack. Sitting next to Sage Cowles, whose husband John owned the magazine, she began popping off with astounding put-downs—the most memorable being, "You're just a cunt!" Willie, on the other hand, found this hilarious, the large allowance he made for writers being extended now to their appendages.

Although this period can be funny to look back on, it was a wretched time for David and me. Willie and I went to a conference at Bank Street, where the director said they were afraid they couldn't help David, for they hadn't been able to solve his old problems: he seldom played with other children and had trouble answering a direct question. Perhaps another school might be better, but when I tearfully asked which one, they had no answer. His teacher said she'd resign if they dropped him, and I think that saved him. But Willie dismissed them all. He simply *would not* discuss the possibility that his son might have real problems.

At the same time, 1968—our last year together—was one of the most wrenching in the twentieth century, and since Willie was putting out a monthly magazine that aimed to speak powerfully to American culture and its role in the world, the year's horrors invaded our personal lives and ratcheted up the tensions. In January, the Vietcong seized the yard of our embassy in Saigon, making a mockery of United States claims to know what was happening, and the Tet offensive not long afterward completed the humiliation. In March, President Lyndon Johnson, the outsized Texan in whose fortunes so many of our friends were deeply invested and who had genuinely believed that his administration could help create the "Great Society," announced that he would not run for reelection. In April, Dr. Martin Luther King was murdered in Memphis, and our hopes for a nonviolent civil rights revolution very nearly died with him. In May and June, rebellion broke out all over France, where workers piled onto the barricades along with students—a demonstration of common cause we knew was highly unlikely in our country—and the imperious President Charles de Gaulle called out his armed forces.

The night before I was to receive my Ph.D. in graduation ceremonies in Bryant Park behind the New York Public Library, Bobby Kennedy was shot in Los Angeles, and our commencement speaker, Arthur Schlesinger, Jr., one of his closest advisers, arrived in dark glasses and cried as he mourned our incalculable loss. In August, the Soviet army invaded Czechoslovakia while the Chicago police assaulted and bloodied student demonstrators and those who sided with them outside the Democratic National Convention. That fall, feminists protested noisily outside the Miss America pageant and were labeled "bra-burners" forever after. Students were massacred in Mexico City, and American athletes at the Olympics gave Black Power salutes. By a narrow margin, Richard Nixon defeated Hubert Humphrey for the presidency, masses of liberals and other progressives having taken the position that there was no difference between them. The Republicans took over the U.S. Senate. And Apollo 8 orbited the moon, which seemed, by the end of 1968, perhaps a safer, saner place to be.

Everything personal was chaos and tumult. Shirley remembers one Christmas when Willie took the roll-away bed into the dining room, closed the doors, and stayed for days. And I too was awful. Once when Willie's mother was visiting in the country, they were driving each other and me so crazy that I crawled under the porch and lay there in the dirt, and though she stood above me frantically calling my name, I did not come out until the neighbors brought David home from a Fourth of July celebration. I could go on telling stories, but the squalor of our emotional life makes the prospect too depressing.

Meanwhile, I was writing my doctoral dissertation on the Arthurian legends, enthralled as I explored the adulterous loves of Lancelot and Guinevere, Tristan and Isolde, and the conflicts these women faced between a grand passion and duty. Only dimly did I realize that the stories as a whole might pull me because they were about the end of a beautiful world. Or that perhaps I was allergic to glamour, as someone suggested years later, for at the party where I was to meet Ralph Ellison, I happened to look down and see that my shoes not only didn't match but that they were both for the right foot.

Finally the Jack-and-Jill problem resurfaced. A year or so after the initial disaster, we were driving home with them from a world-class dinner party when Jill, of all people, started talking about the difficulties of marriage and, once more, the question of swapping leapt onto the table. I had thought I'd done something very nearly unforgivable, but it turned out they did this sort of thing with panache and, as it were, on principle. Jack chimed in that divorce was ridiculous: look at Mailer! All those ex-wives and endless child support.[*]

Since a couple of years on the couch had begun to free up my emotions, this time I could feel my anger, and I left Willie at Jack and Jill's house in the pitch black middle of the night, careening down narrow,

[*] In retrospect, I was stunningly ignorant—and lucky too—for we never encountered at parties the stripping and group sex that Adele Mailer, the second of Norman's wives, would eventually describe in *The Last Party: Scenes from My Life with Norman Mailer*. And the "key parties" that would be memorialized in *The Ice Storm* were still a few years in the future, or so a Connecticut psychiatrist claimed when the film opened. Still, my experience with Jack and Jill meant I shared a cultural moment with a good many others, for in the year I decided to leave Willie, John Updike's *Couples* sped to the top of the bestseller list, and *Time* magazine did a cover story on "The Adulterous Society."

winding country roads in a rage. And I told Willie the next day I would *never* do that again.

This determination led, some months later, to one of those evenings that would have delighted an eighteenth-century comic writer, except that when you don't want to play, it isn't funny. Willie was drunkenly weaving in and out of their house, I was pushing Jack out of the guest bedroom, and Jill was serving as lookout. In the bleakness of the next morning, she said, "You really want your marriage to work, don't you?" I nodded, and we left it there.

But a few months later still, at the Robert Penn Warrens' annual Christmas party, Jack looked at me soulfully and said, "Why don't you and Willie stop by on the way home?" I actually said, "You're demonic!" though I thought I sounded silly even as I said it, and then I waited in the falling snow while Willie stood in the doorway in what seemed an embrace to the death with Jill.

My inner core, which had felt so empty for so many tortured years, had long since begun to fill, for when someone listens to you with profound attention, or its human equivalent, for an hour a day for months on end, you begin to lose your tolerance for someone who doesn't listen at all. I no longer had to buy my way to love with lavish amounts of work and achievement. And finally I understood that Willie might well *love* David and me, but he didn't *care* about us and never would or could. I knew then that his need was bottomless and that it was his to try to fill without me.

We had gone through birth and death together. We had created a precious person who would be hurt by our separation—and angry. I would be giving up a life I had spent ten years building—one that had given me people and places to love, and adventures beyond my imagining. A life so many others envied. A home I treasured. But at last I no longer hesitated.

Shirley and Jerry Wilson had come from California to spend Christmas with us in the country, along with David Palmer, who was teaching for a year at the University of Rochester and brought his wife Pat and their two children. The snow was very beautiful that winter, and I knew it would be my last in the house I had loved so unreservedly. So we had a gala Christmas that went on for several days, and Shirley was the only person I told I was leaving Willie. David Palmer, in fact, was so astounded when I wrote him with the news that for the only time in our lives, he was actually angry with me.

Willie asked me to stay for three social events—the last being a dinner party at Bennett and Phyllis Cerf's for Senator Fred Harris of Oklahoma. I was too drained to object and made it to the afternoon of the Cerf party reasonably intact. Willie had slept until noon and then gone to meet the poet James Dickey for lunch. Dickey had written a fine essay on Edwin Arlington Robinson, whose Arthurian poems had been the focus of my dissertation, and Willie called in midafternoon to say, "You oughta come down to the Ginger Man and meet Dickey! He's really something!" I said I couldn't manage that, since I wanted to spend some time with David before going off to my shrink's. And I reminded him of the Cerf party.

When I got home from Dr. Crouse's, I found Willie with two writers who'd apparently been drinking with him all afternoon. And after asking them to excuse us since we were due at a black-tie dinner, I warned Willie to slow down, to which he said "No problem!"

When we got to East 63rd Street, Bennett stood with his arm around Willie's shoulder, saying that when he told Fred he would invite anybody to dinner whom he wanted to meet, the first person Fred had named was Willie Morris. Ladonna Harris, Fred's gorgeous Native American wife, kept saying "You all *must* come to see us in Washington!" and I kept smiling in what I imagine was a stricken sort of way and mumbling something I trusted was unintelligible.

The "usual" crowd was there: George and Freddie Plimpton, Charlotte Niarchos, Bill and Rose Styron, Lauren Bacall, Gloria Vanderbilt and her husband Wyatt Cooper, Philip Roth, Claudette Colbert, and a handful of others. The introductory chit-chat took place in two elegant drawing rooms, and then we went downstairs for dinner. I noticed that Willie had two drinks upstairs, but there were three tables in the dining room and I was at the one nearest the big plate-glass window that looked out on the garden, which I sat facing. On one side of me was Bob Bernstein. Once before at the Cerfs' I'd asked this freckle-faced, Eagle Scout–looking man what he did at Random House, and he'd said, "I'm the president." So at least I spared myself that embarrassment this time around. But I didn't expect much more of myself than that I keep my head from falling into my plate.

When Claudette Colbert smiled at me and said to Bennett, "Isn't she pretty!" I smiled back wanly and probably mumbled something appreciative. Wyatt Cooper told a couple of weird stories about taking Gloria home to Mississippi to meet Mama, and I nodded at what I hoped were the right places. I looked at the huge ring on Charlotte Niarchos's hand and thought, "People like that don't wear zircons." (In an article about her in the *New York Times Magazine* a year or so later, I would discover that her family called this diamond, which was about 110 carats, the "skating rink.") And so it went.

In the northeast corner of each place setting there was a little crystal saucer with what looked like a bell without the clapper resting on it. When a servant came by with a pitcher of clear liquid, everybody at my table passed, and the crystal pieces were taken away.

After dinner, as I was heading for the stairs, Freddie Plimpton came over to say, "I hope Willie's all right!" When I raised my eyebrows, she told me Willie had gotten up from the table saying he felt a little queasy and wanted to walk around the block. He'd done that and come back, but a few minutes later he had gotten up again, said he didn't feel well, and disappeared.

It turned out that the transparent liquid had been aqua vitae, and since the little glass didn't have a base, it couldn't be put down. Willie had apparently put away not one but two glasses full, and since aqua vitae is about 150 proof, it had finished him. When I called home and nobody answered, I knew Willie was there since the baby sitter would have picked up the phone. I had no desire to be there with him, and since this was to be my last night among the literary and social superstars, I decided to stay.

It was after one when the party began to break up and a gratifying contest arose over who would take me home. Since I couldn't imagine that Charlotte Niarchos had ever gone slumming on the Upper West Side, I chose her, for the prospect struck me as faintly amusing. So we were handed into a gigantic black limousine that cruised in the stateliest fashion across town and up while she went on about what interesting people one met at Bennett and Phyllis's.

When we got to my apartment building, she wanted to make sure I got in safely, but assuring her that the doorman would protect me, I thanked her and waved them on. When I got upstairs, however, I found the door chain-locked, and in response to the bell, Ichabod began baying. Since the roar was coming from our bedroom, he was clearly shut in with Willie and I knew that no matter how drunk, Willie could not possibly sleep through it.

I looked in my purse and found only two dollars. The two friends nearby on whose doorsteps I thought it marginally possible to show up at this hour were too small to have clothes I could borrow. And since I didn't fancy coming home in broad daylight in a long satin brocade dress, I leaned on the bell until it woke David, who came at last to open the door.

I'd become convinced that I could not be a "good enough" mother and stay married to Willie, who made me miserable, and that David and I would both be better off if we jettisoned the illusion of a two-parent family. So when my son said, "That bum wouldn't even let you in!" as he pulled the chain loose, I was mightily relieved, for I knew that ultimately he could handle what was coming.

My parents had stayed together for the sake of their children, while I was going to jettison my marriage for the sake of my child. To be sure, my own self-respect was also critical, for ironically, the pressure to go to bed with a man because my husband wanted me to had finally snapped my stoic resolve. I had told Willie, I'd told the Jacks and Jills, but I knew that as long as I stayed, the pressure would not lift. And so I didn't stay.

Years later, Willie's *New York Days* made it clear that our mutual incomprehension was intractable, for he wrote that I'd left because I was in thrall to the sixties mantra of following one's own bliss. He, on the other hand, had wanted me to find his "demanding yet animating life in the fulcrum of American letters and journalism . . . sufficiently stimulating . . . meeting and getting to know fine writers, dinners at our place in town or in the country with the Arthur Millers, the William Styrons, the Norman Podhoretzes, the Robert Penn Warrens, the C. Vann Woodwards. This was not enough for her, and I could not understand why." Even after the women's movement had changed so many lives, he still thought I should have been content sitting in a room with a group of famous people—or more to the point, cooking for them and cleaning up afterward. He still saw the need I'd brought to our marriage for an equal and complementary life as something that had turned me into a rival.

Willie instructed his lawyer to say he wanted to live with me for the rest of his life, but for almost three months, he refused to see David or call him. David was so hurt and bewildered that I was frantic, and when I asked several of Willie's friends to persuade him to get in touch with his son, the message came back that if David was to have a father, I had to make up with Willie. Nothing spotlighted the gulf between us more vividly than the idea that I would *want* to live with someone who would do that to any child, much less to my son or, for that matter, his own, and a man who had observed Willie closely convinced me that he might well disappear from David's life.

When he finally understood that I would *never* live with him again, however, he got back in touch with David but refused from that time on to speak to me. Over the next few years, I wrote letter after letter that Willie apparently never opened, much less responded to. This meant that whatever I could not handle alone—most notably the responsibility for arranging David's visits—fell on nine-year-old shoulders. For the next eight years, then, David had to take on the adult role in relation to his father, and though I was helpless to do anything about it, I was afraid that David's scars might never heal.

Jean Herskovits, our friend from Oxford who was now living a few blocks away and teaching history at City College, went to hold David's hand and mine on our last trip to our home in the country. Few things have been harder for me to leave, for I knew that I would never love a house or piece of land more than I had loved this one.

I stood in each room remembering how it had felt to the touch and fixing in memory the good things that had happened there. Though it was the dead of winter, I sat under the sugar maple and wept as I looked over a gleaming white home and the rich land I had treasured so. And then I bowed deeply to the house, climbed in with David and Jean, turned the key in the ignition, and drove away to an unknown, but surely very different life.

CHAPTER FOURTEEN

I had come out of a ten-year marriage with most of my illusions shattered and a withering sense of loss and waste, but also with a son I loved, a great dog, and my mother-in-law's top-notch recipe for fried chicken. However belatedly, I was emerging into the sixties, with the era's intoxicating belief that we and our country could be changed for the better. I had a trustworthy psychiatrist, a close friend—Jean—who lived nearby, and a spacious six-room Upper West Side apartment. The Thalia, a treasure trove of old movies, was only a block away. It stank of Lysol and urine, the springs were popping out of the seats, and one day a guy jerked off a few rows away. But with Charlie Chaplin, Greta Garbo, and W. C. Fields for companions, I discovered that you can find the spunk to handle almost anything.

Early one morning, as I walked Ichabod down Broadway, I saw one of our local street people bounding along on the balls of his feet while on his shoulder sat a praying mantis. He was a tall, skinny guy with a beak for a nose who managed to look fervent and blissed out at the same time, and this apparition became a symbol for me; maybe there was no point to it all and life would go on being harder than I'd expected, but the odd moment was charged with energy and little puffs of blessedness.

So David went to school and I, to work—first teaching English at Pace College in lower Manhattan and then commuting over an hour each way to New Rochelle to be an editor for *Change* magazine, which focused on higher education. During my farewell interview with the provost of the CUNY Graduate Center, a mathematician named Mina Rees, I'd confessed to being anxious about getting a job in New York City, or within commuting distance, but she shook her head dismissively and said she didn't worry about me — the unspoken thought being that my successful husband made such problems moot! She *had* said, however, that if she were in my place, she'd find a job teaching ghetto kids — the worthiest possible work, as I agreed, but one for which neither my temperament nor the education over which she'd presided at CUNY had prepared me. By the time I left her, I was swallowing tears, for successful women in those days were often the last to help younger women, and now I was up against a *very* tough system.

When I left Pace after two years, then — the victim of the "last-hired-first-fired" principle as the City University began open enrollment and students fled expensive private colleges — I was essentially blowing my Ph.D. but saw no viable option. I couldn't find another college teaching job in the area and didn't want to leave New York; apart from anything else, David had gone through too many changes and needed to be able to see his father. (I promised myself, however, that if I saw David turning into a younger version of Willie, I'd retreat to a high peak in the Himalayas, shave my head, and live in a cave. Or, in a less punitive mood, I'd imagine taking over the coffee concession on a remote beach on the island of Paros in the Mediterranean.)

So for a very long time, almost everything I'd put into my decade with Willie seemed wasted, including not only my struggle to become a college professor, but my faith in higher education. Vast numbers of students in the late sixties were so hostile that a man who had won national teaching awards told me that if he had been starting then, as I was, he would have been annihilated.

I had a few students I relished. One was a black man who'd had polio and got around with heavy leg braces and crutches. (Irving asked with distinctively Yiddish irony if I thought he might also be a Jew.) Another was an ex-cop who weighed nearly 250 pounds and told me about taking a drug pusher into "the next room" and beating the lard out of him. In those days not long before the Serpico police scandals, he said he had left the force after deciding that if he wanted to be a crook he'd rather do it, so to speak, out in the open.

But the people I taught then were not like the students Shirley and

Sally and I had been fifteen years earlier. For the most part, they were indifferent to "the best that has been thought and written" and sneered at learning for its own sake. They wanted their classes to count toward a better job or a higher salary, and I could hardly blame them.

Our problem was crystallized by a smart young man on scholastic probation who came into my office to complain about having to read *Othello.* Was he going to talk about *Othello,* he asked, at a cocktail party? No, I didn't think so. Was he going to be able to use *Othello* in, say, an advertising job? No, I suspected not. Then he wound up to a grand peroration: "And if my best friend tells me my girl is running around on me, I believe him." So I said, in exasperation, "Look, there's one thing you learn from reading *Othello:* you don't believe him! *You just don't automatically believe him.*"

Still, part of my heart was with him; he was paying good money for a degree that would not be all that valuable because at the time Pace was a third- or fourth-rate college. And I, for one, did *not* believe he had to read Shakespeare to be a decent or, for that matter, even a civilized person.

At the same time, I didn't want to teach people who didn't want to learn, so I experimented with different approaches to teaching, some of which worked better than others. But the problem was structural, as the students of the sixties were busily pointing out, and facing a hostile or indifferent classroom day after day for more than two years cut so brutally into my sense of self that for the next ten years I *literally* could not speak in public.

A part of me I'd counted on since childhood simply shut down. When I tried to stand up or speak out in a group of more than four or five people, no matter how friendly, the muscles in my throat would constrict, my voice would quaver and my skin grow clammy. I was humiliated—and frightened, too—for though I did not know my infirmity would last a decade, I thought it might well last a lifetime.

So I lost what had seemed my most confident and playful side—lost the teacher as well as the flirt, the gang leader as well as the show-off. I had no inkling that the sound part of my psyche had decided, if that is the word, to seal off a part that had sustained such damage from rejection so that I could heal from the inside. But when the breakthrough finally came and I could hold a room's attention again—and have a grand time doing it—I knew that the awful empty space inside was gone, and gone perhaps forever. I also knew I would no longer try to win love through public performance, for the two are not the same order of thing, and confusing them, as I had for so many years, had proved to be a formula for disappointment, if not disaster. Meanwhile, however, I got a prolonged and sobering insight into what it must feel like to be crippled.

As for my personal life, the most deadly blow came from the Rhodes scholars I had loved so dearly, for not one of them came to see us or invited us to come to them. Willie had made it known that anybody who saw me would be cut off his list, though since the dazzling, important job was his, along with the social power, the command was gratuitous. But the falling away of those who had peopled my last few years neither rankled nor surprised me; not only had I understood that I was giving up the glamorous world, I had seen enough of it to last a lifetime.

The Rhodes people were a different matter altogether, and I had assumed that the men I loved would reach out to help David and me through these hard times. But after a couple of calls and a note or two of commiseration from their wives, there was only silence.

Nor did I have the steady stream of "gentleman callers" I had been accustomed to before I married—ardent suitors my old friends and even my psychiatrist seemed to expect for a divorcee who lived just off Broadway in the 90s. It isn't that there were no men, for every two years or so, I would have an affair that lasted seven or eight months before foundering for one quite ordinary reason or another—one of them with Tom Wicker that shattered with the slam of a door but ten years later eased back into a wonderful friendship.

After a few years of this, I wrote David Palmer that for a woman brought up to believe she would realize her best self in relation to a man, the horizon was bleak: "There's a fine black writer who's in love with me, but I told him that getting involved with him would mean [my] committing patricide. Also, he's lived with three women, each of whom has borne him a daughter. . . . He told me my blend of looks and intelligence may destroy me. So much for *Liebe*."

Most divorced women I knew had much the same experience; married men were the plague, albeit on occasion the salvation of our lives, and sometimes we were very lonely indeed. As I wrote David Palmer: "The nights are the worst. Most days I can manage, but at night I often feel on the verge of hysteria. I cook a fine dinner, and sometimes my David likes it and sometimes he doesn't. I make the apartment attractive, and no one else enjoys it. I look good and dine alone."

This world was not the one most people had imagined for me. About six months after Willie and I split up, in fact, I started hearing stories about an affair I was said to be having with Philip Roth, the author of *Portnoy's Complaint*. The stories, for the most part, were coming from Texas, and I was puzzled. For while I was going to parties with New York's literary, social, and intellectual superstars, I had gotten the distinct impression that Roth is a guy who looks over your shoulder to see who in the room is famous. The only time he had actually deigned to talk to me was once when he and Willie and I dined together at Lafayette's, one of New York's swankiest restaurants, and when there are only three people at your elegant table, it is hard to ignore one of them altogether. So this famous author said to me, "If I were you, I'd consider suicide because the sexual revolution is on and men can have thirteen-year-olds." I didn't have to read his work to know that Philip Roth didn't much like women.

So here I was, trying to earn a living in a city I adored but often found bewildering, and struggling as a single mother to raise a son whose father flatly refused even to speak to me. Getting through a day was often hard, and the stories *hurt* me. But for a couple of years, every few months brought a fanciful new version of my glamorous life, some more distasteful than others, some quite ugly.

Then one morning a friend called to say, "Celia, you're not going to believe this, but I was sitting last weekend in a bar in Burlington, Vermont, and some guys at the next table were arguing about whether or not Philip Roth was a fag. And one of them said, 'I know for a fact he isn't a fag because he broke up a marriage at *Harper's* or *The Atlantic*.'" I never doubted that Philip Roth had sex with females, but that's when I knew I had to figure this out. A rumor in Texas was one thing, but a rumor that had traveled from Texas to Vermont was something else.

As I put down the phone, revelation struck. So I picked it up again and called Larry L. King, whom I now saw occasionally, and asked straight out: "Larry, did Willie make up a story about my having an affair with Philip Roth?" And he said, "Yeah, and I went all over Texas tellin' it." Later I heard that certain other male Texas writers had done the same.

This episode taught me that you cannot take rumors personally because they are mainly about the people who tell them, and I settled at last on two explanations for the Roth fantasy. The writers, I thought, had believed it because they could not imagine a woman leaving somebody like them at the height of his social, political, and economic power. I was walking away from a place they had spent years trying to get to. And it was easier, for Willie certainly, to believe that a more famous writer had lured me away than to think that the place itself might not be all that compelling.

As for my old friends in Texas, I think the scandal might have made them feel better in the dark moments when they wondered if they hadn't settled for too little. For by the standards we grew up with, I had taken *big* chances; I had not only married an outsider but a liberal, and I had left the state where I was born. And look what happened: I'd gotten mixed up with a Jew who wrote about dirty sex. It was a story to scare the kids with, to convince them the old ways were best and risks were foolhardy.

Whatever its deeper meanings, the rumor turned out to be tenacious. Almost ten years later, Jeanie Dugger called from Austin to say, "A bunch of people here want to meet you because of your affair with Philip Roth." When I wearily replied, "I didn't have an affair with Philip Roth," Jeanie said, "I know, but everybody thinks you did, so why not relax and enjoy it?"

The Roth fantasy aside, and in the absence of Willie's impossible demands and the deadly erosion of self-respect that marriage had come to mean to me, I *did* gradually relax and enjoy the good things. Walking down Broadway or along the Hudson River made me happy. Working on puzzles and playing games with David made me happy. Bicycling with Jean and David in Central Park made me happy. Reading first-rate prose, or cooking a fine meal, or going to a good movie made me happy. Sometimes even bad movies made me happy, and I remember once, at a double feature of *I Am Curious Yellow* and *I Am Curious Blue,* when a man a few rows back drawled impatiently, "Thank God Sweden doesn't have a *tricolor!*"

For what happened during this hard, discouraging time was that I shifted my hopes for love to my friends, and the analysis was crucial in the shift. Although the pain I felt on the couch was like stripping away filaments of skin without benefit of anesthetic, under Stanley Crouse's quiet ministering, I confronted my tangled family, with its failed relationships and buried aura of desperation. The empty core I had lived with as long as I could remember filled ever so slowly. The self-hatred I had buried under an avalanche of good deeds seeped away, and a whole person emerged—not always charming, easy, or good, but whole nonetheless, or nearly so.

I began to connect with people I cared for at a much deeper level and discovered in the process that there is nothing mystical about it. For when someone listens to you patiently for years, you come to understand in a feeling way that the necessary ingredients in a real human relationship are listening and respect. I responded now to others and they to me because of affinities we shared rather than because of my proximity to someone else's throne. Nobody mediated.

So it turned out that Freud was right at least in this: life *was* about *Liebe und Arbeit*. Love, however, didn't need to be either romantic or sexual love; it could be the love I shared with my friends and my son. Eventually most of the Rhodes people I had missed would come back into my life—after I took the initiative. The telephone helped, and so did cut-rate airline fares. (In far-off years the fax machine and e-mail helped as well.) And since New York was a magnet that drew many people I cared for, we learned to make the most of our time together.

Leaving the guilt for my mother's misery on Stanley Crouse's couch, then, while recapturing the strong ties I'd had with my grandmothers, I began to build enduring friendships with women, and Shirley was the first to weave herself forever into the texture of our lives. Now a professor at the University of Minnesota, she had once appeared to be a delicate lady of the old school, but getting a Ph.D. while surviving a failed marriage and lovers' deaths and betrayals had turned her spine into tensile steel.

Together we shared the play that mends and enriches the soul. One snowy Christmas morning in Manhattan, for instance, we stuffed a turkey and popped it into the oven, put on long gowns, drank champagne and ate pears with Boursin while opening presents, and then went back to bed for two hours, leaving David responsible for basting the turkey. When David and I went to Minneapolis, we would canoe up the Mississippi or walk around a lake, and Shirley introduced us to the Guthrie Theater at a production of the *Orestia* complete with masks. When she married again and had a daughter, she named her Celia.

In San Angelo, Texas, my Theta big sister Pat Hinds Marschall did what she called a little reality testing and discovered that sex could be important to a life. Because of that revelation, along with failures in communication very like mine with Willie, she left her husband and took her two daughters to Cambridge, where she got a master's degree at the Harvard Law School. And when she made a three-day trip to New York, we watched our years of separation dissolve into a friendship that will take us to the death.

When David Palmer wrote that a woman he loved, Diana Kealey, was coming to do a master's degree at the State University of New York at Stony Brook, I invited her for the weekend. And the instant she walked in the door, we felt a rapport that has proved itself in adventures on two continents over almost three decades.

Life, then, became a collaboration among friends. David made a plywood puzzle case about three feet square and four feet high at Bank Street, for instance, and then he and Shirley and I wrestled it onto a dolly and rolled it down West End Avenue from their new building on 112th Street through harrowing traffic to our apartment, where we put it proudly in the dining room. A few weeks later, Jerry Wilson flew in from San Francisco, and we spent all one Saturday upholstering it with an elegant fabric I had bought in London from a friend of Diana's.

I now had sisters for the first time, and brothers to take the place of the one I hadn't known. A wealth of love that had been thwarted for three decades poured out to people who could receive and return it. And over the years to come, I would squander it shamelessly only to find the spring to be self-generating.

So old friends and new got to be part of the same package. Vann Woodward came back into my life, as did John and Billie Maguire, whom I had met at the Robert Penn Warrens' and who now presided over the State University of New York's experimental new campus at Old Westbury. On the odd day off, I would have hilarious lunches with Leina Schiffrin, an eccentric woman who was half English and half Spanish and lived in a penthouse apartment in my building, and she and her husband Andre would invite me to parties. Andre, who was head of Pantheon Books, was beginning to publish a guy from Chicago named Studs Terkel, whom I met on their terrace one evening. We polished off the night in a bar together singing hymns and, over the next few years, became great pals.[*]

---

[*] Decades later, Andre, Leina, and I were invited to be part of Studs's small official "family" when he received one of the ten annual National Endowment for the Humanities awards on the White House lawn. On that occasion Studs wore not only his trademark red-checked shirt and red tie, but also bright red socks, making him comically conspicuous against a sober background of grays, browns, and blacks. As President Bill Clinton put the medal, which hung from a red satin ribbon, around his neck, he said, "Studs, I'm glad to see we got this thing color-coordinated."

Old friends and new created a pattern, and I repeated it over and over—learning along the way that anyone who sentimentalizes friendship does it a disservice. For friends make you live a messy, turbulent life because you have to keep opening yourself up. At its most authentic friendship can mean telling painful truths your friend probably does not want to hear and indeed may not listen to—and listening to them tell you the same without walking out in a huff. Their children, like yours, will demand countless anxious hours, for real friendship means being available even when you have something else to do that may even be urgent. Sometimes it means hurting a lot, for people you love will behave disgracefully, drink themselves to death, and even blow their brains out. You will fail them, they will fail you, as in blood families. But unlike husbands, friends have no more power over you than you are willing to give, and however excruciating it may be to do so, you can break off a friendship when you must without leaving unspeakably large pieces of yourself behind.

With the help of my doctor and my friends, then, I gradually discovered that anger does not kill you unless you swallow it. That loneliness passes. That friends who are worth the trouble may disappear for a time but will resurface. That hunger and fright have their place. That the world is shot through with laughter, challenge, and glory. That all things have their season, and mine might have a long time yet to run.

As for *Arbeit,* when I went to work for *Change* magazine, I discovered that I liked editing and was good at it. And the magazine kept bringing interesting people into my life, the one with the most lasting consequences being a slow-talking southerner from Nashville named John Egerton. John was doing a series of articles for *Change,* and soon we began to sound like two old jazz performers playing riffs with one another.

At the same time, an article I edited for *Change,* along with its aftermath, helped further undermine the trust I had put in powerful men. Pieced together from the manuscript of a book Ronnie Dugger was publishing called *Our Invaded Universities,* it focused on the University of Texas as Harry Ransom took on the challenge of making it a "university of the first class" and as John Silber became dean of Arts and Sciences.

When I came to Ronnie's manuscript in 1974, I was angry at Silber, partly because of an episode more than a decade now in the past. It had happened, in fact, a few months after Willie and I returned to Austin, when John and his wife Kathryn invited us to dinner with Bob Childres, whom John had met in Oxford and who was visiting from Mississippi. My brother Glenn was just going through orientation at the University of Texas, where he'd met several young women John had interviewed for Plan II, and they had given Glenn a somewhat different picture of John than he had gotten from me.

So I'd opened the conversation by reporting that these young women had been startled when Glenn told them John Silber was a friend of his sister. In fact, they'd invariably said they could imagine that he was a brilliant teacher and a fine scholar, but they couldn't imagine anybody being his friend. There was a titter of slightly nervous laughter, while John responded with what Willie called his "shit-eating grin." Then Bob asked, with a curiosity we all shared, "What kinds of questions do you ask them, John?" Jaws then plummeted as John ripped off a string of breathtakingly arcane questions, leaving the rest of us sitting there dumbfounded until I said, "John, I can answer *some* of those questions now, but I couldn't have answered *any* of them when I was seventeen or eighteen." And when Bob followed up by asking, "What do they do?" John answered, from behind the shit-eating grin, "They cry!" The chill that pierced my heart had been so sharp that time has never managed to dissipate it.

Then, a couple of years before I came to Ronnie's manuscript, John had called into question my image of him as a just man who fought the abuse of power. My disillusion had come by way of an article Willie published in *Harper's* called "Yazoo" that included a paragraph of gratuitous nastiness about me:

> I had a wife, a Texas girl, who hated this place, hated the town and its people with a terrible and disparaging contempt. She believed it elementally evil. She hated everything about Mississippi, and once she wrote a graduate school treatise calling William Faulkner a second-rater . . . For her, Mississippi was a symbol of all that was wrong with all of us, so that even what it inspired in the way of literary sensibility was, to any sound and secure academic mind, also an aberration. On the night Martin Luther King was killed in Memphis, as forlorn and grief-laden a night as I have ever lived, she slapped me across the face and said, "you Southern boys have a lot to be guilty about."

As I came to this paragraph, I understood suddenly what it meant to be struck dumb. So much for the decency of "good old boys" or their sense of fair play. In fact, I could recall only one man in Yazoo City I'd thought ill of, but I didn't even remember his name. I *had* said Faulkner wasn't as good as Dostoevsky but had hardly called him "second rate." I recalled pushing Willie rather than slapping him, but in any case he weighed at least eighty pounds more than I did and obviously could be counted on to hit back.

But I could scarcely write a letter of protest and correction to the editor of *Harper's,* and as my wits seeped back, I realized that Willie could go on doing this *ad nauseam*. Still, I thought he might be daunted by the disapproval of people he respected. So I wrote John Silber, who had gone so far out of his way on more than one occasion to tell us both off, thereby demonstrating, if nothing else, his disinterestedness. And I asked if he would write Willie to say, in effect, we don't do that sort of thing.

Instead, he wrote me a preposterous letter, ignoring my plea altogether, accusing me of attacking Willie in front of David, and saying he did not approve of former marriage partners speaking ill of one another. Again I was flabbergasted. Once before I had called his hand on some charges he'd made against me, and he'd confessed, with an ironic laugh, that he might have been 50 percent wrong. Now, by my most generous estimate, he was 98 percent wrong, but the letter seemed so crazy I saw no point in responding.

I *did* ask a mutual friend to tell John the letter had made me angry, and at a breakfast later in New York, when he said in front of Kathryn, "I understand you didn't like my last letter," I merely said, "I was outraged." To which he replied, "All I said was that Willie was still in love with you," an absurdity I let pass by saying, "I wish somebody would make him stop!" They laughed and we left it there.

So when I came to Ronnie's account of the push to make the University of Texas a first-rate institution, John was a man about whom I had mixed feelings. Nevertheless, I took widely scattered paragraphs and crafted a paean to John Silber. According to Ronnie, Ransom had abdicated: " . . . preoccupied with his rare books, a poor administrator, and irresolute . . . [he] melted away as a leader to be relied on." John Silber had perforce taken up the burden.

Though Ronnie noted that Silber's "style of cold logic and hostile contempt toward those differing with him" could lead him as a dean to humiliate people with less power, he presented this largely as a function of his "natural superiority . . . [which] causes envy and insecurity in the less gifted or the less diligent and hate in those who are both." "He is an excellent man," Ronnie wrote, adding, "He rises in comparison with others, he excels." Later John actually called to thank me, saying that it was only when he read the book that he realized what an astonishing job of editing I had done for the article and how well he came off in consequence.

Such Silber-worship as I had left was about to vanish, however. For since John was now president of Boston University, we spoke occasionally by phone on *Change* business, and at the end of one conversation, he asked, "Is Willie unhappy enough for you?"

My eyes turned to glass and my blood to bile at this notion that I might relish the disintegration of my son's father and a man I had loved. But I managed to say, "You're making it a lot easier to say some harsh things I've been needing to say to you!" then slammed down the phone, jumped onto the next train to the city, burst into Stanley Crouse's office, and went into overtime raging against Silber and his appetite for attributing sins to me that he had invented. Then I wrote John that his nastiness obligated him to come for the confrontation he had owed me for several years; I wanted two hours in private, after which I thought it likely we would never want to speak to one other again.

He replied that he was just being funny. I wrote back that it wasn't funny. A few months later, he said his house had burned down and I should get off his back. I replied that I was sorry about the house but not responsible, and meanwhile I was still waiting. The denouement came a few years later still, but the man I had honored above all others as a brave fighter for justice now seemed to me a mixed-up bully. And that was just for starters.

In the early 1970s, just as my trust in powerful men was waning, women's liberation with its core of consciousness-raising groups was blossoming in Manhattan. I had little to do with it, however, for I thought that if my consciousness had not been raised by an hour on a couch five days a week, eleven months out of the year for years on end, there wasn't much hope for it. I read about the 1972 march for women's rights in the next day's newspaper and didn't get to Betty Friedan's *Feminine Mystique* until years after it was first published. So feminists who claim you don't amount to much if you weren't there at the start will write me off.

Luckily, however, one could not escape the influence of feminism, and I first encountered modern-day feminists when two young women came to work for *Change* right out of the Columbia School of Journalism. Their names were Jean and Cheryl, and they were bright, sassy, and committed to women's rights. I liked and enjoyed them, though I found them odd; they fussed when men held doors for women, or stood back while women left an elevator first. And I could not imagine why anyone should despise simple moments of grace.

They were most outrageous, I thought, when they scolded me for letting Gil Moore light my cigarette. Gil was a black man working on an article for *Change,* and in just a few weeks, we'd come close to breaking one of the most powerful taboos in our culture: a black man and a white woman were becoming real people to one another. Meanwhile Jean and Cheryl complained—and not about my smoking, which I would have readily understood.

Gradually, however, I began to get the point. Soon we were talking about publishing a book on campus women, and since we needed someone distinguished to write an introduction, I decided to read Elizabeth Janeway's recent *Man's World, Woman's Place.* Quoting Suzanne Langer's provocative sentence as her epigraph— "We live in a web of ideas, a fabric of our own making"—Janeway begins wonderfully: "If there's nothing more powerful than an idea whose time has come, there is nothing more ubiquitously pervasive than an idea whose time won't go. The division of the world by sexes, challenged a century and more ago by the militants of the first wave of Feminism, still endures and, what's more, still prevails, in spite of new attacks upon it. . . . if women have only a place, clearly the rest of the world must belong to someone else and, therefore, in default of God, to men."

This was language I could understand, and I read the book with the rising excitement you feel when you know something truly important is happening to you.

Janeway lived on the East Side of Manhattan, and so I called about the possibility of her doing our introduction and asked if I could come to see her. Van Ooms was taking me to dinner the night she invited me for cocktails, so we met her together in her book-lined, tapestried drawing room. She was a small, decorous woman about twenty years my senior, with two fluffy cats whose elegant ways seemed very much in keeping.

Her conversation ranged from New York City politics to Greek archaeology to animal husbandry. Books clearly meant to be read were piled in stacks of varying heights on a large square glass coffee table. Aside from Helaine Newstead, I hadn't had a female mentor, but by the time we left, I knew I had found one.

So Elizabeth wrote the introduction and I began to read books about women—biographies, histories, theory, psychology—each one leading to a dozen more. Parts of my life began to connect that had never even made sense before. Things I had taken to be personal failings looked far from unique in the context of other women's experiences. Patterns and meanings emerged. And a woman whose most treasured compliment had been that she was a red-blooded egghead's dream girl began to see things rather differently.

All through college and graduate school, I had learned things because men had defined a body of knowledge and told me I should master it. Now I was thrilled to find myself at the center of my own education; *I* would ask the questions and then figure out where to look for answers. While the "best that has been thought and written" did not lose its value as a category or a spur to excellence, I was no longer sure what that category did and did not include—nor was I convinced that anybody else knew. And that shift was tantamount to intellectual and personal revolution.

On the subject closest to my heart, however, the answers were not forthcoming: I was a single mother with an adolescent son, and compared to my struggles with David, everything else faded in significance. Dr. Crouse had taken the position that the stronger I was, the better David would be, but no matter how sure-footed I got, the word on David continued to be mixed. Every time he pulled himself out onto the beach, he seemed to stumble again and get sucked back into the bog.

When Bank Street said he needed professional help, I found a child psychiatrist who ranked among the best in New York, but David refused to talk and the doctor's three suggestions to me were impossible: I should remarry, stay celibate, or send David to boarding school. I didn't know anybody I even *could* marry, much less wanted to. My sex life was meager but I was in my prime, and I could hardly see how taking a vow of celibacy for David's sake would help my zest for coping with the world or, for that matter, with my son. Nor would I send him off to boarding school unless he wanted to go, and he most definitely did *not* want to.

So I wrote two women who worked with children and had been close to David and me, and begged their counsel. One replied that nothing was wrong with David. The other remarked coldly that he'd become so rude and self-absorbed that she had washed her hands of him. Neither offered concrete suggestions.

On one level, our dilemma was insoluble; I couldn't stop being what I was—a vital woman in her thirties who liked men. Unless Freud was a deluded fraud, the bond between David and me was bound to be laced with sexual tension. Years later, a woman who had raised two sons saw a picture of us together when David was about sixteen and wrote reflectively about a handful of similar photographs of herself and another friend with their sons: "No wonder these boys are struggling with a new version of manhood and no wonder they hook up with strong women when you look at these mothers, lithe and sexy and—obviously—on some kind of make, not necessarily sexual, but certainly the boy would see it that way." And then she added: "Well, our place in history demanded it."

Fortunately, David turned out to have his own plans. He bought a camera, signed up for courses at the International Photography Institute, turned our tiny back bath into a darkroom, and began staying up till all hours developing negatives and printing pictures. He was a night person while I loved the dawn, and after a few years of spilled chemicals, foul smells, and boring shots of brick walls, peeling paint, and falling plaster, I began to wake up to pictures that looked like he might be on to something.

Still, after a string of triumphs, he would plunge into a sullen funk. I spent those years as a mother being impatient, thrilled, bored, angry, frightened, baffled, amused, resentful, happy—in no particular order and for no predictable duration. He would do fine creative work—stunning wood-block prints and watercolors of places we'd seen in Italy, a paper on Beethoven that was better than anything I'd done until I was a senior in college. Then he would stubbornly insist on dressing like the local beggar, turn churlish and rude, and wonder why he was lonely. He would defiantly do something I had warned him against and be miserable at consequences I had predicted. If I held my tongue, the same thing would happen, and since Willie was unavailable, I bore the anxiety alone.

But Willie multiplied it. His worst betrayal of David came after we left Ichabod with him on Long Island while we spent the Christmas holidays with Shirley, and he refused to give Ichabod back. Six months later, I wrote him irately, "Most people just can't believe a man would steal his own son's dog," and told him David had "talked of getting a court order and getting up a petition from his friends to make you [give Ichabod back]." Two weeks later, David called from his father's, sobbing so hard he had to say it twice before I understood: Ichabod was dead. Willie had let him run loose and he'd been killed by a car.

If I had had the chance, I'd have hurt Willie very badly at that moment, or at least tried to. He was not merely careless with things and people I loved; he was reckless and stupid. And for a long time I hated his guts. I didn't feel righteous about what he had done to me, but for what he did to David I would have wrapped him in chains if I had had the power. And the fact that I could do nothing whatever did not improve my disposition.

In his last year at Bank Street, David's teacher and the school psychologist told me a handful of boys were picking on him. When I begged them to make them stop, they said he was asking for it and the only solution was for him to change. So I spent the whole year yelling at him—an experience I loathed—and at the end of school, he practically stole the show in the class play. He was marvelous.

Everybody was thrilled, and when they asked what I had done, I simply said I'd yelled. But I was emotionally bruised and baffled, and, in fact, I never *would* know whether his problems stemmed from incompatible genes, a learning disability, my early misery, permissive child-rearing, the conflicts between Willie and me, some combination of those things—or something altogether different.

He had applied to eight or nine high schools but had appeared to be so morose when he went to look them over that only two accepted him. (When I said his looking sad worried people, he insisted hotly that he wasn't sad. Full stop.) So he spent four years at a school that struck me as barely adequate but where he seemed happy enough; he made good friends, and I found him gifted tutors when the need was dire. He played the recorder for a while and then the flute, and when I bought us both guitars, he was the one who learned to play and for a few years, at least, enjoyed it.

Being David's mother was a humbling experience, for it taught me a great deal about my own limits. We were not at all alike, as my father and I had been, but I learned more from my child than Daddy had from me. The "I" who was a mother was not always someone I recognized, much less admired, but gradually I came to trust her. And David taught me to listen to people who are different, to see that good intentions and common sense can take you only so far, and to know that when they fail, despair is not an option.

Ultimately it seems futile to try to describe the deep bond between a mother and her child, for the sentimentalists fail by making it look pretty when it isn't. But I remember his glee when I high-stepped around a panhandler on Broadway and the victory sign he flashed as I joined him on the way to one of our delicious adventures—Marcel Marceau, perhaps, on 52nd Street. I remember the time in Bologna when he said, "Watch out, Mommy, here comes the Italian army!" and then caught up my hand and held it high as he shouted to a brace of Italian men in uniform, "She's mine!" We laughed and cried through so many things together, we screamed and pouted but refused to break, we failed each other time and again and came back for more. The moment after I flounced away over what had seemed his latest folly, I would see that child's face appealing to me and know the sentence was for life.

Still, more than anything, I wanted to live in the Middle Ages when people sent their sons to someone else's court where they were taught manners and learned how to be happy if they had it in them to be. Despite the obstacles, I think I was a "good enough" mother, but I shall always believe that David needed more than I could give—or something perhaps altogether different. The stronger Celia of twenty years later would surely have handled some things better, but she wasn't the one on duty during the sixties and seventies. And in the pitch black of the night when the soul is rawest, it doesn't help to know that mothers in our culture are called upon to do the impossible. For I remember the burbling, mindless bliss of holding my lovely baby in the Nuffield Infirmary in Oxford, and then I think of my David, at three or four, at ten or eleven, with pain jammed behind those big brown eyes. Pain I cannot touch or lift. And there is no solace.

CHAPTER FIFTEEN

The *Liebe* in my life, then, came largely from David and my friends, and as the years passed, our bonds grew deeper and more enduring. Stanley Crouse had taught me that listening could bring solace, and when I realized that most people did not have my mother's bottomless need, my home and heart gave shelter from many a storm. When I got ready to leave New York, Pat Marschall went into mourning, for my apartment had become the place she counted on to be there whenever she needed it. It took us a while to discover that wherever the heart was, the home was too, and in this process, Pat and I were not alone.

Meanwhile my friends and I sustained our trials together. One lost a baby to crib death, and after her husband knocked her around one time too many, she divorced him and went on a spree to make up for the sex she had forgone as a loyal wife. She would meet a man at a bar at some seaside resort and go with him to make love on the dunes, and then go back to the bar to find somebody else for a return trip. One summer she slept her way through one of the more dynamic foreign countries and almost emigrated, but as her rage and frenzy eased, she found a gentle, worthy man who made her happy and has gone on doing for more than a quarter of a century.

A man I had been hopelessly fond of grew impossible at last, beat his wife with his fists, then married another woman who belatedly discovered that he was bisexual. And not long after his second divorce, he died painfully of a peculiarly cruel disease. A more upstanding friend took up with his secretary, whereupon his former wife married an ex-heroin addict who beat her, so her youngest child grew up without a father.

Another friend had an illegal abortion I arranged to have done in my apartment, and I sat in the back room while the doctor was with her, beating back the terror that she might die. John and Billie Maguire lost their eldest daughter Kelly after she spent two months in a coma induced by insulin shock; John and Ann Egerton's family was traumatized by a horrible neighborhood murder. And just after my fortieth birthday, my mother finally drank herself to death.

But good things were just as much a part of the mix. One summer Jean Dugger brought her sixteen-year-old daughter Celia to stay, and we jump-started one of my sweetest relationships. By the time they left, Celia Dugger had truly become my namesake, and in the years since, I have watched her move from one happiness to another, from one triumph to another. Once I told her, "I don't think anybody has the right to say 'I'm proud of you' except to their own children, but if you wouldn't mind, I'd very much like to say 'I'm proud of you!'" And, as it turned out, she didn't mind.

So within a few years of my divorce, I had replaced a derivative life amidst celebrated company with something far more authentic. Through the hard parts and even the tedium, my friends stood fast, and as I prepared to leave the analysis, I shifted my trust that someone would be there when I needed them from my doctor to my new family. For the cavity that had yawned where my sense of self should have been had all but vanished under a skinny redhead's care. Stanley Crouse hadn't promised me a rose garden; he hadn't even promised that I would be happy. But he *did* say I could most likely handle whatever came next, and in this modest promise he has proved very nearly correct. For all the setbacks I'd suffer in the years to come, he had saved my life.

If the *Liebe* was good, the *Arbeit* was promising. Sometime in 1973, John Egerton called from Nashville and said, memorably, "I've just run across a dazzling woman, and her name is Fanny Wright." He was doing a book for the University of Tennessee Press on four nineteenth-century communes in that state, and one of them was Fanny's Nashoba. Because she had descendants apparently living in New York City or its environs, he asked if I could help him with some preliminary research.

He hoped one day to write a novel about Fanny, whose essays had already caught my eye, and I was intrigued.

For Fanny Wright was the first woman in this country to act publicly against slavery and the first to speak before what was then called a "promiscuous" secular audience—one of men and women together. She was the first to say that women were men's equals and should act as such and be treated as such in all the business of public life. The privileged, upper-middle-class daughter of a highly stratified class society in Great Britain, she spent half her adult life in the United States, casting her lot with working people and doing what she could to encourage Americans to live up to the promise of the Declaration of Independence. Since taking Thomas Jefferson literally meant being truly radical, to be called a "Fanny Wrightist" in the 1830s was roughly equivalent to being called a communist in the 1950s.

My research on Fanny began, then, with a tryst at St. John the Divine Cathedral with a man who'd told me he'd be in the right bay in long white. He had succeeded Fanny's grandson, William Norman Guthrie, as pastor of the historic Episcopal church St. Mark's in the Bowery, and by the time we met, I knew enough about her to know that as an eighteenth-century rationalist, she would be stunned, if not appalled, to discover that her two grandsons were both Episcopal rectors.

Through this interesting cleric, I located Guthrie's eldest daughter, who invited me to tea in Riverside, Connecticut, where I also met her sister, who was visiting from Charleston. They were both in their eighties, and I discovered that the thread of resemblance had spun out very thin indeed. By this time, I had read two biographies of Fanny Wright— one of them published in 1924 by William Waterman, and the other, in 1939, by Alice Perkins and Theresa Wolfson—and I knew that Fanny was as radical as people get, in this country or anywhere.

Fanny's great-granddaughters, on the other hand, were proper ladies who bent daintily over translucent cups and referred often to Poppa, as in "Poppa said Miss Perkins lost the trunk with all those papers." Or "Poppa didn't approve of Miss Perkins's book, and neither did Mama." There was the matter of a possibly illegitimate daughter, and the Guthries did not take to plain-speaking. I already knew more about Fanny Wright than her descendants did, and as I made my way home, I thought about what a rollicking good time John Egerton had before him.

A few months later I got fired from my job at *Change* magazine, and so, in the midst of a phone conversation with John, I said, "I need a good idea. I'm not very good at getting them, but not bad at working them up." To which he said, "I'll give you Fanny!" I was struck dumb; I couldn't imagine *anything* more generous than one person's giving another his or her idea. And I thought the prospect of writing the biography of Fanny Wright for my generation the most exciting and valuable thing I could possibly do for the next couple of years.

On top of that, I was ready. During my four years at *Change*, I'd learned as much as I was likely to learn there, but after the third year, I'd begun to slide into a bristly, unpleasant relationship with my boss. When he fired me, I thought to myself, "If I'd had the power, I'd have fired *you* a year ago." And since I hadn't failed or even hesitated to do anything he had asked of me, I insisted on three months' severance pay rather than the two weeks' salary he'd intended. A number of our most distinguished writers, among them the Harvard sociologist David Riesman, considered me a top-flight editor, so I had a strong bargaining position. And when I won, I banked the money, signed up for unemployment insurance, and plunged into nineteenth-century American history.

Funds were tight, for after Willie lost his job in a celebrated showdown at *Harper's,* I had implicitly waived alimony but insisted that he keep paying child support because David and I could not do without it. Months might pass without a check or even a vow to send one—six months in one particular year—and several times I threatened to take him to court.

Now and again I applied for jobs, but so did hundreds of other editors and teachers and nothing ever panned out. So for almost two years, David and I lived frugally, but with a certain flair, while I turned myself into a historian. In 1974, I applied for a fellowship from the National Endowment for the Humanities and didn't get it. So I asked if there were a rule or bias against my applying again. When they said no, I asked where my application had fallen short, spent the next year trying to fill in the gaps, and got the fellowship on my second try.

Meanwhile I had a friend who designed wonderful clothes, and since I wore a standard size 10, I could buy her display dresses at season's end for ten and fifteen dollars apiece. David took up cooking, while I learned to knit and crochet to make the sweaters and coats we needed. We bought opera and ballet seats in what was colloquially known as the vertigo section and, after the curtain rose, moved down to find empty places in the orchestra. Pat Marschall lent us eight silver goblets in which I served cheap Spanish wine. When our building went co-op, Daddy lent me the money to buy the apartment.

And I read. And read. I sat in on two history seminars at the City University on 42nd Street and found out what it means to crave answers to a set of complex questions.

At the time I began trying to come to terms with Fanny Wright, I thought history had a great deal more to do with facts than I would discover it did or even could do, and I had yet to realize how profoundly being a woman shaped a person's life. For Fanny was so inflammatory that many stories about her were bizarre and some were flatly incredible. She was physically intimidating—almost six feet tall in an era when the average man inducted into the French army was less than five feet five inches—and so well educated and articulate that she stunned audiences whenever she spoke. Because she had become a myth—and a figure to frighten other women with—sorting out truth from fancy would be hard.

My first piece of real research was at the New-York Historical Society, where I sat scanning the New York City newspapers for 1829 and 1830. At the end of that long, gloomy day I must have looked ashen, for an archivist asked, "Lady, what's wrong with you?" And I said "I've just read the most vicious attack I've ever read on anybody." I later found one on Rachel Jackson that was marginally worse—Andrew Jackson's wife had been widely called a Jezebel who would corrupt the nation's women—and when I realized that in the violently partisan wars of the day, the press was not above attacking the loyal, kind-spirited wife of the most powerful man in the country, I knew Fanny had been doomed from the outset.

For Andrew Jackson was bitterly convinced that the press had literally killed his beloved Rachel, who died just before he was inaugurated president. And at a time when propriety forbade women to use a word like "corset" in public, a woman who wrote that miscegenation was the way to solve the race problem and spoke of sexuality as the source of the best joys of human existence was letting herself in for it. So from the beginning, I knew I was dealing with someone who was either inspired or crazy—perhaps a measure of both—and working through that quandary would be one of my challenges. But I had stumbled onto a woman who asked all the questions I did—about race, sex, power, work, money—more than a century before I was born, and the study of history took on a relevance I hadn't felt earlier.

First I had to find the primary material, and the key source was apparently a trunk full of letters and manuscripts that both earlier biographies had depended on heavily. Fanny's great-granddaughters thought Miss Perkins had taken the trunk, but I discovered that William Waterman, the 1924 biographer, was still alive and drove up to Dartmouth College in New Hampshire to see him. A courtly octogenarian, Waterman told me he'd had to use Alice Perkins's notes, for Guthrie kept promising to show him the trunk itself but never produced it. So the trunk had apparently disappeared even before 1920.

So who was Alice Perkins? Nobody knew, including *Harper's,* which had published the 1939 biography. Who was Theresa Wolfson? Nobody knew that either. For more than a year, I pursued one will-o'-the-wisp after another to what began to seem inevitable disappointment, and in the process I became obsessed.

In such a state, one babbles to anybody, and at a cocktail party, I was going on about my dilemma when a guy I had never met said, "Oh, Tess Wolfson; she taught me economics at Brooklyn College!" I was momentarily speechless. Then he said she'd died, but he thought her husband, Austin Wood, was still alive. The next morning I found Wood, who told me he had given all of Tess's papers to the School of Labor and Industrial Relations at Cornell University.

At least it wasn't somewhere in the Midwest, I thought ruefully, but at the time I had the impression that Cornell was a college that did animal husbandry and hotel management—one of the last places I'd have thought to look for Fanny Wright. Still, I called the library and found a kindly archivist who said that yes indeed, he'd driven a van to Brooklyn and brought back forty boxes of papers that had been Theresa Wolfson's. Forty boxes! I felt like my room had suddenly filled with noxious gas, and as I gasped for breath I heard him, faintly, saying he thought they included material from the Wright biography, but I would have to come up and see. After I hung up, I lay for an hour staring blankly at the ceiling.

A few days later, I took the bus to Ithaca and found my way to the library, where the archivist, Richard Strassberg, sat me down in front of four boxes he thought held most of the Fanny material. For the first ten minutes or so, I found only things like postcards from Hawaii and recipes for *boeuf bourguignon,* and I was about to conclude that Cornell really *was* about the domestic arts when I found the first notes about Fanny Wright.

They were on 5x7-inch paper that had been fastened with a straight pin, long since rusted, to a regular 8x11-inch sheet. Some of the notes were in pencil, lots were mere fragments, and Perkins had used a good many abbreviations. I estimated the boxes contained maybe fifteen hundred sheets like this, so I was excited and overwhelmed at the same time. I was grateful to Alice Perkins for spending what must have been months in Sewanee, Tennessee, sometime between 1900 and 1920, copying from letters, documents, essays, and plays that were in Guthrie's trunk. The notion that he had *lost* a trunk, however, with letters from the Marquis de Lafayette, Thomas Jefferson, James Madison, Andrew Jackson, and so on was confounding. I told Richard I would be back later, climbed onto the bus for New York City, and when I got home drank, as I recall, quite a lot of bourbon.

Within the next few months, however, I made two more trips to Ithaca and brought back more than five hundred photocopied pages that then had to be arranged and interpreted, and in the course of this I discovered discrepancies between the notes and what Perkins and Wolfson used in their own book! They had changed words when it suited them, in ways that sometimes altered the meaning. They had left out passages and whole letters I found significant.

By now I had blanketed Tennessee, Ohio, New York, Connecticut— wherever I had reason to believe Guthrie had been—with letters asking libraries and historical societies if they knew anything about the trunk, but I found nothing. For years I would live with the nightmare that as soon as my book was published, somebody would find the trunk and the whole thing would have to be written over. But meanwhile I had to face the fact that my work would rest on a source I knew was shaky; it was my first chastening lesson on the imperfect nature of what we call "history."

The next quest followed from a book on Fanny called *Commune on the Frontier* that was written by Richard Stiller for adolescents and published in 1972. Citing letters held by one Cecilia Payne-Gaposchkin, the author made claims about Fanny that hadn't appeared in the earlier books. When I somehow found Stiller and went to see him, he said the papers dealt largely with Nashoba, Fanny's Tennessee commune, and were owned by an astronomer at Harvard whose great-great-grandmother, Julia Garnett, had been one of Fanny's closest friends.

My beloved Celia Dugger was now a freshman at Harvard, so I made an appointment with Dr. Payne-Gaposchkin and took myself up to Cambridge. At the time I was not above imagining astronomers as people who wore pointed black hats with spangles, and so I was not altogether surprised when I got to the Harvard College Observatory and found a rather formidable woman I took to be in her seventies with wispy white hair going in all directions. She had an English accent, and though it was November and the air was crisp, she was wearing plaid wool socks with wide-thonged leather sandals and smoking a long black cigarette in a holder. She scowled.

Her letter to me had seemed querulous; she imagined that I wanted to publish her cache of letters just when she'd found the time to edit them for publication. And so I had to assure her that I wasn't interested in stealing her avocation, but since I hoped to write the biography of Fanny Wright for my generation, I had to see letters she'd made available to a man who was writing for adolescents. Her husband Serge Gaposchkin, a refugee from the Russian revolution and also an astronomer, came into her office to tell me in a twinkly sort of way that "Mama" had her heart set on her project, and I assured him too that my designs were honorable.

After an hour or so, Dr. Payne-Gaposchkin seemed convinced that I was both determined and serious, and so she said I could see all of Fanny's letters, along with her sister Camilla's, but stipulated that I could not see *any* that were written about them. She knew as well as I did that it couldn't rest there, but this concession would be good enough for the time being. So the Houghton Library made photocopies for me of twenty-two letters, and I spent almost a month bent over my typewriter transcribing them, letting their meanings and allusions sink in as I worked.

A few months later, after visiting David, by then a student at Hampshire College, I was back in Cambridge, staying with Celia in the Harvard Yard, which resonated so wonderfully with romantic stories from the American past. Dr. Payne-Gaposchkin was out of town, and when I stopped by the Houghton, I discovered with a glee I instantly suppressed that the librarians didn't know that I was *not* supposed to see the whole collection. She had counted on my honor, which vanished on the instant.

Freezing the expression on my face—or at least trying to—I asked them to begin bringing me ten letters at a time. I then rented a typewriter so old I wouldn't have been surprised to find a key representing the Anglo-Saxon thorn, and I typed so fast a man came over to ask if I'd do some typing for him. While I worked, I kept imagining that a white-haired woman brandishing a walking stick would descend on me wailing tremulously, "I said you couldn't see those papers!" And late every afternoon for three days I ran across the Yard through the falling snow and hid my notes under the mattress. Truly I did.

Now I found out what learning *really* ought to be, for nothing in even my best classes had come close to the excitement I felt in pursuing Fanny Wright. I was learning things because I needed to know them to reach a goal I'd set for myself—not because some person in authority had said I should. My years of psychoanalysis had taught me something about the human psyche, and that experience was paying off in ways I had never anticipated. I had to weigh a huge amount of information, using my psychological insights and political savvy to interpret what had happened to a woman in a very different world from the one I lived in.

So I was doing two things at once—tracking down every scrap of information I could find about a person I needed to understand and at the same time steeping myself in the history of her period. I knew that at some point the two would have to come together, but for years I had not the slightest idea how or when that would happen.

I wrote Diana Kealey, who was working now in Manchester, to ask her to find a historian who could help me locate Fanny in Great Britain, and she put me in touch with a wonderful and intellectually exciting woman named Jill Liddington. Jill in turn found a genealogist in Edinburgh who tracked some intriguing connections of Fanny's in Scotland, a historian at York University who could illuminate Britain's radical movements in the 1830s and 1840s, and an archivist in Devonshire who could help me understand the cultural milieu of Fanny's adolescence.

And so it went; one person would lead to two or three more, each of whom might open several doors through which they would show me into a network of corridors, potentially *ad infinitum*. The process could be tedious and enthralling at the same time, and somewhere along the way I discovered that the biographical passion could be a terminal disease.

Ultimately I went everywhere I knew Fanny Wright had gone except to Haiti and did most of the things she'd done except go walking in the Scottish Highlands. I even chugged down sections of the Ohio and Mississippi Rivers on a barge. I traveled to libraries, courthouses, and historical societies all over the eastern and southern United States and made three trips to New Harmony, Indiana, a town the Scottish industrialist Robert Owen had bought in 1824 for roughly $150,000. Two women there, Alene Cook and Josephine Elliott, guided me through a rich collection of letters at the Workingman's Institute where I could never have made much headway if left to my own devices, and Josephine became a good friend. (I made one of those trips because Alene told me I should come back to read a letter she'd finally persuaded the owner to let me see. When she called to propose it, I thought she was daft: a thousand miles for *one* letter? But since I had come to trust her, I went, and she was right.)

Then there was Cincinnati. Fanny was buried there, and the historical society had documents I needed to see. Ray Farabee, my old University of Texas friend said, "If you're going to Cincinnati, you have to call Ceil Waldrip," and when I did, she invited me to stay and sent her seventeen-year-old daughter to the airport to meet me in a jazzy little sports car.

Wendy Waldrip took me to one of those amazing mansions with probably twenty-six rooms and twenty-five fireplaces, and a few minutes after we arrived, Ceil and the rest of her family got home from a trip to Canada. In tight faded blue jeans, she was one of the most beautiful women I'd ever seen—a redhead with stunning blue-gray lavender eyes a year or two younger than I. She had grown up in Archer City, Texas, with Larry McMurtry, who'd lived in her house for a couple of years while in rebellion against his own parents. In fact, she was said to be the model for Jacy in *The Last Picture Show,* but the resemblance was merely physical; Ceil was generous, kind, and vitally interested in almost everything. (The contrast between Ceil and Jacy taught me that a novelist's characters are far more likely to reflect his or her nature than the people on whom they are ostensibly based.)

The following summer, Ceil came to New York with her youngest son, who was understudying the boy's lead in *The King and I,* and she took so happily to David's and my life there that she decided that going back to Cincinnati would feel, as she put it, like jumping into a bowl of warm oatmeal. So she stayed and in the first year lived in fourteen different apartments. Eventually she and her husband divorced, and she took the name Ceil Cleveland (her family was somehow related to Grover) and won many prizes during the ten years she put out Columbia University's graduate magazine. Within a year or so of our first meeting, Ceil too had turned into my sister.

While tracking down Fanny, my only bad experience came at the hands of the French aristocracy in the person of the Count de Chambrun, a descendant of the Marquis de Lafayette and owner of La Grange, Lafayette's former chateau some forty miles outside Paris. Fanny had been a disciple of the general's, and though he was old enough to be her grandfather, she may also have been his lover. After World War II, sixteen rooms full of material had been discovered at the chateau—letters, manuscripts, portraits, and so on—and I wanted to know what they might tell us about this peculiar relationship.

Chambrun's wife was the daughter of Pierre Laval, who had been executed by the Allies after World War II for collaborating with the Nazis, and I was told that Chambrun was hostile to Americans. Nonetheless, in the summer of 1977, I got an appointment, and when I was ushered into his office on the Champs Elysées, he was clearly ready for me.

He started by telling me how busy he was as president of Baccarat, rattled off some statistics about the company, showed me two books from the collection at La Grange that Fanny had inscribed to Lafayette, talked portentously for several minutes on the telephone, and then said he had to leave in a minute for a luncheon appointment and wondered how he could help me.

When at last I had a chance to speak, I told him I would like to see the letters at La Grange, and he said that was impossible: only Andre Maurois had been allowed to use the collection, and he had been doing a biography of the Marquise de Lafayette. When I asked to see La Grange, he said I could write some months ahead and perhaps could join one of the rare tours. When I pointed out that I lived on the other side of the Atlantic and could not make the trip easily, he gave a slight shrug of the shoulders and bowed me out. I was furious.

It had been a polished performance, and I suspected that the phone conversation had been part of the act—a buzzer under his desk no doubt signaling his secretary to call him at a given moment. Two years later, I confirmed my suspicions when I went back with a new husband who was a member of Congress and Chambrun went through precisely the same routine, including the two books and the telephone call. I had hoped my companion's eminence would soften the old bastard, but at least Chambrun was consistent. My husband was apoplectic.

On that second trip we got a driver from the American embassy to take us to La Grange, the grounds of which, according to the tourist brochure I showed Chambrun, were open to the public. He had hotly insisted the brochure was incorrect and must have phoned ahead, for his butler was waiting for us; when we parked the car and stepped out, the man loosed two enormous dogs. Three people never turned more quickly into trees. Another huge animal was howling ferociously from its kennel about a hundred yards away and throwing itself frantically against what seemed a highly dubious fence. So when the dogs snapping at us backed off, we jumped into the car and acknowledged defeat.

Eleven years after my book was published, the Count de Chambrun made a deal with the Librarian of Congress to allow the library to photocopy the entire La Grange collection. By 2010 or shortly thereafter, the material should be available to scholars, so it is just as well I did not wait.

Meanwhile, things were better than I had ever imagined they could be: I loved my son, my friends, my city, my work. Discovering that my book on Fanny Wright would inevitably fall short of telling the whole story had only sharpened my curiosity for what I *could* know. Impossible goals had been banished, hopefully forever, and life was sweet. So I decided that the time had come to confront what I'd come to think of as the last big threat that shadowed my life.

CHAPTER SIXTEEN

*I*n November, 1975, Jean Herskovits and my son David threw a gala fortieth birthday party for me, and Pat Marschall Spearman came up from North Carolina after I assured her she would almost certainly never be called upon to make the trip for a wedding. And that night, for the first time in public, I called myself an alcoholic.

The subject was so intensely painful I had discussed it only with my doctor, who was also a close friend. Veins in my mother's neck had burst six weeks earlier and she was in the hospital dying horribly. And though my father had asked me not to come to her deathbed, I didn't need to sit beside her there to hear the stark warning. The disease was probably hereditary, my doctor had said, and then he'd given me a bottle of bourbon and a book on alcoholism—a canny way of pointing out that the temptation would always be there and nobody else could resist it for me.

I was standing at the party talking with the feminist scholar Catharine Stimpson, my old drinking buddy Larry L. King, and Jean Herskovits when I said it, and Jean looked dumbfounded. She had never seen me drunk, and since I probably spent more time with her than anybody else—we'd even driven from Paris to Pompeii and back together—she knew my habits well. I seldom kept hard liquor and rarely drank more than a bottle of wine a day. When I told Pat, she was as startled as Jean.

But for years I had spent very nearly every day trying *not* to drink too much. When Willie left, the temptation to drown myself in alcohol had lifted, but the urge to drink had not. Too often I had ended up sleeping with the wrong man, and one horrid morning I'd lain in bed staring at a fat brown spider making his way across the ceiling while I told myself I'd die of alcohol and didn't much care.

Still, I *did* care. In fact, I was adamant about *not* dying of it, and I thought that using the "A" word to people I cared for was a first step toward giving it up. In this, I think I was right, but the struggle would be far more tortuous than I had imagined.

For a few days later, a man who had been a hero of mine for almost twenty years called from Washington and asked to come see me. It was Bob Eckhardt, who, along with Ralph Yarborough, had been a leading liberal Democrat in Texas and one the *Observer* treated with something like reverence. A dissenter—perhaps by nature but certainly by conviction—Bob was a labor lawyer in a state with right-to-work laws. He had also been involved in the early school desegregation cases and regularly took on Big Oil and other giant corporations. He was even a cartoonist of biting wit and, in general, a class act. In fact, in *North Toward Home,* Willie had begun with him when he talked about the good men who redeemed the experience of watching state legislative folly:

> [He was] a gentle and learned man, undoubtedly one of the outstanding men in state politics in America. The role of the anecdote, the story, is a powerful one in Southern politics, and Eckhardt was a genius in the milieu; his humor was usually sad and quiet, like Lincoln's. He . . . told the story about how a voter in Houston walked up to his mother . . . and said, "Mrs. Eckhardt, we're favorably inclined toward your son, but we're worried about his views on the race issue." She replied, "Oh, I'm afraid that's my fault. I raised him to be a Christian."

Willie went on to say that the lobbyists for the big corporations would be warned about Bob when they were sent down to testify: "There'll be a fellow . . . named Eckhardt, with a drawl like a dirt farmer, but when he starts asking questions, you'd better stop and think about the answers. He knows more than we do."

Not long after I left Texas for Stanford, Bob had married Nadine Brammer, Bill's former wife, and in 1967 he had been elected to Congress from Houston. I had stayed with Bob and Nadine in Washington in the early 1970s and had even written a will making David their ward if I died before he reached his majority. But I'd eventually learn from Bob that Nadine had flown retrospectively into a rage one night he and I had stayed up to read Mark Twain aloud after she'd gone off to bed. She wrote me two harsh letters I found excruciating, though I suspected that somehow I'd dropped innocently into a roiling domestic cauldron and was being used to shore up a shaky marriage. And nothing I said could repair the shattered trust.

So when Bob called, I was wary. Nadine had moved back to Houston, which suggested a break of sorts. Still, I put him off a time or two, until finally I said he could come the following weekend.

We agreed to meet at Zabar's around noon on Saturday, and at the appointed time I spied him across the crowded delicatessen in a wide-brimmed felt hat and long, shabby tweed overcoat. He was looking blissfully at a counter with about twenty different kinds of salami, and as I came up, he said with wonder, "Celia, how is it that everybody knows I'm from Texas?" When Bob comes out with that kind of sentence, it sounds like there are about eighteen words instead of ten. (He once said he thought he should be given more time on the floor of the House than his eastern colleagues because he couldn't talk as fast.) I was captivated.

He was a big man, twenty-two years older than I, with masses of longish, dark brown hair streaked with gray, a craggy German face, and large, square hands crisscrossed with bulging veins like my father's. A little over six feet tall, he wore a bow tie, suspenders, and vests more often than not, and his clothes were always a little mussed except when he had on the three-piece white suit that made him look like an understudy for Big Daddy in *Cat on a Hot Tin Roof*. His exercise came from riding his bicycle—a habit that inspired a good many stories and more than one cartoon and landed him on the cover of a magazine for cyclists. Once a guy in a television studio asked a member of his staff, "Where'd you get him? Out of Central Casting?"

His voice had the old inflections I had loved in childhood—the languorous sentences, the soft vowels—and encased as he was in romantic myth, I found him beautiful. At the drop of hat or pin, Ronnie Dugger would wax rhapsodic about him, keening over his first wife's suicide or regretting his pain over his second's alienation. So Bob was not only a fine man, but prime for rescue.

That Saturday we chatted and laughed as we walked slowly back up

Broadway and then sat at my dining table with the winter sun flooding through a row of windows over a leisurely lunch of brie on sourdough, with "love and garlic" salami, a mixed green salad, and generous amounts of Pouilly-Fuissé. Later we wandered around the second-hand bookstores and ended up at the Strand on lower Broadway looking for a first edition of Mark Twain's *Roughing It*.

It wasn't until midnight, when we had moved on from a little French restaurant in the West 60s to a bar across from Lincoln Center that I asked: "Eckhardt, what are you doing here?" And he said, "My marriage is a legal fiction." I told him I wasn't overly concerned about the conventions, but I had been rolled over by the Eckhardt Mack truck once before, and it was not an experience I was eager to repeat. "I'm free to do what I want," he said, for he and Nadine would stay married merely for their daughter Sarah. So, not much later, trailing ties and shirts and stockings from the sofa through the hall to my room, Bob and I went to bed together, which made us both very happy. And an hour after he left on Sunday, my father called to say that Mama had died.

The next day I sat in Daddy's living room in the Hill Country and shuddered at the story of my mother's wretched end—the blood soaking the rug, the tubes, the pitiful sobs, the diapers. I'd spent most of my adult life being *not* like her, and now, in this fatal way, I knew I might well be her heir. Friends gathered in a gentle, protective circle, but my joy came from seeing Thelma Hamrick, the blithe spirit of my childhood. In a fit of self-pity, I had written her years before that I wished she had been my mother, and when she whispered, "You think too highly of me," I could only say, "I'm too old to change now."

Bob called me at Daddy's, who minded far less than I expected that a notorious liberal was once more connected somehow with his daughter. With a few eloquent words of consolation, Bob seemed so tender that tears began trickling down my cheeks for the first time since Daddy had called. I could *feel* more when I didn't have to be strong all the time, and I realized gradually how hurt I was—and how tired. And having a good man in my life fed the hope that I would no longer have to fight my battles alone, as I had done for so many years now.

When we met in New York a few weeks later, I knew infatuation could deepen into love, and all my professions of self-sufficiency began to seem like so much bravado. For the idea I had grown up with that a woman was incomplete without a man had far more weight in my imagination than mere rationality could lift. In my years alone, I'd had enough sexual experience to know that sex could be little more than a happy time between friends, but I also knew that when it was right, it could be transforming. And the sex between Bob and me was right.

The physical thrill and tenderness ministered to our sense that we were kindred souls; we loved so many of the same things—books, the theater, walking down Broadway holding hands, bicycling through the park. And whenever we were together, we seemed to be playing; he wrote spirited doggerel and drew witty caricatures of people in bars; he quoted the odd, rather than the obvious parts of Shakespeare, such as the bastard Edmund from *King Lear:*

> *Why brand they us with base?*
> *Who in the lusty stealth of nature*
> *Take more composition and fierce quality*
> *Than doth within a dull, stale, tired bed*
> *Go to the creating of a whole tribe of fops*
> *Got 'tween sleep and wake.*

Tight metal bands I did not even know I'd had burst from around my heart, and it swelled with such delight I could have flung open a window and sung Puccini to the crowds below.

Everybody who knew him had at least one choice Eckhardt story, for he was also eccentric and forgetful. One of mine came when I told him that Nora Ephron had just interviewed me for a story on John Silber. After listing things Nora had written, I ended my thumbnail sketch by saying, "And she's married to Bernstein of Woodward and Bernstein." There was a long silence until Bob finally asked, "Are they the people who do the sex stuff?" If a Montana sheepherder had said it, I wouldn't have noticed, but coming from a man who had written an *amicus* brief for his fellow members of Congress in the Pentagon Papers case, I thought it was pretty funny.

From time to time, he would disappear to Houston and once came back with an awful black eye he said he got when his horse reared up and his head hit the saddle horn as he threw himself forward to keep from falling off. We were expected that evening at Andre and Leina Schiffrin's, and I said, "If you think I'm taking a Texas Congressman to a New York cocktail party with a crazy story about getting a black eye from a horse, you'd better think again." So he amused himself and enthralled a long line of New Yorkers with dire accounts of angry lobbyists and estranged wives.

Nadine heard sooner rather than later about our liaison and called for Bob at my apartment over the Valentine's Day holiday—an event he would subsequently refer to as the Valentine's Day Massacre. The idea of a competitor had rekindled her interest, which whetted his, and for a few months I waited anxiously for him to choose. Meanwhile, the singer in my head was Ethel Merman, the song was Cole Porter's, and the subject was Bob Eckhardt:

> *You're the top!*
> *You're Mahatma Gandhi,*
> *You're the top;*
> *You're Napoleon brandy.*
> *You're the purple light of a summer night in Spain,*
> *You're the National Gallery,*
> *You're Garbo's salary,*
> *You're cellophane!*

When he finally chose, he chose me. And Nadine filed for divorce.

David had another year of high school by the time Bob became a real presence in my life—a year of second- and third-hand fights with Willie and anxiety that centered on college. The first time David took the college boards, his scores were so low they caught even Willie's attention, and he started blaming me for sending our son to an inferior high school and then huffed and puffed about getting him into a string of fancy places; Reynolds Price would help him out at Duke, Neil Rudenstine at Princeton, and so on.

I knew that David couldn't do good college work if those scores fairly reflected his verbal ability, and once when I chanced to get one of Willie's famous writer friends on the phone, I yelled that what Willie was doing was called castrating the kid, and if he didn't stop, I was coming out to East Hampton and cut it off! After days and nights of tears, it was a moment of delicious release.

Then I found David a remarkable tutor named Cathy Lipkin, and after working with him for several months, she tested him to discover that he was above average in every category and off the charts in more than one, but he was nonetheless reading slowly at an eighth-grade level. I fumed at Bank Street, though I knew it was a pointless exercise, while with her help, David's reading skills gradually improved and the possibility of his handling college work increased exponentially. The key question then was which college would be right.

Willie was still going on about places like Wesleyan and Yale, but at *Change* I'd learned about less traditional liberal arts colleges where David's strengths would have greater play. So he and I went up to Amherst, Massachusetts, to see an experimental place called Hampshire, where students set their own goals and designed their own curricula. Since it was part of a consortium with Amherst, Smith, Mt. Holyoke, and the University of Massachusetts at Amherst, students could take courses on the other campuses. Hampshire's motto was *Non satis scire,* "To know is not enough," a maxim I thought put my life's experience to date into a neat little capsule.

Writing the Fanny Wright biography was giving me strong convictions about what real learning means, and as David and I sat on opposite sides of a room listening to faculty members explain how the system worked, we caught each other's eyes and grinned. In the belief that there are as many ways to measure competence as there are ways to excel, they had been undaunted by his low SAT scores. The place was strong in theater and photography. The faculty were chosen for teaching well. Hills covered with apple orchards and a gentle river valley looked like a grand place to come into adulthood. And so Hampshire was it! David was exuberant, I was thrilled, and we seemed to be emerging from a pit of underfed vipers.

In the midst of all this turmoil, however, I drank more rather than less. Bob loved to sit around drinking wine and eating cheese, and so did I; of all the pleasures we enjoyed together, that was one of the most delectable. Wine warmed me when I was cold; it soothed me when I was frightened; it calmed me when I felt like my arm was being twisted behind my back or a plastic bag tightened over my head. It blurred my misery and ballooned my happiness. After twenty-odd years, it was so woven into the texture of my life that I began to suspect it would take a major effort to break its hold.

So I finally confessed to Bob that I considered myself an alcoholic. I could scarcely look him in the eye but forced myself to say I had to stop drinking and would need his help; I didn't want to come to him under false pretenses. We were picnicking on a little road in upstate New York at the time, and in the face of my shame, he couldn't have been more tender. He took my hand and promised to do anything within his power to help me. That big, strong, gentle body seemed to enfold me, I felt immensely relieved—I'd told the awful truth and found a protector— and then we finished the bottle of wine.

A politician living in what his opponents would call sin was thumbing his nose at the fates, so marriage was assumed and Bob expected his third time to be the charm. His first had been a marriage of the spirit and intellect; the second, of the passions; and the third would combine the three. In turn, I saw a second chance to help a man whose values I shared do the hard work that gave those values a fighting chance in the real world. And while I wondered if I shouldn't leave a longer space between my life with David and a new life with Bob, the fact that he was already over sixty argued for haste. It was hard enough to admit that in the natural course of things, I was likely to live many years without this man I loved so deeply, and cutting our time at the front end seemed misguided, if not downright foolish.

So I put my apartment up for sale, we started looking for houses on Capitol Hill, and I talked quite a lot about how to make our contributions to our new life together roughly equal. Since for the next couple of years, I would be writing my Fanny book, I'd have no income beyond modest stock dividends, so I would use whatever money I realized from the sale of my apartment as the down payment on our house. And then, of course, I would do the work of running a busy establishment and being a political wife. As deals go, this one struck me as fair enough.

One Sunday morning in the spring of 1977, when I had gone down for the weekend, Bob found a notice in the real estate section of the *Washington Post* about a row house on Third Street directly across from the Library of Congress in a block he had always found charming. I thought the price too high, but we got on our bicycles and rode over to check it out. We both had on torn blue jeans and tacky sneakers, and as we chained the bikes to a graceful cast-iron fence, I felt absurdly out of place. And when we walked into a long, narrow living room with two fireplaces, crystal chandeliers, and glass shelves full of porcelain *objets,* my throat began to constrict. It would have made a perfect setting for an Anthony Trollope novel.

Bob, however, was enthralled. It was a two-story house with high ceilings, a master bedroom, dressing room, and bath on the second floor in front and two small bedrooms with a bath at the end of a long hallway in back. The location was spectacular—three blocks from the Capitol and the Longworth Building where Bob had his office—and it had wonderful old wooden floors. And though the kitchen was a disgrace, there were valid permits to push the back wall out six feet and architects' drawings for an extension.

Still, I was worried, and not only about the cost. Even my New York apartment was bigger, and I thought we needed another room; the back bedrooms would have to be set aside for children and friends, and I would have liked a separate study. After ten years of being on the eleventh floor with light pouring in from banks of windows on two sides, a narrow row house felt too dark. The kitchen was so bad a friend would call it "the tragic kitchen," though Bob assured me that we'd make it right by extending the back of the house. When Jean Herskovits saw it, she was appalled.

But Bob ambled through those rooms with a look of sly glee. During his first decade in Washington he obviously felt he'd had the right setting for a member of Congress—a grand three-story Georgetown house a block or so from Jack Kennedy's—and he could see himself presiding here with the same flair. So I gulped down my doubts with the reminder that a biographer whose home is directly opposite one of the world's great libraries would be living out a scholar's fantasy.

We agreed to buy it.

I sold my apartment for just under $40,000. (Just a year later, as New York real estate skyrocketed, it sold again for $125,000, while two years later still, one like it sold for well over $200,000.) And I began the dreaded process of leaving my son, my beloved city, and people who had become my family. I quipped that I would miss my butcher and the New York City Ballet the most, but the real list was very long indeed.

All through April and May, I pared down my possessions, evoking old memories and ghosts with each thing I discarded. A dress would remind me of places I had gone and people I had loved; a cup or plate, of celebrations long since silenced. Jean was so upset at my leaving that we plunged into an emotional bog from which we never emerged. David took to his bed or flew out the door to play frantically with his buddies, our next-door neighbor went into mourning, and I went into shock. Twenty years later, the emotions of that time were still so vivid that Ceil Cleveland could write to me that she'd been "*devastated* when you moved to Washington just as I got to New York. . . . I didn't *want* you to get married again. I loved your independence and your great Westside apartment, and your big oval wood table, and your place, as I saw it, in the literary society of New York. You were my 'Green-witch Village' of that period! *Why did you have to go?*" It was a sentiment I would come to share myself, and sooner rather than later.

But in the end, our lives were dismantled. The gas and phone were turned off and the lights went out, David blustered away in a late adolescent fit of not caring, and I sat down to wait for the movers. I waited a week. Even the can opener was packed, and I had to use my neighbor's phone. Meanwhile I sat amidst piles of boxes in dreary rooms surrounded by dead walls with smudged outlines where pictures had been. Every day I called the dispatcher and he assured me they were working on it. Late one afternoon, more than five days into the ordeal, I called Bob and burst into tears.

The next morning, the dispatcher said, "Lady, you gotta lot of pull, don't you, gettin' a congressman to call." I said "Yeah, but the question is 'Has it worked?'" He said, "Can you believe it? Not yet!" I said, "I believe it."

But by the next day, the moving company had found a long truck to block half our street while they loaded my worldly possessions. And after they pulled away, I sat on the floor in the empty dining room and gave thanks for my time there, time that, to be sure, had been full of pain, but also yeasty, rich, and wonderful. Within those walls and against the odds, I had raised a son I thought would be a good and useful man and had redeemed my own life. "Grateful" scarcely touches the emotion.

With my household gods tucked, I trusted, safely under my arm, I locked the door to 11G for the last time, shook hands with porters and doormen who'd been good to me, and walked solemnly out of 250 West 94th, where Elizabeth Cady Stanton had spent the last years of her life and where, no doubt, her spirit had strengthened mine. Then I rounded the corner, ran down the subway stairs and jumped on the Broadway express to Penn Station, where I climbed aboard the train for Washington and my new life.

A week later, the virus that would ultimately destroy my second marriage made its first big hit. I had flown to Minneapolis to be with Shirley while Bob went to Houston for his second divorce, and he called one evening in grand spirits to announce the deal: he had signed over their two houses to Nadine, along with six acres of land; taken on their substantial debt; and committed himself to almost three times the child support I had had in New York City, which cost a lot more to live in than Houston, Texas.

I said "You did *what?*" and he was clearly stunned, for I probably said it as Medea might have when Jason told her he was marrying King Colchis' daughter. When I had tried to talk to Bob about a fair settlement, he had not been forthcoming, so I had simply trusted him to take care of it. After all, he was not only old enough to be my father, but notoriously mingy about money—witness the tacky jeans, old suits, and torn hats—and I had assumed he was at least prudent.

But this felt like a disaster. As a congressman, he had to have a Houston residence, and now, apart from a barn and twenty acres of land, he had no property other than his salary. *Never* had he mentioned carrying a debt—a category I loathed so intensely that David and I would have lived on thin gruel to avoid it. This debt was double any annual salary I had made and well over the amount for which I had sold my New York apartment.

Why had he given Nadine their second house, known as the "shack"? Well, it was too close to the "big house," he didn't want to be under Nadine's eye, and besides, he wanted to build another place. Well, where did he think he was going to get the *money* to build something else? I was irate, to understate the matter very considerably. And what about the extension of the back wall on Third Street and the new kitchen? Well, obviously we would have to wait on the Washington house, but we'd get around to it eventually.

From that day on, instead of figuring out how to get his finances under control, Bob blamed me for reacting badly, as though blaming me addressed any problem whatever.

Shirley tells me we talked about whether I should abandon the marriage and go back to New York, but all I remember is taking two Valiums and going to bed with a large tumbler of bourbon. I had been counting quarters, if not pennies, for so long that my mind simply could not get itself around what seemed to be a terrible folly.

That summer I was doing research in Europe, where I expected Bob to join me after attending a conference. So we had noisy rows when we met in Switzerland six weeks later and then again in Paris, when I argued that he should sell enough land to cancel or at least cut his debt and then cover the costs of whatever he built on his property. He felt like an elephant heading stolidly toward a cliff with a thousand-foot drop while I was a mouse dashing to and fro, trying to deflect his course without getting crushed. On he went, *thud, thud, thud,* as the edge drew nearer.

In September, in our new house, just after he said emphatically that we would build the bookcases when he got good and ready, I threw a glass of ice water at him and then ran upstairs and fell on the bed, where I lay sobbing for a quarter of an hour. I could not work *at all* until my books were on shelves where I could find them, and I could not do *good* work in the midst of chaos. Eventually he came and sat next to me, stroked my hair and asked tenderly if I would rather *not* get married after all.

But there I was in Washington, with all my worldly possessions, having already spent a great deal of time and money, not to mention emotion, leaving one life behind and committing myself to another. Now and whenever in the future I would steel myself to bring up the subject, Bob insisted: "You'll have a house and a lifetime pension when I die." Since his loan was secured by his Houston property, and I obviously wasn't marrying for money, I tried for years to believe that what struck me as financial recklessness could not injure me.

Still, the truth was simple enough: I didn't have the nerve or spirit to turn around and go back to New York, to abandon this man with whom I had known such happiness, whose aura was so bewitching, and whose public life I was so proud to join. Nor did I have the heart to put aside my biography and look for a job that would take me from work I had spent the better part of three years preparing for.

Most important, it was unthinkable that Bob Eckhardt would take advantage of me.

So on September 6, 1977, Fanny Wright's 182nd birthday, Judge Gerhardt Gesell married Bob and me in his chambers. Gesell was a crusty, courtly man whose daughter Patsy had been one of David's best teachers and whose front-page decisions in the Pentagon Papers case we had all followed with great excitement. Not only did the good judge not ask me to obey, he required so little that I wondered how we could be properly married.

Bob's oldest friend, the legal scholar Charles Black, came down from Yale to be the best man and our sole attendant. A man of extraordinary versatility and many parts, he also gave away the bride, played the wedding march on his harmonica, and caught the bouquet. The Yale University Press had recently published a book called *The Tides of Power: Conversations on the American Constitution between Bob Eckhardt and Charles L. Black, Jr.*, and Judge Gesell commented that he had found their mutual monologue quite interesting—an insight so subtle its value escaped me for more than fifteen years.

From then on, I worried acutely about money. About two months later, when I again brought up the possibility of his selling some land, Bob shoved his face into mine and shouted fiercely, "I'm going to keep it all!" Shaken at losing control, he stayed home the next day and we bought some cheerful plates to signal a rapprochement. But for serious thought about how to use our resources well and fairly, I might as well have talked to an iguana.

CHAPTER SEVENTEEN

*W*hen I ask myself what I liked best about being married to Bob Eckhardt, I think first about his daughter Rosalind and the grandchildren. But that isn't fair, for the best things were between us and they were very plain. Sitting before the fire talking. Walking down the street holding hands. Sleeping with someone I expected to live with to the death, arms and legs entwined. Bicycling to Georgetown and wandering in and out of the shops and down the C&O canal. Cooking for a man who liked whatever I made. (Bob came home almost every day for lunch, with the dire result that soon we looked like Tweedledum and Tweedledee.)

I liked to sit and watch him, for his look and gestures pleased me. Nothing in my parents' lives or in mine had prepared me for the sweetness of such days. Slowly I began to know what serenity meant, and in the beginning and in patches, I was so happy I might as well have been on laughing gas.

At the same time I was effortlessly absorbed into the smooth-running operation that flowed out of Bob's congressional office, talking every day, and often several times, to the capable women who'd been there since he came to Capitol Hill about invitations, schedule changes, or a projected trip. And the people on his various professional staffs were almost as much a part of our lives. That year he was head of the Democratic Study Group, which had shaped policy issues for the liberals for more than a decade, and its director—articulate, smart, and hard-driving like my best Rhodes friends—had been one of the first people I'd met on the Hill. Walking through the tunnel between House office buildings, he had asked, "What do you do?" And when I asked in turn, "What do I do *where?*" he broke into peals of laughter and then grinned every time he saw me coming.

Bob also headed a House Commerce subcommittee staffed by lawyers more nearly my age than his—dedicated professionals who were in and out of our house and became my friends. Though I couldn't always understand the argot, they were fighting what I took to be the good fight. Our house was their base and I ran the house, so I felt like part of the team. Competence has its satisfactions.

Finally I had the chance to meet Barbara Jordan, whose district was adjacent to Bob's, though I was so intimidated by the God-voice and her awesome presence I probably babbled. Pat Schroeder, who could have been a stand-up comic, was more approachable; when her husband extended a business trip in Europe, she'd cabled, "Have joined the Moonies, Children with Mother." Then there was Lindy Boggs, a gracious southern matriarch who gave me a recipe for gumbo, and Millicent Fenwick, who really *did* smoke a pipe. Texan Betty Dooley was just beginning to put together the research arm of the Congressional Caucus for Women's Issues, and through Betty I would eventually work with most of these women.

But of all Bob's colleagues, I was most taken with the outrageous Phillip Burton of San Francisco, unacknowledged leader of "The Group," a collection of liberal Democrats who had led the civil rights, consumer protection, and environmental crusades in the House since the 1960s. A man who had come within one vote of becoming majority leader, Phil repeatedly used his genius at redistricting to enhance the power of politicians who cared about plain people and the earth we live on. He loved to take on the big corporate interests, and if his techniques were arcane, his attitude was not, for his motto was "Terrorize the bastards!"

Brilliant and adroit, a man of gargantuan appetites, Phil descended, politically speaking, from Huey Long and Lyndon Johnson; he believed in tricking people into doing good as he defined it. A *Los Angeles Times* reviewer of his biography would write: "Important people have gone on record as believing he may have been the greatest of them all in his field. His effect on the life of this land is profound, and yet most Americans would not recognize his name."

He was so canny at drawing the lines of legislative districts that while he was alive, the proportion of Democrats in California's state assembly and its congressional delegation far exceeded their overall voting strength. In fact, he designed a district for his brother John so bizarrely shaped that it snaked in and out of three counties and Phil called it his contribution to modern art. (At "The Master's" memorial service, Willie Brown, then Speaker of the California Assembly, told about a district in the southern part of the state that against all odds Phil had carved in such a way that a Democrat could win it, and he concluded: "That's when I found out you could count ships at sea.") A few weeks after we met, Phil said, "Celia, I want you to promise to call me if Bob is ever in political trouble," a pledge I made happily because Phil had the aura of a man who could fix damn near anything.

The man himself was out of proportion. Loud and unpredictable, he smoked unfiltered cigarettes incessantly, swore constantly, drank at least a fifth of whiskey a day, maybe more, and his whisper was as loud as the average person's speaking voice. Though he lived only a few blocks away, he kept a bottle of expensive Russian vodka in our freezer in case he wanted to stop off on his way home. His table manners were appalling—when he ate corn on the cob, the kernels sailed over a six-foot area—and you would *not* want to be around if the main dish was lobster. I never knew anyone of remotely comparable eminence who was so untamed.

The other congressmen I came to know through the Group were men of principle and spiritual generosity. They were also fighters and splendid company. Five years after I moved to Washington, people of my political persuasion—and for that matter, most Democratic staff members on the Hill—would look back on them as among their all-time heroes and on these years as the last of their golden time. Jimmy Carter had not completed his first year as president when I married Bob, and nobody knew that the good days for our side were almost over. So I had the luck to sit in the House of Representatives' family gallery at a time when Bob could still call on Phil, and they could rally their troops on the floor to slip something past the opposition.

Though I begged off any deeper involvement until I finished my book, Sala Burton, Phil's wife, took me to an occasional function for congressional wives, most of whom were sharp, astute, and well informed. In the years to come, they would often be patronized by younger women who thought they had settled for too little, but when the bond between husband and wife was strong and honorable, it seemed to me they had the best of both worlds: they were doing the key work of democracy and home-building at the same time. A good many of their husbands would neither have won nor been effective without them; the congressional seat, in fact, was often a mom-and-pop operation. Some had independent careers and some did not, but all were likely to give even more than the average wife did to her husband. Like Lindy Boggs, in fact, many could have taken their husbands' seats as she did Hale Boggs's when he died, and gone on to similarly distinguished careers.

So the threads of my life connected in a new and alluring way. I was doing thrilling work I thought was important; I was married to a man I loved and honored; I was part of a community whose members I liked and whose business in the world I considered vital. Whenever I could blank out my anxiety about money, I imagined myself so lucky as to be blessed.

My marriage gave me two other gifts I prized beyond the telling, one centering on Bob's daughter Rosalind and her son Robert Stanley. Once on the escalator at Bloomingdale's with Bob, I had pointed to a mannequin wearing a slinky red satin dress with spangles and an undulating fringe and said, "Good grief, can you imagine anybody actually wearing a dress like that?" And Bob had said "Yes: Rosalind." I was intrigued.

Rosalind had been living in Austin with an architect named Stanley Walker, whose father had been a famous editor on one of the New York dailies, and Bob loved to tell how she came to Houston one weekend to say, "Daddy, I'm pregnant." Two months later, when she'd come back to say brightly, "I'm getting married," he claimed to have replied, "What's your hurry?"

He took the position that Rosalind had connected with Stanley for the sake of his genes, for she had wanted a baby. And sure enough, not long after the thrilling delivery of a beautiful boy, she had unceremoniously dumped Stanley Walker's things on the lawn and commenced life as a single mother. I thought of Rosalind as a woman marching bravely in the vanguard of a new era for women who'd *never* again be treated as the second sex, and for years, I found her attitude to childbearing and her timing hilarious.

By the time I met them, Robert Stanley was ten months old and they were living in a place commonly known as Rosalind's tree house, for two improbable stories had been added to a conventional bungalow from which the inside walls had been removed and the plaster stripped to reveal the wooden shell. It was a helter-skelter sort of affair where sprites and faeries seemed likely to be, not to mention Charlotte of *Charlotte's Web*—a home filled with sunlight that embodied the spirit that dwelt therein.

I met Rosalind in late summer, 1976, in Austin's Zilker Park at an outdoor production of *As You Like It,* the play in which Shakespeare unites two women, Rosalind and Celia, in an intimate friendship. I had brought a box of barbecue, and Robert Stanley lay grinning on his blanket while nibbling from time to time on the sausage in his fat little hand and smearing himself happily with sauce. I had never seen a sunnier child or a woman who seemed more natural and serene.

Though a nursing mother, Rosalind was the image of a sixties flower child, with an open, trusting face, an outsized smile, big brown eyes, and long dusky blonde hair, and I imagined her in a garland of flowers and interwoven vines. She wore faded blue jeans or full, print skirts down to her ankles, and sandals or laced-up boots, depending on the season and occasion. A potter who had studied with the internationally known Ishmael Soto, she had big, capable hands and an evident disdain for making what most people would think of as a living. Instead, she had learned to make do with very little money, and she did it so cheerfully that in her presence one wondered why anyone should do life differently.

I fell in love on the spot. And I was captivated by the prospect of having Rosalind and Robert Stanley as part of my intimate family.

The second priceless gift my marriage to Bob made possible was that I reconnected with Texas. By the fall of 1977, I had not been to Houston in fifteen years, and I flew into a place that had been transformed. The downtown buildings I remembered were floodlit like the Coliseum in Rome and seemed to take on its aura of antiquity, while the new skyline was breathtaking. The Medici process had clearly been at work, and a place I had fled as a cultural wasteland was now truly interesting.

We stayed with Bob's oldest daughter Orissa and her husband Larry Arend, who lived in West University Place not far from where I'd grown up. Larry was finishing a medical internship, and they had two children: the older, Jonathan, was a ravishing five-year-old with black hair and blue-violet eyes who would some day undoubtedly be death to women; their daughter, Rebecca, was Robert Stanley's age and very like him—

blonde, blue-eyed, and pixie-faced. Seeing the two cousins together, in fact, I was forced to wonder how the difference between boys and girls could be cultural, for Robert Stanley was as typically a boy in the old-fashioned sense as Rebecca was a girl. She flirted and wheedled from the time she could walk, and I quickly became one of those she could effortlessly twist around her finger.

As Bob's wife, I saw a different Houston from the one I had grown up in. Since his constituency was largely working class, I met men and women active in labor unions whom real, if unacknowledged, class divisions had kept me from knowing. And since Hispanics and African Americans were crucial to the coalition that elected Bob, I could build friendships with people of color the normal way—by working and playing together.

By now, my mode of dealing with race had gradually evolved from a commitment to certain abstract notions of justice and fairness—inter-mixed with a large dollop of rebellion—into fondness and respect for certain people, some of whom I'd come to love. Indians and Africans at Oxford. African Americans, for the most part, in Austin and New York. People toward whom any incivility seemed unthinkable. Being married to Bob meant being far more closely identified with the fight for racial justice than ever before—in the city where so many people I grew up with took the other side—and when I went with him to black churches as part of the standard campaign ritual, I got caught up in the energy and the throbbing music, mesmerized by the synergy between preacher and congregation.

Not only did I enjoy myself, but I also learned from those occasions. Several years later, I was the keynote speaker at Black Emphasis Week at Meredith College in North Carolina, and after they got over the fact that I was white, the students were curious. One asked, "How did you learn to do that?" by which she meant to speak with rhythm and em-phasis, and I answered, "By listening to black preachers."

The best thing about being back in Houston, however, was that I could stop denying or apologizing for the place I came from, which was embedded, after all, in the rhythms of my heart. New York would al-ways be my favorite city, and I would choose to live in a different part of my country. But Texas had been my home for almost a quarter of a century. Its imprint had been indelible. And being there again opened springs of feeling that had been so deeply buried I had forgotten all about them.

CHAPTER EIGHTEEN

*L*ate one afternoon, some two weeks after Bob and I had taken joint custody of our house on Third Street, he called to say, "Guess who's coming over at five?" This is the sort of question that sets you up for being surprised, but when he said "John Silber," I was not only astonished, I was anxious. For my quarrel with John had moved onto a new plane with the current issue of *Esquire,* which featured an article about him by Nora Ephron, including a story from me that he was bound to dislike.

Nora had listened for hours while I talked about John, but after my verbal purge, I'd been stricken with worry. For I had met her only once at dinner at Elizabeth and Eliot Janeway's and knew nothing about her except that she was sharp and funny. So as I pursued Fanny Wright around Europe, I had obsessed about what she would do with what I'd said.

When I got back to Washington, I had literally dropped my bags in the house and run across the street to get a copy of *Esquire,* and I'd been immensely relieved to discover that Nora had not, in fact, taken advantage of my naiveté or abused my confidence. She had included my story about the exchange at John's when we asked how students he was interviewing for Plan II responded to his appalling questions and he'd said, "They cry!" But she had not used anything else, and I thought she had written a balanced article.

So when Bob said John was coming with one of his vice-presidents,

I decided that if he brought up the article, I would say, truthfully, "She didn't include any of the good things I said about you, but she also didn't include most of the bad." But I wouldn't volunteer anything.

When they arrived, Bob was not yet home and, with packing cases standing here and there, the house was barely functional. Still, John was at his best. He had been in every home I'd had for more than twenty years, and now he wandered about in that familiar way of his, picking up the corners of rugs and peering at the underside to see how they were made, and looking around with that appetite for the undiscovered that I considered his most engaging quality. I had told Nora that if you enjoyed someone who cared about the sounds fish make and could re-create them, John Silber was your man. So long as power was not an issue, John could be a delight.

So I put out all the cheese I could find, and we were deep in conversation when Bob arrived. The spirited talk went on and on. Among other things, we discussed the question of whether old people should live with relatives, and the three of us ganged up on John, whose sentimental generalities we each shot down with a personal example of how a well-intentioned plan had turned to grief. John took the rebukes like a debater, as though that is the way the game is played. Despite the depressing stories, everybody seemed in good humor, but since we had nothing else to eat, I kept wondering why they were staying. They barely gave themselves time, in fact, to catch the last shuttle to Boston, and only after they left did I realize: John had been waiting for me to apologize.

His silence, in fact, turned out to have masked his fury, and he later told a reporter that I had lied to Nora. The reporter, however, happened to be the son of David's Hampshire adviser, and when he told me, I replied in a state of high dudgeon, "You call Willie Morris. . . . " My voice was trembling as I told him that Willie was said to keep his phone in the refrigerator or off the hook, "But if you can get hold of him, he'll confirm that story!" Years later when I heard that John went around saying I hated men, I told a friend, who looked at me thoughtfully and then said, "If you hated men, your life would have been a lot simpler." Which I took to be a fine instance of understatement.

Meanwhile, I put my old Royal Standard on a table in our bedroom and began writing about Frances Wright, the woman who had been destroyed more than a century before I was born for fighting for so many things I believed in. I saw this biography as a precious chance to discover how principles played out in the real world, while at the same time resurrecting a woman whose circumstances had been so different from my own.

It was not long before I discovered that reading hundreds of books did not teach you how to write one, and sometime in December, I walked into the Library of Congress and was suddenly dizzy at the thought that at least one human being had written every book there. The work was alternately thrilling and tedious. Others have no doubt discovered better ways than plunging in, and other methods must be less wasteful. My way seems to be to plunge, however, and as I sat staring at the paper, ideas would come, facts would arrange themselves, revelation would strike, and I'd begin typing. Pages would pile up, and then I would get the scissors and tape and begin editing my copy and rearranging paragraphs.

Sometimes I spent the day tunneling into what felt like a dark hole with a dead end and woke the next morning with a way out. In the process, I found that I needed skills like those of a National Security Agency investigator, which are, according to a recent *Washington Post* article, "a willingness to endure tedium, a stoical tenacity when faced with dry holes or disappointments and, above all, an ability to gaze at often purposefully obscure documents and discover a story line." I had no idea that this first draft would take me more than two years to finish.

I found myself having conversations with Fanny, demanding irately, "*Why in the world* did you do *that?*" Or commiserating about how much some slight must have hurt, or wondering what she'd thought about this person or that. I would imagine her in a rage over something I had written, insisting, "I didn't do it that way!" or launching into an erudite monologue on, say, the Second Bank of the United States. I would hear myself telling her to go away and come back fifteen years younger, or older as the case might be, and eventually I said to myself, "Celia, maybe you need a rest."

It was the most fascinating work I had ever done, and while women who later became close friends were gathering in Houston for the First National Women's Conference, I was sitting in my bedroom/study learning my feminism from a woman who had died in 1852. I don't remember giving a thought to this momentous occasion, though it was held in my hometown and not far from my husband's congressional district.

But it transformed many women's lives, including mine, and produced a Plan of Action that, if implemented, would go a long way toward making women more nearly equal in American society.

Almost a century and a half had passed since Fanny Wright had preached women's equality in the late 1820s, and only now were American women sufficiently aware of the task before them and well enough organized to come together to figure out how ideas like hers might be implemented. And it was a measure of how hard and unyielding our problems were that in 1977, those women in Houston didn't know a thing about Fanny, and I, in turn, knew virtually nothing about them. All this would gradually change, but like Fanny before us, we would find it *much* more difficult to translate rhetoric into reality than any of us imagined—though Jill Ruckelshaus had a good idea when she addressed the National Women's Political Caucus:

> We are in for a very, very long haul. I am asking everything you have to give. We will never give up. You will lose your youth, your sleep, your arches, your strength, your patience, your sense of humor, and occasionally the understanding and support of the people that you love very much. In return, I have nothing to offer you but your pride in being a woman, all your dreams you've ever had for your daughters and nieces and granddaughters, your future, and the certain knowledge that at the end of your days you will be able to look back and say that once in your life, you gave everything you had for justice.

Not long after Bob and I married, Daddy called to say he had cancer. Less than a year after my mother died, he had married a woman who was brassy and vital in a way Mama hadn't been, and he'd told me before the event that he had never been happier. I suspect his decades of sexual denial had left him somewhat unhinged, for his choice proved a nearly immediate disaster. She had persuaded him to build an eighty-thousand-dollar house on her property, though his lawyer, my friend Sam Perry, warned him: "Rudy, if you build a house on her land, she'll have homestead rights." But Daddy told Sam he was grabbing at his last chance for happiness.

So he went for it and lost. A few months after the house was finished, she kicked him out, and he moved into an apartment in Austin, started divorce proceedings, and was diagnosed with cancer. The last time I had been with him at the ranch, we had had a quarrel so violent that I had asked Tom and Sally Leach to come out and get me, and I was so hurt and upset I wasn't sure that I would ever see him again. But the instant I found out he was seriously ill, the old primary love flooded back like the surf pounding on Galveston beach.

He came to spend Christmas in Washington, for my brother Glenn was living in Virginia and he could split his time between us. I fixed Christmas dinner, and afterward he sat as the sun paled and talked about his life. He was proud of his work; it had been challenging, and he'd done it well and been rewarded. He had seen things a poor boy from Galveston, Texas, did not usually get to see. Been places, known good people. But no woman had ever loved him, that was his great regret—the one thing he had truly missed.

His voice was quiet and mournful, and I was sitting in the candlelight trying to hold back tears that came nonetheless. It no longer mattered that he had made it so hard for a woman to love him, that he had done more than his share to build walls no one could penetrate. For he was the father I had waited for at the bus stop in childhood, whose face had lighted up when he saw me, who had carried me out of hospitals and made sand castles on the beach, who had been so puffed up at my triumphs. And I was desolate at the prospect of losing him.

As we went upstairs, Bob asked, "Is your father usually that open?" And I told him I had never, ever heard him talk that way. But when he saw me in my new home, I think he believed I was properly settled and he could let down his guard and rest.

Late one evening in mid-January, 1978, Daddy's next-door neighbor called to say he was back in the hospital and in intense pain. The cancer was taking him much faster than I had expected, so I made a reservation to fly to Austin the next day and then called Mickey, Daddy's kid brother who had been his favorite and mine.

Mickey had retired and was living with his wife Teka in Dime Box, about an hour and a half from Austin. Though I had not even seen them for more than twenty years, I cried when I told him the doctors said Daddy might be dying and asked if they would meet me at the hospital the next afternoon. Without a second's pause, Mickey said yes. Then I called Sally and asked her to pick me up at the airport in Austin.

The next morning I got on a plane that was delayed on take-off, and as we approached Dallas, it was unclear whether I would make my connecting flight. I started to sob with the wracking kind of cries that hurt your chest, and when the flight attendant hurried over, I burst out, "My father is dying, and I want to make a plane that leaves in thirty minutes." She said, "What can I do?" I asked for straight vodka, no rocks, and she brought me a triple shot. As soon as the plane touched down, she ran back and said, "When the door opens, run!" And I made it.

Sally got us to the hospital and into the elevator while I gave myself a lecture on self-control. So I was dry-eyed when we walked into Daddy's room, where he was sitting on the edge of the bed talking to Mickey and Teka, and I put a good measure of fake cheer into my voice as I asked, "Daddy, what are you doing here?" He was weak but beamed as he said, "Why, Celia!" I hugged him and then turned to Mickey and Teka, and that is how it all started.

It went on for five weeks. At one point Mickey said, "You got one Ph.D., and now you're getting another," and I answered, "This one's a whole lot harder." He and Teka drove in at least twice a week, and without their practical help, their solace, and their counsel, I don't know how I would have got through it.

For several days, I stayed with Tom and Sally across the lake, but driving Daddy's 1977 Chrysler felt like driving a building, and to get to their house, you had to go for miles on a narrow, winding road with corkscrew turns that killed people every year. One night I got lost, though I had been on that road hundreds of times, and when I stopped to borrow a phone, the people were alarmed. I was sober enough to know they thought I was too drunk to drive, and to know they were right. But I was drunk enough to do it anyway. Later I came to think it was a miracle I hadn't killed myself.

So I moved into town with Rosalind and Robert Stanley, whose tenderness seemed all-enveloping. I would spend the day with Daddy in the hospital and then come back to what felt quickly like home. Robert Stanley would climb onto my lap and I would rock him or read Dr. Seuss books he was too young to understand. He would grin with that magical smile, and I would believe despite the pain that I had found peace at last.

Daddy grew more gaunt, and once, pointing a spidery finger at the wall beyond the foot of his bed, he whispered that soldiers with fixed bayonets were climbing over there. The doctors had told me to be straightforward and tell him if he was having a hallucination, and so I tried to be matter-of-fact. He looked quizzical and unconvinced, but lay down and stared at the ceiling.

He queried the doctors about the medication they gave him and once refused to eat for three days because they put him in a cozy that tied him to the bed. One irate doctor took me aside and said Mr. Buchan had three problems: one was his sarcoma, the second was his weakness, and the third was his character. I looked him straight in the eye and said, "It's his body and his life and his death. I'm proud of my father." Six weeks later, I sent the doctor a copy of Dylan Thomas's "Do Not Go Gentle into That Good Night" and told him I was glad that my father had raged against the dying of the light.

He was sixty-nine years old and had been smoking unfiltered cigarettes since he was nine. Lung cancer was not going to keep him from smoking now, but his hands shook so badly he asked me to light his cigarettes. Since I had not smoked for several years, I dreaded it but did it anyway and got hooked again. With the alcohol and cigarettes, along with the anguish, I was soon a mess but promised myself to do something about it later. One night I slept sitting straight up on a barstool at his apartment, leaning against a wall, and it defies all probability that I didn't fall over and splinter some bones.

Most weekends I went to Houston to see Bob, who was campaigning in the 1978 primary. And one Sunday afternoon he took me to my first black church, Antioch Baptist, for a birthday tribute to Martin Luther King. We were sitting in the minister's office and I had just met Mickey Leland, who was running for Barbara Jordan's old congressional seat, when I heard a woman singing "The Battle Hymn of the Republic." She had such a magnificent contralto that I went out and stood looking at her from the back of the church. Then I went back to ask Floyd Williams, the minister, if he knew her, and he replied, "Her name's Lillian Mitchell, she's a good friend."

When the time came, I walked with Bob and Mickey down the aisle behind Reverend Williams, and the ushers seated us on the front row of the dais facing the congregation. Bob was to follow Williams in paying tribute to Dr. King, and midway through Williams's remarks, I began to cry. I sat there willing myself to stop. I bit my lip and shifted in my chair, but nothing helped; the music, the greatness of the man, the cruelty of racism, my misery at losing my father—all of it came together. The tears kept coursing down my cheeks, and when Bob got to the lectern, I was resigned to making a spectacle of myself. By the time he finished, I faintly wished someone would call an ambulance.

A few days later, I called my uncle and asked if he'd mind a black woman singing at Daddy's funeral and he said, "I think that's great!" I said I didn't care what anybody else thought, though I was quite sure that Daddy would die again if he knew and that his friends would be appalled. But funerals were for the living, and if it was all right with Mickey and Teka, that's the way I wanted it. They said, "Fine!"

So I asked Lillian Mitchell if she would sing, and when she said yes, I decided on four songs. One was "All My Trials, Lord":

> *Hush little baby, don't you cry*
> *You know your [poppa] was born to die,*
> *All my trials, soon be over . . .*

Another was an old folk song, "Old Gospel Ship":

> *I'm gonna take a trip on that old gospel ship,*
> *I'm goin' beyond the sky,*
> *I'm gonna laugh and sing until the bells are gonna ring,*
> *When I tell this world goodbye . . .*

One was from a poem of Byron's, "We'll Go No More A-roving":

> *So, we'll go no more a-roving*
> *So late into the night,*
> *Though the heart be still as loving,*
> *And the moon be still as bright.*

> *For the sword outwears its sheath,*
> *And the soul wears out the breast,*
> *And the heart must pause to breathe,*
> *And love itself have rest.*

> *Though the night was made for loving,*
> *And the day returns too soon,*
> *Yet we'll go no more a-roving*
> *By the light of the moon.*

And the last was "Abide with Me":

Abide with me
Fast falls the even' tide;
The darkness deepens,
Lord, with me abide.
When other helpers fail
And comforts flee,
Help of the helpless,
Oh, abide with me. . . .

It was a horrible time. About ten days after the King memorial service, a nurse came into Daddy's room and said I had a call at the nurses' station. When I picked up the phone, I was surprised to hear Bob's voice but thunderstruck when he said, "Wendell Hamrick has died." Wendell was my second father, and I simply could not believe that he and Daddy would both go together. By the end of the next two weeks, Bill Brammer had died of a drug overdose and Ronnie Dugger's father and brother had died within three days of each other. I was tempted to turn mystical with Rosalind and say the planets were out of kilter. Mainly I felt wretched.

Bob flew in for Wendell's funeral service, and as we walked down the aisle to sit with Thelma, titters ran through the congregation. Wendell had been president of the Harris County Medical Association, a bastion of conservatism, and the idea that Bob Eckhardt was being decorously received at his funeral was too much for some frayed nerves to take.

Two weeks later, the same core of people stood around Daddy's casket for a graveside ceremony in Houston. David had flown down from Hampshire, and he and Bob and I had driven over from Austin. On the way to the cemetery, I had bought a huge bouquet of flowers but was startled to find so many people who had come to say goodbye to my father. My fifth grade teacher was there, and the man at whose house we were dining when the phone rang with word of Pearl Harbor, and a couple who'd lived on Rutgers. They were frail, most of them, and shrunken, but still the same somehow. The place was full of ghosts.

Though it was the middle of March, the air was chilly and the skies were overcast. Lola Williams, Floyd's wife, was standing to one side with Lillian and the minister who would conduct the ceremony. The casket was held by straps stretched over the open grave, and I'd asked that it be lowered while Lillian sang "Abide with Me."

As if at a signal, all of us began to gather around the casket, and then I walked around the circle handing each person a flower from an armful that turned out to be barely sufficient. Then I faced the casket again with David on one side and Bob on the other, each holding my hand, as the minister began. I barely listened, for his words had no power, but instead looked dully at Thelma, who had just lost her husband and now one of her oldest friends, and at my old playmate Wendell, who, like me, had lost his father and second father, and Mickey, who had lost his brother, and Glenn, who had never been close but now seemed so alien that he had not only lost a father but perhaps a sister as well.

Then Lillian began to sing "We'll go no more a-roving," and Bob, who was holding his hat across his heart, began to cry. Once again, she was magnificent—*her* words *did* have power—and I watched the music sweep through the people clustered there. Then, as she began to sing "Abide with Me," I gave the signal for the coffin to be lowered and stood there for a second while the pulleys shrieked horribly, for someone had forgotten to oil the chains. Finally, as the coffin sank below the rim of the earth, I stepped forward to toss my flower after it, David threw the second, Mickey, the third, and then everyone followed. The flowers covered the coffin; Lillian sang one last "Abide with me," and the service was over.

Weeks later, back in Austin, Mickey and Teka asked what we were to make of Glenn, who had not spoken to me at the funeral. I told them I knew it must have been hard on him when people asked, "Are you Celia's kid brother?" but when I'd tried years later to talk that over, he'd turned away and told his first wife, "I wish Celia would shut up."

So I did not know, and probably never would, what made Glenn tick, but for me, the experience of helping my father die had been rich and terrible. When Daddy's neighbor took my hand and said, "It meant a lot to Rudy for you to be here," I managed to reply, "It meant a lot to me too." Many good things I have and many good things in me I owe to my father, and in the end I had been able to thank him. The love had overwhelmed everything else that had gone between us. And I knew that when it counted, I had not failed him—nor had I failed myself.

After Mickey and Teka and I finished clearing out Daddy's apartment, we faced each other for yet another parting. And I said, with a heart that had grown a size and a half bigger in the past three months, "I've lost a father and brother, but gained an uncle and aunt, and for that last, I am *very* grateful." For now I was building another primary family.

CHAPTER NINETEEN

After Daddy died, I moved slowly for a long time. And months later, when I came back to myself, I began to realize how different my life was now. I had made one new friend, Claire Foudraine, who promised to have the kind of presence in my life that Ceil and Diana did. A psychotherapist a few years older than I, Claire had married two psychiatrists who turned out to be impossible and had escaped the first with a child in each hand, the clothes on their backs, and a garlic press tucked in her purse. (Italians, I find, tend to have their priorities straight.) A native of Carmel, California, she had grown up reading books in an apricot tree, and they were as vital to her as to me.

But apart from Claire, the people I met in Washington seemed mainly to discuss practical politics—the mechanics of a coming election or the intricacies of a current piece of legislation, the strategies that might lever a bill out of committee or even get it passed. I missed New York and the tumultuous dinner tables where I might be the only goy and everybody interrupted everybody else because they had so many ideas and cared so passionately. Here nobody sat on the floor and talked about Mark Twain—or even the Wobblies. The narrow focus could bore you witless, and when a friend from Barnard who was a leader in the burgeoning women's movement came for dinner, she whispered, on leaving, "I don't know how you can stand it."

I cared less about having to learn a new way of thinking, however, than about an ominous clash between Bob and me over alcohol. When the tension of sitting at Daddy's bedside dissipated, I went back to taking my disease seriously. But it was *much* harder now; for almost a decade, I hadn't kept liquor in my apartment, but Bob's supply was always more than ample. When I begged him simply to drink before he got home, he was indignant; on his own hearth, he'd do precisely as he liked.

Visions of my mother's last years weighed on my spirit. I knew nobody could do it for me, but Bob had *promised* to help. If he hadn't, I wasn't at all sure I would have married him, and now he not only drank in front of me while I was trying so hard to stop, but from time to time he would even talk about how wonderful it tasted.

Claire tried hypnotizing me, but that didn't work. And whenever I chalked up a few dry weeks or months and seemed to be ahead, I would get cocky and take a sip of something or other, and the whole thing was there to do over. Larry L. King was now living around the corner, engaged in his own heroic stand against the bottle, and we lost a skirmish several times in each other's company—most memorably the night his daughter Lindsay was born, when Larry pitched off our porch into the holly and then toasted the arrival in our living room until three in the morning.

Finally I got scared enough to swallow the remnants of my pride and ask Stanley Crouse to recommend a local psychiatrist, but the new man turned out to be useless. And so the stand-off continued for months that would stretch perilously into years as Bob sat clinking the ice in his scotch and I got more frightened and resentful.

In the spring of 1978, United Nations ambassador Andrew Young flew into Houston for an Eckhardt fund raiser at the Shamrock Hotel. Young and I had close mutual friends in John and Billie Maguire, and I was looking forward to swapping Maguire stories when Bob seemed to choke on his breakfast and ended up in the hospital.

A doctor had noticed the commotion behind the dais and run backstage, where she checked him out and then gave him nitroglycerin. Though she didn't think it was a heart attack, she recommended immediate tests. And since every television station in Houston had a truck parked in front to get shots of Andy Young, we asked the ambulance to meet us at the back entrance and took him out through the kitchen in a wheelchair.

Just as the orderlies bent to lift Bob and the wheelchair through the open back doors into the ambulance, I looked off to the side to see a television camera filming us, and with an instinctive passion for privacy, I ran up and put my hand over the lens. The cameraman jumped back, mumbling something; Bob disappeared into the ambulance; the doctor and I climbed in after him; and Orissa got in front with the driver. I leaned forward to ask them not to turn on the siren or rotating light, and after I'd made sure Bob's color was good and he was breathing normally, looked out the back to see the television truck right behind us.

The hospital was only a few blocks away, and when we came to a stop, a bevy of doctors and interns stood poised at the door and the television truck was pulling alongside. So I jumped down and ran over to block the lens again, and when the cameraman shouted, "We *have* to do this!" I shouted, "*No you don't!*" Orissa had climbed out and was moving forward to block another camera when one of the television crew members took her by the shoulders and shoved her aside. Just then Bob was being lifted down in a stretcher, and he raised up from his litter, pointing his finger, and roared, "*Get your hands off my daughter!*"

And sure enough, there was yet another camera on the opposite side that recorded this wonderful scene of the wounded lion tending his young, and it played several times that evening on the local news, obscuring all mention of our distinguished visitor and puncturing the balloons of politicians who'd spent the intervening hours planning to succeed Bob as congressman from Houston's Eighth District. He was released in good spirits, with the understanding that he would come back as soon as possible for further tests.

He did not find time until after the fall election, which he won with a much narrower margin than he had expected. But early one winter night, as I was dining in Washington, he called from Houston to say that Denton Cooley would do bypass surgery at seven the next morning. And then, as my heart thudded to the floor, he went on to chat—something about the election, I think—about mending a fence with some labor people in Pasadena.

I made a reservation on the last flight and called Rosalind to ask her to meet me at Houston Intercontinental Airport at one in the morning. And after three or four hours sleep, the two of us walked into Bob's room just after they had given him the first injection. He was propped up on his pillows doodling, and when he saw me, his smile was as sweet as a five-year-old's who'd just gotten the rocking horse he wanted. He held out the drawings—a doctor with beetling brows, a large wart on his forehead, and a truly amazing nose; one nurse who was skinny and another who was fat—and I made what I hoped were appropriate noises while holding very tightly to his hand. Rosalind was standing on the other side of his bed, and we chirped like demented crickets when the men with the gurney rolled noisily through the door, loaded him on, and wheeled him away.

Four hours later, a ginger-haired doctor in green with the commanding air that Rommel must have had in the deserts of North Africa burst through double doors and stood looking quizzically around the waiting room. This had to be Denton Cooley, and so I jumped up and introduced myself. I had put my vital organs on hold and remember staring anxiously at the surgical mask pulled down under his chin while he told us that he had done a triple bypass and all was well. Moments later, a surgeon in his entourage took me aside and said that without that operation, we would have lost Bob within the year.

So I was already in a mild state of shock when I walked into the hospital room Bob had been assigned, looked around at what had to be St. Luke's equivalent of the presidential suite, and said out loud, "We can't possibly afford this!" But when I finally got the right person on the phone, he said Bob had been put there for the convenience of the hospital; so many people would be in and out, so much attention would be paid. . . .

And he was right. Within a few hours there were as many as twenty-five bouquets and a stack of telegrams. The phone rang every few minutes, and for the next ten days, we were treated like Bob had invented penicillin. I slept in a small room adjacent to his and kept the vigil. Those who have done it know how demanding this work is; you simply turn your life over to someone else for the foreseeable future. I was scribe, answering service, stand-up comic, hand-holder, reader, intermediary, and all-purpose drudge. I wasn't a saint, but I came as close as I thought I was likely ever to do. For an indefinite period the alcohol question was put on hold, and to "be there" once more for someone I loved touched me in ways I had not expected.

For the second time in eight months, I spent my days and now my nights in a hospital, and it was more than two weeks before we could fly back to Washington. But we got home at last, late one afternoon just after Christmas, and as Bob was changing his shirt in the thin, watery sunlight, I noticed that the fresh scar running down his chest seemed inflamed. With one hand on his forehead, which was hot, I called Houston. They told me to keep an eye on his temperature, which climbed above 102 within the next hour, so one of Bob's staff drove us, at Cooley's command, to the Naval Hospital in Bethesda.

Within an hour and after a flurry of phone consultations with Cooley, they decided he had a staph infection and they would have to open up his chest again. Since the last plane for Houston had already left, it would be done in Bethesda.

So once more I sat up, this time alone, until they wheeled Bob into the recovery room, where I stayed until he was out of danger and could be transferred. The operation had been straightforward, for the infection was confined to a relatively small area, and he could talk well enough to say there were times in his life when he had felt quite a lot better.

And when they took Bob to his room, I saw we were in now for a very different experience. This was the sort of place where they say, "You want a pillow? Bring it!" The rooms were plain, the walls were bare, they were accustomed to the powerful and were mightily unimpressed. "Cough!" meant "Cough hard!" and nobody connived with Bob when he wanted to shirk or hide. I loved it.

For the next ten days, two Capitol cops picked me up every morning at seven and brought me back every afternoon at six. While aides moved in and out and the business of Congress resumed, I knitted most of a sweater. Then we turned the house into a congressional office until finally Bob was able to spend a few hours a day at the Longworth Building.

By then I had had enough of "being there," and one cold afternoon, I almost despaired when I had retreated to the farthest bedroom for a half-hour nap only to hear the doorbell and then a loud knocking. Suddenly I remembered that a delegation from Great Britain was due and ran down to let them in. While they were waiting for Bob to get back from his office, a man with a Yorkshire accent began studying the bookshelves and concluded: "I look forward to meeting the congressman; we seem to like the same authors." When I commented dryly that most of the books were mine, he looked startled, and when Bob came in and chewed me out for not having a fire going, I wondered about reclaiming my life.

Through all this, my greatest joy sprang from Rosalind and Robert Stanley, who came to help and stayed for several months. While she seemed to waft from one room to the next, he barreled along or bounced like Pooh's friend Tigger. But either could burst in and smile, and life for me would be full of blessedness. When the heavy day came that would take them back to Austin and Rosalind looked down and said, "Poppa and Celia are going to miss us very much," he looked at her thoughtfully and said, "Then maybe we'd better stay." And I would have loved it.

The downside of helping someone is that if they are a certain kind of person, they come to take it for granted, and Bob turned out to be that kind of person. Once I said in a fit of more than usual exasperation, "You act like you were brought up by servants," and he replied, "I was." Later a man who grew up with him told me that his mother had picked up constantly after her husband and three sons, and whether this was inherited or learned behavior, I was paying for it. He was even worse than Willie, and I began to wonder if I was caught up in some weird form of fatal attraction.

If Bob were frying an egg three feet from the garbage can, the shell would fall onto the counter next to the skillet. Left to his own devices, remnants of cheese would molder on a plate, dirty glasses would stay on the table or the floor next to his chair, his clothes would lie wherever he was standing when he took them off. Once when we were staying at Ceil's New York apartment, sleeping on a roll-away bed in an elegant living room, I turned as we were walking out the door to see his shorts lying in the middle of a lovely Bokhara rug.

On top of the trail of debris he left in his wake, he lost or misplaced something at least once a day and took it for granted that somebody else was going to find it. When compelled to do it himself, he left the drawers open and the closet doors ajar. If he was not a class five hurricane, he was at least a three.

This time I tried everything, but it was as though the relevant piece of Bob's brain was missing and he would look puzzled as though he could not quite grasp what I was saying. When I complained that I wasn't a body servant, he would chuckle and remind me that his father used to say, "Bobby, I'm gonna have to get a little Negro boy to be your brains." Which I did not find the least bit funny.

Here I was, well into a second marriage with a man I had loved and honored more than anyone in the world—a man with whom my sexual rapport had been splendid—and I had three *big* problems: money, alcohol, and order. Though I'd made fun of the romantics, I had been a romantic myself: I'd thought the only real question was whether my heart was right, for it had *not* been the first time and I knew the failure of my marriage to Willie was not merely Willie's fault.

So I went on another quest down a good many paths that led nowhere until, with Shirley's help, I found another psychiatrist I trusted. I'll call him Roger Painter, and though I had hoped to find a woman, I had the sense from the beginning that he was nice to his mother. This, I thought, showed *some* progress on my part: the first time I had wanted a doctor who was smart; this time I wanted one who was kind. At least I had my priorities in better order.

Dr. Painter's office was across town, almost to Chevy Chase, which meant taking the subway and then the bus—a trip that ate up nearly an hour each way. Committed to going twice a week, I kept my expectations modest: my goal was to stop drinking and to persuade my husband to give me an equal say in financial decisions that affected me equally. My marriage was fine, I told the good doctor, except that Bob's way with money frightened me.

In less than a month, Dr. Painter told me I should go back into analysis, and when he said it, I sat there staring like a woman who had just been sentenced to five years in solitary. As the shock wore off, I felt petrified at the prospect of subjecting myself again to that kind of pain—and angry too, for I had already spent years on my psyche and devoting any more struck me as monstrous self-indulgence.

So I fumed and cried and argued while Dr. Painter listened patiently. After several hours of this, however, he said that if I didn't make the decision soon, I'd have to do the analysis with someone else, for we were perilously close to establishing quite a different relationship. At last I agreed, with the proviso that I would come four days a week rather than five. So on the following Monday, I caught my breath, lay down slowly, stared up, and steeled myself against the pain.

Amazingly, it did not come! And sometime in the second week, it dawned on me that I had left that anguished core *forever* on Stanley Crouse's couch. As I let my breath out and the light grew softer, I began, slowly, to smile—until at last I could burrow down to do the work I had come for.

It took less than a year to see that my problems with Bob were more substantial than I'd been able to admit when first I came. I had to see, for instance, that once again my husband's interest in my work was more rhetorical than real. High above the Atlantic on the way back from a NATO meeting, I wept bitterly because he simply could not get around to reading what I had written about Fanny and looked blank when I told him why it mattered.

For I'd had a disastrous experience with Oxford University Press; four years earlier we had signed a contract, but in the spring of 1980, the vice-president who'd shepherded it through many stages with a string of flattering comments had turned it over to a copy editor who evidently hated it. And at what he'd led me to believe would be a celebratory lunch, she handed me a nine-page, single-spaced critique in which she said *not one* good thing about the manuscript while he sat shamefaced and quiet.

I'd told myself the debacle had something to do with the politics of the Oxford Press and ultimately had withdrawn the book. But now I faced not only the problem of finding another publisher but the struggle to sort out what was valid in her criticism from what was pique. I needed help in doing that, so I'd asked Bob even more urgently than before to read it.

But he had not. One weekend, in fact, he'd come back from Houston and said he must have left a chapter in someone's bathroom and then stood there waiting for me to laugh. I was incredulous. Who was this person who professed undying love but couldn't find an hour here and there to do something my soul needed? What had happened to this celebrated liberal's sense of fair exchange?

So I took another precaution; in years to come, a shrewd friend would notice that whenever I was in trouble I found a therapist and sanded a floor. And in 1980, the year I would choose as runner-up to Stanford for "annus horribilis," I not only spent four days a week talking to Roger Painter but months in torn, paint-speckled clothes doing something I loved. For since Bob had reneged on his promise, I used my share of Daddy's life insurance to extend the back of the house six feet and make a new kitchen.

After spending a year battling the District bureaucracy to get new permits and months wrangling with local carpenters, I threw up my hands and called Jeff Spinks, a Houston carpenter in the Charlie-and-George-Burton tradition. And I asked, "Jeff, would you do something to make me very happy?"

Jeff Spinks is an attractive man, about fifteen years younger than I, who was working on the 150-year-old log cabin Bob had bought in East Texas and moved to his land on the outskirts of Houston, and he laughed before asking, "What did you have in mind?" I said, "I love to cook and want this kitchen built in the spirit in which I want to live in it. So would you fly up and build it for me?"

After the briefest pause, he said, "I've never been to Washington, and I might like to do that. Call me back in two days." When I did, he said "Yes, ma'am," and two weeks later I borrowed a car and met him at the Baltimore International Airport. Carting a gigantic tool box, he came intending to spend two weeks but ended up spending nine. And when we got down to it, we made something beautiful together and had a wonderful time.

Whenever someone insisted "You can't do that!" Jeff would figure out how. We turned the house into a workshop, and if there was nothing I could do to help him, I'd paint a door or scrape a window frame. So Jeff was there to measure the damage and console me when I did stupid things—the worst being the time I backed off an eight-foot ladder on the front porch, went into a slow roll in the cool air, and bounced down the brick stairs.

For a few seconds I sat there stunned while my blowtorch sputtered out in the ivy, and after I made sure I could move and gave a little time to contemplating the fact that I might have ended up a paraplegic, I started calling for Jeff. It was a long way back to the kitchen, and at first my voice was thin and shaky. But finally he heard me and came running.

We exchanged one of those "How-in-the-world-did-we-get-into-this-mess?" looks, and then he sat down beside me and chatted quietly while he slowly picked up an arm and watched me move it. Then he gestured to my legs and I bent my knees one by one and lifted them gingerly. Finally, with Jeff's arms under both of mine, I managed to stand up and then to move slowly. And a few hours later, after lowering myself carefully onto Roger Painter's couch, I began to talk, for I suspected that what might seem a moment's carelessness was a warning that my coping mechanisms were breaking down.

The current crisis was even more peculiar than those that had driven me back into analysis, for this one was about Bob's own political well-being. After years of barrages from well-heeled conservatives, both Democrat and Republican, he'd come so close to losing the Democratic primary that I'd asked pointedly, "How are you going to like practicing law again?" Subsequently I'd been the channel that key supporters had used to warn him of imminent defeat and tell him what he'd have to do differently to win in November. But as far as I could tell, he had ignored us.

Politics is not astrophysics, and over the course of three years, I'd learned a good deal about what works politically and what doesn't. What Bob was doing didn't work and wasn't going to. The campaign stagnated, and on trips to Houston he was apparently giving a speech or two and then retreating to his cabin.

On the issues I cared most about, Bob Eckhardt was a fine public servant. I believed that electoral politics mattered. I was as close as anyone could be to the candidate. And I could *not* get him or his daughters to hear me. To my hand-wringing about tasks left undone and feuds unreconciled, Orissa said, "Maybe Daddy wants to lose," to which I replied, "Then he shouldn't have asked so many of us to work so hard for him."

Though the analysis kept me from spending weekdays in Houston, I'd done as much as I knew how to under the circumstances and offered to do scores of things nobody organized, while David was taking a year off to work in the campaign as photographer, chauffeur, and all-purpose fetcher. The need to help Bob had triumphed over my ten-year anxiety about public speaking, and my ham instincts had rushed back so strongly that I'd ad-libbed a speech in Baytown that had a roomful of men bent out of shape with laughter. From a merely personal standpoint, this was exhilarating; the years of feeling crippled were suddenly over.

I had called Mickey Leland, who thought of Bob as a political father, and said, "Mickey, if you and the blacks don't help, Bob is going to lose," and he'd said, "Oh my God, I thought they just didn't want *me* there!" I had called Phil Burton and said, "Bob's in trouble," and Phil shot back: "Have the unions maxed out?" I said, "I beg your pardon?" And after he explained the verbal shorthand, I'd found out which unions could still give more money.

I kept sounding the alarm, and three weeks before the November election, three members of Bob's committee staff took vacation leave to fly to Houston to do whatever political hackwork might be helpful. Panicking at the disorganized campaign they found, they persuaded an advertising genius to come down and cut ads. And Jim Hightower left his post as editor of the *Texas Observer* to put in sixteen-hour days in the campaign office.

A terrific organizer for the steelworkers took over as campaign manager. I flew down for the last two weeks, and a bunch of good people working frantically together nearly pulled off a political miracle. With a very funny man who belonged to the railway workers union, I ended up going to a string of topless bars and "ice houses." At one of the latter, I started my spiel to a couple of guys sitting on barstools when one asked, "Lady, are you a Democrat or a Republican?" And his buddy said, "Ain't no Republican gonna come in a dive like this."

Ron Dellums of Oakland, the leader of the Congressional Black Caucus, flew in for a fund raiser at Dominique de Menil's, where in 1958 I'd been astounded to see a Braque in the bathroom. When she lent us her limousine for the occasion, I said *sotto voce* to Dellums, "I hope you understand that we're treating you in a style to which we are *not* accustomed."

Ted Kennedy came for a packed rally at a union hall, and we spent the last Sunday before the election following Andy Young to black churches. I hadn't known it was possible to give an enthusiastic speech for President Jimmy Carter, but Young not only did it—he did it three times without repeating himself. (Between campaign stops, he told us his wife Jean had said, "Andy, you better get your black self out there.")

If we'd had two more weeks, we might have done it, but the nation's political temper had shifted. As the returns dribbled in and, one by one, Democratic powerhouses began to go down all over the country, David took one shot after another of very glum Texas liberals. On the near side of midnight, blubbery people began drifting out of campaign headquarters to lose themselves in booze or sex—or both, depending on age, timing, and constitutions. By four in the morning it was clear that Bob had lost—and to a facile kid with blow-dried hair whose only elected office had been the student presidency of Baylor University. Bob was grand in defeat, and exasperation so quickly gave way to pity that I even agreed to spend a night sleeping, or trying to, on the floor of his log cabin.

Not only my husband, but my side had lost badly; the Democrats' margin in the House was drastically narrowed, and the Republicans took control of the Senate by defeating such stalwarts as Frank Church of Idaho, Birch Bayh of Indiana, and George McGovern of South Dakota. The consequences, both personal and political, would be monumental.

So I was *very* angry when we got back to Washington, where I vented my spleen by writing a note to a multimillionaire oil man named Jack Warren. We'd entertained Warren from time to time until the day he said to me in parting, "If you can't get Bob to vote with us, we're just going to have to beat him." And as a member of the Democratic National Committee, he had subsequently used DNC letterhead stationery to raise money for Bob's Republican opponent.

Never had I abandoned decorum with such fierce conviction, for I wrote as follows:

> Well Jack,
> You finally bought yourself a congressman: an ignorant man who lies and cheats. I'm sure you're proud of what you did for your country.
> Celia

Three years later, I discovered that Jack had framed that note and displayed it in his office; he'd even made a point of showing it to Tom Edsall, a political writer for the *Washington Post*. And when I got over being astonished, I was intrigued.

I asked Bob what he made of it, and he said, "Oh, I think Jack just wants people to know he can buy a congressman." Which seemed likely, but nonetheless not quite enough of an explanation. So I asked Democratic National Committeewoman Billie Carr what she thought, and Billie said, "I think Jack likes sassy women." Which also seemed likely, but was still insufficient.

So I wrestled with this question until I came up with an explanation that struck me as adequate: Every politician in Houston who aspired to an office higher than justice of the peace was likely to show up at one time or another in Jack Warren's office. The message he used my note to convey was: "I make you, and I break you, and moral outrage doesn't touch me." And the person for whom the message would be most biting was the man described in the letter. Jack Warren had provided my most unforgettable lesson in hard-ball politics.

Nursing Bob through the loss of his congressional seat turned out to be even more emotionally demanding and time-consuming than nursing him in the aftermath of bypass surgery. What I didn't count on was that in years to come, Bob would blame me for his loss. But by the time he'd said it so often I realized that he actually believed it, I knew that this was the least of my problems.

226

CHAPTER TWENTY

*Y*ears later, a knowing therapist put my core problem succinctly: "On a narcissism scale of one to ten," she said, "Bob's a twelve." In 1980, however, I'm not sure I'd heard that word except in the story of a Greek boy who gazed into a pond and fell in love with his own image—a pretty tale, to be sure, but too silly, I thought, to take seriously. It would be years before I realized that the messages we need may be buried in those old stories, but first we have to recognize the ones that apply and then translate them. In my case, the Wolf has usually eaten Red Riding Hood before I've realized that I am wearing a bright red cape.

After the 1980 election, I felt overwhelming pity for Bob—a man I had loved enough to change my name and leave my beloved New York for—a man who had lost the work he did so splendidly—the work for which I, along with so many others, had honored him. As with all true sorrow, it was quite beside the point that I thought he'd brought so much of it on himself, and when I saw him sad and lost, I wanted only to ease the pain. We went into mourning together.

And I still felt the pull of a family; Rosalind and Robert Stanley came for Christmas and stayed three months, and my love for them was as potent as ever. Rosalind had been flat on her back in a body cast after an operation on her spine and Bob had been sitting beside her when her mother's corpse was carried past their window. People who hold each other's hands through a trauma like that have a special bond, and her tenderness now salved a wounded spirit and was lovely to watch.

Then there was Robert Stanley, who could crook his head and say, "Poppa, are you sad?" or "Poppa, let's go for a walk," and you could see the gloom lift. A tow-headed cherub in a scruffy cap, he once boomed out in his four-year-old voice as we walked down M Street in Georgetown, "Celia, my penis is hard!" He sounded not only puzzled, but irked, and two guys coming toward us burst into laughter as I giggled and said, "Don't worry, darling, it'll be okay." In company like that, a bruised soul heals.

Which is a good thing, for by the time they left, the debris Bob attracted was all piled in our house, along with whatever came out of his congressional office, and it was clear that we now had to face the question of our relationship. For I woke in the midst of a frosty night with a frightening thought: "Bob expects me to be Frances, Gloria, Alma, Judy, Jocelyn, and Ann—his core personal staff in Congress—all in one, but I can't. And I wouldn't even if I could."

Our most immediate problem was money, the subject that had prompted me so often to insist, albeit fruitlessly, "I'm your *wife*, not your mistress or a staff member!" Apart from handing over the money to run the house, he'd simply ignored me. With an aristocrat's disdain for tradesmen's bills, he always seemed faintly surprised that he might be expected to pay up. When I discovered that he owed Jeff Spinks a substantial amount for work long since done on his log cabin, and that he'd reduced Jeff to calling every few days to dun him for money, I was beside myself.

The cabin that had been the lightning rod for our quarrels had now become superfluous, for Bob no longer needed a residence in Houston. But there it sat, giving a new dimension to the term "white elephant." Bob had told me he would spend, at most, thirteen thousand dollars to move it from East Texas and fit it out with modern conveniences. In three years, however, he'd tripled his debt, spending more than forty thousand dollars on the cabin alone, though it still had no running water, no kitchen, no bathroom, and no furnishings other than an army cot. (Eight years later, it still had none of those things, and the amount poured into it by then exceeded fifty-five thousand dollars.)

Except for the mortgage payment, we had *not* spent our money on the house in Washington. We'd put nothing aside for a new roof or a furnace to replace one that looked like it had gone in with General Pershing. We had laid *nothing* by for the future and given *no* money to causes we believed in. I *detested* spending money on a playhouse nobody went to rather than a furnace in Washington, a shelter for abused women, public radio, or People for the American Way, and I was irate at being forced to.

I begged Rosalind and Orissa to help me persuade their father that he couldn't afford to keep all his property. But Rosalind pleaded, "Oh Celia, let Daddy keep the land," and Orissa said, "It makes me angry when you want me to change my father." Alice was plummeting farther down the rabbit hole, and I thought ruefully of the Thurber quip that marriage is an institution that links two people—one of whom cannot sleep with the window open, the other who cannot sleep with the window closed.

Sired by an Aggie with a passion for order, I found myself married to the most profoundly disorderly person I had ever known. Frances-Gloria-Judy-Alma-Jocelyn-Ann, it turned out, had been retaining walls, and when they were removed, the contents of the structure spilled out onto whatever was around. It was not that Bob hit anybody or did anything openly dramatic besides throwing a few tantrums. But he left behind a trail of hats, screwdrivers, cigar butts, bookmarks, old cheese, pencils, paper, shoe polish, broken crackers, nails, chicken bones, books, envelopes, doodles, glasses, stale bread, hammers, newspapers, ties, and most preposterous of all, file folders.

And night after night, while I was trying to find an Alcoholics Anonymous meeting that worked for me, he would sit there smacking his lips over his latest find in scotch or a new Beaujolais. Long afterward, a man who grew up with him said he had always been a unilateral guy, so perhaps this was merely the quintessential Bob.

Finally, I said flatly, "I won't live in your mess, and I won't clean up after you." I told Bob I would leave him unless he agreed to go with me to a therapist, and so for almost two years we went to a sensible woman whom Bob refused to take seriously. When he said ultimately he didn't think she was smart enough for us, I suggested that he find someone who was, but nothing came of it.

Abandoning the distance psychiatrists traditionally maintain, Roger Painter finally said I should leave Bob, gently pointing out that I was nearing the time when men would no longer find me attractive. But I was not prepared to walk out on a sixty-nine-year-old man who had lost the job he loved most in the world, and since this didn't leave us much more to say, we ended the analysis. After almost twenty years and despite the dreadful things that happened later, I still don't see how I could have decided differently; leaving a thirty-four-year-old man at the height of his personal and professional power had been something else altogether.

But as I approached fifty, my financial situation was precarious. A good deal of my money was invested in our house, and I'd given a huge part of five years over to being Bob's wife. I had a Ph.D., a wide range of practical experience, and my Fanny Wright book was finally under contract with Harvard University Press. But you cannot eat prestige, and the chances of my finding a paying job that used my peculiar combination of talents and skills were dwindling.

Quickened by the outrage and insights that come from being taken for granted and undermined by *two* husbands now whose public personae had promised fair dealing, I was furious at Bob for being oblivious to my well-being, or for that matter his own. And as my hopes for the joint therapy dimmed, I felt more and more like my head was being held under water. But as I stubbornly raised it and shifted my focus from holding up a marriage to working on behalf of women, I realized that anger is an underrated emotion.

In 1982, while teaching a course at the Institute for Policy Studies on the American women's movements, I discovered, among other things, that those nineteenth-century crusading women seemed to have found the formula for long life: Elizabeth Cady Stanton died at eighty-seven, Susan B. Anthony at eighty-six, Sarah Grimke at eighty-one, Angelina Grimke at seventy-four, Margaret Sanger at eighty-seven, Jane Addams at seventy-five, Alice Paul at ninety-two. Many less illustrious women had stormed indignantly alongside them into their eighties and nineties, and their example was contagious.

During class, I held myself responsible for talking about the first women's movement, which ended as a mass movement in 1920 when women got the vote. To discuss the second, which had begun gathering force in the 1960s, I invited women from Washington's activist community to discuss aspects of the problem—class, economics, race, organizing, and so on. One woman was a demographer from the Children's

Defense Fund, and the statistics she gave us about the perilous state of women and children in the world's richest country were so staggering that, figuratively speaking, we crawled away.

A week later, I went to a conference sponsored by the research arm of the Congressional Caucus for Women's Issues, and when the same statistics came up again, I had yet another pagan mystical experience, or moment of truth: not only were the figures revolting, but I *personally* had to do something about them. And within the week, I'd begun to see what that might be. For I went to a fund raiser on Capitol Hill for the Highlander School in Tennessee, where Rosa Parks had learned about civil disobedience, and there I met a tiny woman with white hair named Millie Jeffrey who was wearing a button that said "Women Vote!" A fresh-faced blonde a few years younger than I named Lael Stegall was standing beside her with the same button. They were both sprightly women—blue eyes sparkling and chins high—and when I asked about the buttons, they invited me to the second day of a two-day conference. By then, we knew that women were voting differently from men on several key issues, and that the power of organized women could therefore amount to something. And by the end of the next day, I had decided to see if I could organize a Women's Vote project in Texas.

So began another of my transforming experiences. I started welding pieces together from different parts of my life—the passion for plain people I got from my grandmother, connections with friends I knew from growing up in Texas and attending the state university, activists I had met through Bob, ideas I got from reading, and the inspiration of Fanny Wright. I was moving away from being a private person toward being part of a movement.

My hidden agenda was to decide whether I could go on living with Bob, but only Shirley knew that. I wanted to protect his dignity along with my own pride, and so I simply told people I was moving to Texas for a year to register poor women to vote.

Day after day I began doing things I not only had never done before but never dreamed I might do. For instance, Lael asked whether I could raise thirty thousand dollars in three weeks, and I was vastly relieved that we were talking on the phone so she couldn't see the expression on my face. I simply answered, "I don't know," but within six weeks, I had raised it. Lael was the director of the Windom Fund, whose money came from Ellen Malcolm, who'd go on to form EMILY's List, and after

I'd proved I was serious, Lael and Ellen gave me ten thousand dollars. In the year that followed, I discovered that if you believe in something enough, you can be utterly brazen, and I learned to walk into people's homes and offices and ask for ten thousand dollars a shot.

During a three-week exploratory trip to Texas, I talked to a wide spectrum of women and began putting together a board with Barbara Jordan as honorary chair and State Treasurer Ann Richards as a key member. It was one of the first statewide boards on which African American, Hispanic, and Anglo women were all represented; labor sat alongside the League of Women Voters and Business and Professional Women, Republicans with Democrats. The project, in fact, would be nonpartisan because it depended on tax-deductible money, and Democrats could only hope that the people we registered would vote in what we took to be their self-interest.

We limited our scope to five major cities—Austin, Houston, Dallas, Fort Worth, and San Antonio. Since I knew the first two reasonably well and virtually nothing about the others, I began taking my information wherever I could find it. While sitting in on a hearing at the state capitol on indigent women, for instance, I began chatting with a woman named Harriet Griffin who turned out to be from Fort Worth. After an hour's conversation she said she would do what she could to help, and some six weeks later, she introduced me to a group of women there who became the core of our project.

So in September, 1983, I moved back to Austin to share an apartment near Zilker Park with Jocelyn Gray, a woman a few years older than I who'd worked for Bob. We picked a name—Texas Women for the '80s— designed a sleek logo, and had hundreds of T-shirts made that read "Texas Women Vote!" Having fled Texas years earlier to avoid getting stuck in another sorority meeting, I began to sit through women's meetings by the dozens and realized that women I had been inclined to mock twenty years earlier were the ones who knew how to get concrete things done for real people who needed them.

Convinced that I was allergic to the telephone, I'd spend hours a day with that black plastic receiver tucked under my ear. Sure that I hated to drive, I put twenty-seven thousand miles on my late father's 1977 Chrysler in the course of a single year. Unable to speak in public for a decade, I now began giving an average of five speeches a week. A private person who loved books turned into an organizer.

The board in each city chose its own organizer, each of whom would be paid, like me, fifteen hundred dollars a month. Each city set its own goal for the numbers it would register and designed its own strategy to achieve the goal. Jocelyn became the state treasurer, and I began driving from city to city, coming to know Texas far better than when I'd lived there.

And I started connecting with the people who have been making this country work since the seventeenth century—the "little old ladies in tennis shoes" who've done the fund raising, the knocking on doors, the petitioning—in short, the hard, tedious work of democracy. The people whose names don't make it into headlines or textbooks but who show up to work day after day. I grew close to an amazing man named Willie Velasquez, a legendary organizer within the Hispanic community who ran the Southwest Voter Registration Project through which, for tax purposes, our money was channeled. Willie had dedicated his life to helping poor people gain political power, and he not only gave me access to Hispanics and communities I hadn't known before but also taught me how much struggle goes into any significant political change.

To be sure, some of the women connected with Texas Women cheated and others lied. Some were garrulous and boring. A little clique in one big city fought for control of an organization that had no money, no power, and no future as though they were fighting for AT&T. I liked to end my speeches with Sojourner Truth's great line, "If the first woman God ever made could turn the world upside down all alone, these women, together, ought to be able to get it right side up again." But whatever romanticism I had about women did not survive the 1984 election. Nor did my conviction that no one could be more stupid than an intelligent person, for the stupidity of a stupid person turned out to be breathtaking. There were times I wanted to hire a hit man.

But so many women I came to know were feisty, tenacious, and generous with themselves and their time. I met women in their seventies and eighties who'd been the backbone of their communities for half a century and were still hard at it. I met women who could pick up the phone and get twenty-five people to a meeting where they would persuade them to make common cause. I made friends for life.

One was Ruth Bowers, the angel behind *Roe vs. Wade,* who used a fortune that derived from the legendary Spindletop oil rush for causes she believed in. After we met in a corridor while attending a conference,

I sent her a sheaf of information about Texas Women. And when I called a few days later, she said, "I like what you're doing so much I wonder if you could do the same thing in East Texas. I'd like to pay for a black organizer there." I said, "If you're willing to pay her salary, I'm willing to find her."

So I called Jean Dugger Marshall, who had just lost her second husband to cancer, and I said "Jeanie, how would you like to drive with me into East Texas?" She said "Fine!" and so we set off in Daddy's ridiculous car, which by accident had been painted bright red, and in four days we drove a thousand miles in and about the region, talking to people who led us to other people who led us to still others.

When we got back to Austin, I called Ruth to say, "I found four women who might work, so why don't you and I and two black women from Houston meet in Tyler to choose between them?" Ruth said that sounded fine. So I asked, "Then how about my driving down, picking you up, and heading for Tyler?" But Ruth said quietly, "Well, I have a plane."

That was also fine. When I asked if we could pick up our friends in Houston, she said the airport there was impossibly congested, so she'd pay their way to Tyler but would stop off in Austin for me. So on the appointed day, I went out to the little airport for private planes and watched while a sleek little Cessna landed and Ruth climbed down with an engaging grin and her hand outstretched. She introduced me to her pilot, Henry, who had worked for her for twenty-odd years, and then we took off for East Texas. They had boxes full of sandwiches and cookies stashed under the seats for the four of us to eat when we all got together, and by early afternoon we had started interviewing our candidates.

Pat Lamar, the woman we chose that day, turned out to be our best organizer, for by November of 1984, she had cheerfully worked her way through four counties and signed up record numbers to vote. I stayed with her in Marshall for a couple of nights—to the consternation of a black community that clearly wondered what a white woman in a big red Chrysler could be doing there. We broke a good many unwritten rules and had a lot of fun, while Ruth helped shatter my prejudice against rich people, for she and I, who look a bit alike, became so close that people sometimes take us for sisters.

Another woman I met then who would weave memorably into my

life was Taunya Banks, who was teaching law in Houston at Texas Southern University, a historically black college. Ten years younger than I and a native of Washington, she'd joined us that day in Tyler. Taunya is an unusually beautiful woman, and I never knew whether people stared at us in Houston restaurants because she is so striking or because she is black and I am white. On more than one occasion, she reamed out some local women who were endangering not only our tax-exempt status but that of an important colleague by making partisan comments, and she helped me acknowledge that being soft-spoken is not always a virtue in women.

The range of my experiences that year might have made Balzac jealous. I slept on sofas cats had peed on, as well as in a four-poster, canopied bed that had belonged to a governor of Texas. I stayed in cottages and garage apartments, as well as in a twenty-room mansion on one of Dallas's grand boulevards, and coaxed ten thousand dollars out of J. R. Parten, an enthralling, cranky multimillionaire in his eighties. I caught road fever and loved to take off down those wide highways, and several times the cops caught me going eighty. A car I'd hated because it felt like driving a building became a cherished friend I called Big Mama, who introduced me to mechanics all over the state. A famous pro football player I gave a lift to thought she was such a piece of work that he said, "Lady, if you ever want to get rid of this car, just call me." Though people snickered at Big Mama and me, we carried big cartons, piles of yard signs, and even a pair of Siamese cats from one city to another, and had many adventures together. An ill-starred animal, probably a raccoon, met us at 3 A.M. in a rainstorm thirty miles outside Houston, and we had a flat in 95-degree weather not far from Buda, the desolate place Katherine Anne Porter remembered when she wrote "Pale Horse, Pale Rider." Once in Bastrop, when I had locked my keys inside, a trucker used a coat hanger to jimmy a door and then asked offhandedly if I fooled around on my husband.

Texas Women for the '80s became the biggest vote project in the country aimed at women, and Joanne Howes, the director of the national Women's Vote Project, flew down to see how we were doing it. Helen and Swanee Hunt, daughters of the late, infamously right-wing H. L., were enthusiastic enough to give us ten thousand dollars. House Speaker Jim Wright gave a windy, well-meaning speech at our kick-off rally in Fort Worth, and Congressman Jake Pickle climbed up the four flights to our attic office in Austin to wish us well and give us one of his trademark pickle-whistles. We got good stories in every daily newspaper in the cities we worked in and even showed up in a picture on the front page of the *Houston Chronicle*.

All the stories took note of the fact that Bob Eckhardt's wife was the driving force behind Texas Women, and Bob, in turn, found it disconcerting that the "Eckhardt" in the headlines referred to me rather than him. But the attention that counted was from ordinary people, and the high point for me came when the Texas Women's Political Caucus named me their Woman of the Year.

In late October, Jean Marshall asked a guy who was helping us change a tire how he was voting, and he said, "For Ronald Reagan, of course; we're all Christians here." Democracy had seldom felt more tenuous, for the gulf between us was so deep it seemed miraculous that we shared a common language. Ultimately, Texas Women for the '80s registered about forty-five thousand people to vote—some ten thousand fewer than we had hoped but a respectable figure nonetheless. A good many of them may have voted for Reagan, if they voted at all, and I resolved never to do anything nonpartisan again because it was too hard to stand by while the other side trounced us.

But I had had a wonderful time in Texas. I had resurrected old friendships and met scores of new people I valued—many of them people a little white girl growing up in West University Place had been unlikely to know. I had taken risks that sharpened my faculties and taught me a good deal about the country I lived in. I had learned how to do things I hadn't known I could manage. I had gotten lost, baffled, frustrated, indignant, hurt, discouraged, and angry and emerged none the worse for all that. I had survived palace coups, mean-spirited women, flat tires, indifferent friends, lazy and/or lying organizers, a bad transmission, boring roads and loved—if not every minute—at least most of them.

Best of all, I had been my own person, and by the end of the year I knew I could never again accept the demeaning and even dangerous terms Bob Eckhardt had set for me as his wife. I'd told him my life was at stake in my battle with alcohol and called my mother's squalid death to witness, but he had never taken me seriously. Though he would literally go down on his knees and promise with tears in his eyes to do things differently, he'd done that too many times and I knew now that, for whatever reasons, he simply couldn't.

I'd had very little to drink that year and, on David's birthday, had sworn a vow I intended to keep: for 350 days of every year, I would have no alcohol, but on the other 15, I could have whatever I liked and as much as I wanted. Gambling that those few days of freedom or license would hold in check my instinct for defiance, I thought I could do it.

So one black Sunday afternoon, weeping bitterly for the failure of a dream that had been so precious, I wrote Bob to say I could never live with him again. I told him how proud I had been to be his wife and asked if he wanted a divorce. Four years later I reread the letter and wept again over the tenderness I found there.

CHAPTER TWENTY-ONE

*B*ob did *not* want a divorce, so I moved back to Washington late in 1984 to set up an odd form of marriage—eccentricity appealing, as it did, to both of us. I found a small apartment ten minutes away from what we called "the big house," where we would take turns living. Since he'd go first, he agreed to pay me six hundred dollars a month, or the equivalent of interest on the money I had invested in the house. With a separation agreement that spelled out the terms, we seemed at last to have mastered the art of negotiation and the skills of problem solving.

I took so little from the house that it was hard to tell anything was missing and, with a little sofa bed and bookcase I bought in Georgetown, set up housekeeping on the fourth floor of a small building a half block off East Capitol. The great dome that dominates Washington loomed down the way, and I realized how fond I'd grown of this part of the city, where narrow row houses were painted in soft greens and yellows; roses and clematis trailed along black iron fences; bells rang from old brick churches; masses of peonies and hydrangeas filled little front gardens; magnolias, cherry trees, and crabapples lined the streets. It was the first time I had ever lived alone, and I liked it.

Just under me lived a slim, elegant curator at the National Gallery of Art. Two doors down was a tall, forceful woman I'd met when she worked for Phil Burton. And around the corner was a wiry Austrian sculptor who taught at the Corcoran. The women were both magnificent cooks; the man did wonderfully strange pieces he occasionally lent or sold to us; and every few weeks we would meet at one or another's place to feast together.

Often Bob joined us, and he usually slept over once or twice a week. After he agreed to bring in a woman to clean regularly, I went occasionally to the big house. Meanwhile, he'd set up a law office on Capitol Hill and hired Gloria Cochran, a loyal and loving woman who'd been with him from his first term in Congress. I trusted her to bring what order could be brought out of chaos and counted on her to see that I got my check regularly.

For I had found that if I were extremely frugal, I could live on dividends and the interest from my investment in the house, and I wanted to write another book. *Fanny Wright: Rebel in America* had been nicely reviewed in the *New York Times Book Review* the week it was published, and subsequently on the front page of the *Los Angeles Times Book Review*. It got a full page in the *Village Voice* and the *Toronto Globe and Mail*, the largest and most influential newspaper in Canada, and I did an hourlong radio interview with Studs Terkel that he syndicated. Studs had said "it reads like a house on fire," and Senator Pat Moynihan had called it the best biography of the year. All but one or two notices were complimentary, and the only sour note was that Irving Howe wrote Harvard to say they had edited the book badly and told someone it would have been splendid if it hadn't been for the feminism. At last I was excited about what my own mind might come up with, and I'd found work I believed in and could do indefinitely.

In the wholly unpredictable way I had come to expect, though obviously not to count on, my past interceded with the present, for Joe Goulden, whom I had known as managing editor of the *Daily Texan,* invited me to join a writers' lunch group with Rod MacLeish, Judith Martin, Sophy Burnham, Les Whitten, Abigail McCarthy, Pat Anderson, and John Greenya. And after I got over being intimidated, I began to enjoy myself hugely. So sparkling and raucous were these occasions that we actually got asked to leave one restaurant, though the place was usually empty because the food was wretched. Over the next few years, they helped me take to heart Les's verdict on the writer's life, "so full of treachery, disappointment, and brutality but still the best life there is," as he wrote in a *Washington Post* article.

So I began a period of what Hampshire College calls "creative floundering"; for six months or so I experimented with a book about political women in Washington, interviewing people like Millie Jeffrey, Bella Abzug, and Catherine East, who had played key roles in the current women's movement. I went to New York and found a classy new agent, Ellen Levine, and we submitted a proposal to several publishers before finally deciding that for various reasons that project was not going to work. By the end of the year, I was leaning toward doing a book on miscegenation that would be, in effect, a follow-up to my work on Fanny Wright.

But this was not a subject that got you notices in *People* magazine or brought in handsome advances, falling as it did somewhere between academic and commercial nonfiction. It challenged me intellectually and stretched me emotionally in directions I had been moving since adolescence. But for the privilege of doing that kind of work, I would have to pay. So I did ghostwriting for congresswomen and a little editing, but spent most of my time reading books and finding new recipes for cheap, nutritious soup.

Through Texas Women for the '80s, ironically, my Washington world expanded to include a remarkable group of activist women. One was Mildred Wurf, who represented Girls, Inc., and whom I had watched move unwieldy meetings from one stage to the next with a deft comment or question. The widow of Jerry Wurf, who'd made the American Federation of State, County, and Municipal Employees Union into one of the most dynamic and important in the country, Mildred knew everybody in Washington connected to liberal causes, and soon we were going to movies and the theater together and I was spending weeks at her house in Wellfleet on Cape Cod.

Then Joanne Howes, who had been national director of the Women's Vote Project, invited me to join a reading group made up largely of women who'd met in the early 1970s as staff members of the National Women's Political Caucus and were still committed to the practical political work that makes democracy real. Lael Stegall, who had asked so memorably if I could raise thirty thousand dollars in three weeks, was involved, and nine of us began meeting once a month at each other's houses to read women's fiction together.

The first year we read contemporary novels by such writers as Nadine Gordimer and Toni Morrison, and the second we decided to go back and read the classics. Discussing books with adult friends is entirely different from reading them with academics or adolescent students, and one of my happiest moments came when we were reading Jane Austen's *Emma* at my house. Doris Meissner, whom Bill Clinton would name to head the Immigration and Naturalization Service, came in late and confessed breathlessly: "I thought it was a terrible idea to go back and read these old books. And when Celia told us we were going to love this one, I thought, 'No way!' And then I started reading and couldn't bear to stay in my office! I wanted to find out what happened next." And then she asked: "What do you think? Did Emma and Mr. Knightley have a good sex life?"

Every year we read something a man had written about a woman — *Tess of the D'Urbervilles, The Portrait of a Lady, Madame Bovary, Howard's End,* and *Anna Karenina* being only the most famous. We got to know writers from India, the Middle East, South Africa, and the Scandinavian countries as well as from the more obvious places in Europe and the English-speaking world. Now and again we dipped into biography.

As Nancy Mairs puts it in *Voice Lessons,* for me this meant reading women "whose writing has aroused me and nurtured and chastised me, each one drawing me on, teaching me to love her, to love myself in her, to love myself, to love: To write." Meanwhile our little group scrapped, cajoled, explained, puzzled, argued, and laughed together. In each other's company, we made a remarkable number of discoveries — about the conditions under which women had lived and what had been expected of them, about books, writers, ideas, and feelings — and for the most part we had a fine time.

All of us skipped meetings now and then, Lael dropped out for a while, and after a couple of years we added two more people. We spent long weekends in Maine and Wisconsin at members' summer homes, and several of us became close personal friends. Some ten years or 120-odd books after we started, we got dolled up for a formal dinner in the Ulysses S. Grant Room at the Willard Hotel to celebrate our first decade and toast the pleasures of those to come.

I took Bob along to everything I did that was not just for women, though sometimes he was the only man, and he usually enjoyed himself. He went with me to North Carolina, for instance, when I spoke during Black Emphasis Week at Meredith College, and at lunch, when a professor commented that it was refreshing to see a man who wasn't intimidated by his wife's success, he quipped, "Who's not intimidated?" Still, he not only went with me to Hampshire when I was chosen to give the commencement address at David's graduation but actually bounced up and down when I got a standing ovation and then beamed as I got to present David with his diploma. He sat with Thelma when I gave the keynote address to the first Texas Women's Scholars conference and boasted that I was also a pretty good cook and sensational on a bicycle.

Though he had no social life to speak of apart from mine, he told a friend he liked living alone, especially since Texans like Ronnie Dugger used the house as their base in Washington. From time to time, he rented the back rooms to our friends' children.

For more than two years we managed our peculiar arrangement with good grace, and the crises were fewer and less exhausting than when we'd lived together. When I wanted my turn in the house, however, he flatly refused but guaranteed, in an official letter to a mortgage company, to send me six hundred dollars a month so I could buy the apartment.

But trying to talk with Bob about money was still like shouting to make yourself heard from the cave behind Niagara Falls, and once when Orissa was in Washington, I told her that since Bob might well be a candidate for debtor's prison, I wished she'd help him understand the danger. Subsequently I wrote the same to Rosalind, but they both responded, in effect, with what I considered the trademark blank stare.

Nonetheless, I was exhilarated, for when I didn't have to watch Bob drink night after night, I had no trouble keeping my pledge to David, with whom I now had a happy relationship; several years earlier I had finally broken through his resistance to therapy, and he'd come out of it a far more responsive, happier person. After doing a fine photographic essay on Vietnam veterans at Hampshire, he was working as a newspaper photographer in Mississippi and Tennessee, and we talked often on the phone.

Every few weeks somebody or other was tucked away in the sofa bed, for my beloved old friends breezed in from time to time—Shirley and Sally for a couple of long weekends, Diana Kealey and Pat Spearman for longer stretches. Ray Farabee, John Maguire, and Tom Wicker would come to town occasionally and take me to dinner. Nancy and Norm Richardson would drive down from Gettysburg and we'd go to the Arena

Stage. And when my Aunt Bernice gave me a striking painting for my fiftieth birthday, I was thrilled to discover that I had a real artist in my own family. It was a peaceful time filled with solid, promising work and the love of friends.

Then on April 2, 1987, my telephone rang at four in the morning; it was Capitol Hill Hospital saying my husband was in the emergency room and may have had a stroke. I pulled on my blue jeans and ran five blocks—oblivious to the dangers of nighttime Washington—and when I burst in, I found Bob with eyes wide but talking gibberish. Grabbing his hand, I struggled to make out what he was urgently saying, for the sounds themselves were clear but the combination was a jumble.

The next few days are a blur, though I remember stumbling to the house awash in tears. For the admitting physician had implied that although Bob's body did not seem affected, much of his brain was, and the loss might be permanent. So in the next few hours, I summoned Bob's family, talked to doctors, and made scores of calls to friends who might help.

By late afternoon, a makeshift team had assembled. Men and women who'd been staff lawyers were scrubbing toilets and vacuuming floors, for we found the house very nearly a wreck. Friends were taking turns answering the phone and making the airport run. Members of my book group were bringing food, and everybody was holding everybody else's hand. Late that evening, when something like fourteen people were sitting around the table over plates piled with barbecue, I looked up and saw a giant cockroach scurrying across the ceiling, started laughing, and couldn't stop. Bob's youngest brother Norman pulled out his flute and began a tune I vaguely remember as "Nearer My God To Thee." Everyone was borderline hysterical, and "crazy Eckhardt" tales dominated the table.

The camaraderie of the next few weeks was so breathtaking the years of strain and disillusion dropped away. Bob's youngest daughter Sarah and I had had a falling out, but in a taxi between two hospitals, she said "Poppa really loves you," I said, "I really love him too," and we hugged and made up. Rosalind was pregnant again, and my old love for her came flooding back. Orissa gave me a wonderfully gaudy tote. Norman played his flute at likely and unlikely moments and told a string of hilarious stories about bars he'd played in and women he'd wooed. Another close relative acted like Dmitri Karamazov, breast-beating and all, while everybody looked away and waited for the fit to pass. Ronnie Dugger came from New York and stayed at my apartment while I directed the troops at the house, and one night he and I got drunk together while weeping over the parlous state of this man we both had loved so dearly.

But Bob was tough, and he surprised even the doctors by the speed of his recovery. People would stand around while we played a sort of word game; he would draw something to give me a clue and I'd start guessing the word he couldn't remember. Since our decade of intimacy involved so many shared experiences, we were good at this, and I usually came up with the word he wanted. Once the answer was "Don Kennard" when we'd started with John Brown and Harper's Ferry, and when I got it, Bob beamed and the room burst into applause.

After a couple of weeks, my stepdaughters went home, the other relatives having left rather sooner, and the hard core rescue team, meaning me, dug in. Bob's troubles had dissolved the armor his hurtful ways had thrown up around my heart, so I worked tenderly and with an openness to him I hadn't known in years. There were therapists to see, tests to take, medicine to be administered, doctors to confer with, dozens of forms to sort and fill out, bills to pay, and well-wishers to entertain. I spent weeks closing his office, distributing assorted belongings to the appropriate people, and packing and sending twenty-five boxes of official papers to Rice University. My separate life was on indefinite hold.

Not long after Bob came home from the hospital, Rosalind sent Robert Stanley to cheer up his grandfather and help with the care-taking, since he was almost ten now and very responsible. And I took his being there as an opportunity to figure out Bob's financial situation, for it now seemed unlikely that he could lobby in the future and we needed to know what resources he would have available.

So with Gloria's help, I went through Bob's files, coming across two- and three-year-old checks worth several thousand dollars that I got reissued and deposited. I discovered about twenty thousand dollars in a non-interest-bearing account and promptly switched it. By the time I finished, I'd discovered that he had spent more than twice his annual salary on the cabin and his Houston property during the years we'd been married, and for the past five or six years had had an annual shortfall of at least three thousand dollars.

244

I sent summaries of what I'd found to Rosalind, Orissa, and Norman, for Bob's daughters would inherit the Houston property that secured the loan, and Norman, who'd made a fair amount of money on real estate, might give good counsel. I'd consulted a therapist who said that after the kind of brain damage Bob had sustained, he shouldn't be given a bewildering array of choices. His doctors had said he shouldn't live alone. And since even before the stroke, he'd left the gas in the kitchen on from time to time, a fire under an empty pot, and the doors unlocked at night, I agreed with the doctors, for I didn't think either he or the house was safe if he was alone in it. So I wrote Rosalind and Orissa asking that we think together about his future and suggesting several options.

Bob was to go to Orissa's in New Orleans for two weeks in June, and I waited for word from her or Rosalind before giving him the sobering news, hoping we could narrow the options down to two before I had to spell out the problems. But I heard nothing and, as I waited, my anxiety began to rise. With intense foreboding, then, the day before he was to leave, I sat down with him, spread out the charts, and slowly made my way through the figures. Finally I got to the end and paused, and when he broke his silence at last, he said he would stop paying me the six hundred dollars a month!

I was thunderstruck. So deeply had I been immersed in helping him that *this* possibility had never occurred to me. I stared at him witlessly and kept on staring until I managed at last to say, "You *can't* do that!" And then: "You're legally obligated to pay that money—you sent a letter to that effect to my mortgage company." After another long silence, as he looked obsessively down at the figures, I added, "That money is the interest on *my* investment in the house *you* live in." I was behind Niagara Falls, however, and he was not listening.

For the next eighteen hours I moved in a slow daze as I expect someone might who'd been given electric shock treatments, but surely, I told myself, sanity would return in good time. When putting Bob on the plane the next day, I did what I could to hide my fright. But a week later, Gloria left a teary message on my answering machine that ended with: "Celia, what's all this about?" And when I called, she sobbed as she told me Orissa had asked her to find Bob a divorce lawyer!

From then on, and for almost a year, I found myself trapped playing Cordelia in a modern version of *Lear*, though no loyal Kent told the king he was betraying himself. The only option that would have been acceptable to Bob's two elder daughters, it turned out, was my moving back into the house permanently. As I didn't offer to do that, Rosalind shouted at me when I telephoned; and then, as I heard my own soul wailing piteously in a huge echo chamber, the step-daughter who'd written, "I can't bear the thought of anything coming in the way of our love for each other," dropped me from her life as she had Stanley Walker.

The unthinkable had happened; the man I'd honored and trusted beyond anyone *had* taken advantage of me, breaking promises without which he knew I would never have married him. And while insisting repeatedly that he didn't want it, he filed for divorce because I refused to change the title of the house so he could squander more of our money. The charge was desertion.

Such an accusation was not only insulting; from a layperson's point of view, it was patently untrue, as a glance at my calendar book for the two weeks before his stroke made clear. We had given a dinner party at the house for John and Billie Maguire and Peter and Marian Wright Edelman; dined at the home of *Washington Post* writer Tom Edsall; gone to a play at the Arena Stage; joined a retirement party at the Willard Hotel for a favorite professor; had dinner at my place with Nancy and Norm Richardson and Kate and Fred Michelman shortly after Kate took over as head of the National Abortion Rights Action League; and celebrated Ellen Malcolm's fortieth birthday. All of these were people Bob had met through me, and as always, I'd been the social secretary, cook, and organizer.

Scores of people had watched me care for Bob, and many had helped simply because I'd asked them to. My attempts to persuade him and his daughters to take his financial problems seriously were documented in a sheaf of letters, along with his oft-repeated promise that I would have a house and lifetime pension when he died. But when I met with a prominent lawyer who'd been a friend and protested that I would *never* desert someone in trouble—*and had not*—he laughed awkwardly and said, "Oh, that's how the law lets people get out of marriages they want out of for other reasons." So if Bob chose to say the contrary, nobody was going to stop him. Facts and the truth simply did not matter.

When I got the first letter from Bob's lawyer spelling out my dreadful options, I climbed onto the train for North Carolina, where I spent a long weekend with Pat and Bob Spearman. Not only were they both lawyers, but Pat taught family law, and after reading through the documents, she said, "You did everything anybody could to make that marriage work!" and then became my most trusted adviser. Her bottom line was "Don't go to trial!" for trials cost a fortune and justice is too rarely done.

I was not only outraged, I was humiliated. When I married Bob, I was writing about Fanny Wright and wondering why she had failed to negotiate a prenuptial agreement, as her own sister had, to protect her property. But I had trusted Bob so entirely that I *had not even thought* of doing that for myself, and despite his many broken promises, it had simply *never* occurred to me that Bob would go back on his promise that I would have our house and a lifetime pension when he died.

For months it felt as though my brain cells, not to mention my nerve endings, were inflamed, and from time to time I had trouble catching my breath. I wrote voluminous letters to my lawyer, indignantly protesting this miscarriage of justice and explaining my intricate relations with Bob though I knew by now that the law didn't care. To friends who hoped I would moderate my rage and grief, I snapped that I didn't want to be Julie Andrews; I wanted to be Anna Magnani.

Still, I was determined to come out of this with my power to love and trust intact, and above my computer I put the quote from Aeschylus that Robert Kennedy had found so consoling: "Even in our sleep, pain we cannot forget falls drop by drop upon the heart until, at last, in our despair, against our will, wisdom comes through the awful grace of God." For months and even years to come, I turned to it as to an incantation.

I saw a therapist in New York who specialized in grieving and another in Washington who specialized in families. When I said to the latter, "I need to put the anger behind me," she commented dismissively, "That's just the jargon of the profession. You'll be angry for a long time. But don't shoot yourself in the foot." This was all the reality check I needed—good, common sense that calmed me until I felt stronger to face what I had to.

I kept getting reports that Bob was miserable, for he didn't want the divorce but wouldn't let go of the demand for money. Pat came up from North Carolina to assure him that my latest offer was my last—and took the opportunity to say she'd lost respect for him because he was leaving me so much worse off financially than I would have been if I hadn't married him. He told her he would give anything to undo what he'd done—but of course did nothing.

As far as I know, nobody else sat Bob down and said, "What you're doing is cruel." Or "What you're doing is wrong." Or told him he would lose the esteem of people he cared for. A good friend asked me if I wanted him to find a hit man, and others said they would cross the street rather than speak to Bob. But the liberal community, for the most part, treated him like a hero whose high-mindedness had got him into trouble and the *Observer* keened for the great man fallen. Two prominent columnists asked people to chip in to help him out, and when one said the debt was political and I wrote that she had apparently been misinformed, she did not reply. An Austin fund raiser for him brought in twenty-seven thousand dollars.

Meanwhile I was left with two choices: I could remain solvent or keep my home. Since I'd already given up two homes I loved for men—the old farmhouse and my New York apartment—I couldn't bear being forced to do it again, and so I told my lawyer I would give up a fourth of my inheritance to keep the house on Third Street. At fifty-two, my professional options had radically narrowed. But the separate life I'd had when I married Bob had grown richer during the marriage, and now I was free to live it fully at last.

David came up from Mississippi to hold my hand through the awful proceedings, during which Bob now and again cried. I could not have had a more loving or generous son, and I was terrifically proud of him and astounded at what we had managed to get through together.

When I got back in the house, it looked like something on Tobacco Road. The back gate had burst its hinges, three doors had fallen off theirs, five sockets had to be replaced, there was a huge hole in the tile wall in one bathroom and another in a ceiling through which rain had poured. Water stains had spoiled a corner of the newly painted living room ceiling. The roach infestation was so grim the exterminators had to come monthly for a year, and I had to pay five years' back termite protection. Bob had gone off with almost two hundred of my books, four large boxes of my papers, and the wedding album from my marriage to Willie, the latter of which I never saw again.

But friends were grand. Tom and Sally Leach, along with Tom's mother Molly, paid their own money to fly up and spend two weeks helping me get the house in good order. Tom built a wonderful window seat in the living room while Sally planted a garden of impatiens, columbine, and ferns. Sally and I sanded the dining room floor while Molly spent two days pulling up a grungy rug from the little dressing area off my bedroom to discover a lovely old pine floor we then refinished.

Jerry Wilson flew in from San Francisco with his bejeweled magic wand—Jerry had become a "wizard"—and we had a gala exorcism party with about sixty people. Nancy and Norm Richardson showed up with an original Rowlandson etching from the early nineteenth century of a woman in a plumed hat and plunging bodice who is asserting her domestic authority, for the caption reads, somewhat ungrammatically: "Who's Mistress Now." Drawings and sculptures friends had done, and two of my Aunt Bernice's paintings with their bold colors, proclaimed the new era. Along the top of one living room wall I'd hung a row of large photographs of my feminist heroines. My writers' group, my reading group, and a motley assortment of people from hither and yon crammed in while Jerry pronounced the words that released the evil spirits and we toasted to the good times rolling.

Two weeks later, the man who came to make cushions for the window seat walked in and caught his breath, saying, "I remembered this house as rather dim." And I said, "Not any more!" for sparkling in fresh, rich colors like the old farmhouse, it looked like the new place it was and its spirit now was mine.

Bob moved to Austin, and some eight years later, I got a last glimpse of the quintessential Eckhardt when *Texas Monthly* published an article about him called "Last of a Breed." In his opening, writer Jan Reid described the "80-year-old patriarch of Texas liberals" as he "shambled forth in grimy blue jeans" to order a margarita at ten in the morning.

Declaring that "among lawmakers from Texas, he ranks in importance with Lyndon Johnson, Sam Rayburn, Ralph Yarborough, Lloyd Bentsen, and Phil Gramm," he noted that Bob could never be elected today. Observing that "excess and eccentricity are out," he went on to say that "Eckhardt uses tobacco, he drinks too much, his three marriages have failed, he's a liberal, and he is unabashed on all counts." As for the marriages, Reid wrote that after Nadine had discovered "the patent impossibility of living with the man," Bob had married me: "It was all very inbred, if not incestuous. But they were the royalty of Texas liberals, and Eckhardt pedaled his bike at the head of the parade."

In his yard in the Clarksville section of Austin, Reid wrote, Bob had built a tree house where he liked to sit while drinking scotch and watching the sun go down. ("I suppose a man of Eckhardt's age and accomplishment," Reid wrote philosophically, "is entitled to break his own leg.") Of the house itself, which "was filled with scattered newspapers, Bibles, assorted hats, pots and spoons frozen in dry muck of forgotten meals," a woman said, "One look at the place and you could tell what his wives must have gone through."

The article was so masterful that even I managed to laugh, though less heartily, I suspect, than those who'd had the option of observing from a distance. And it prompted me to give silent, but heartfelt thanks that the clean-up, if there was to be one, was long since someone else's responsibility.

CHAPTER TWENTY-TWO

On the afternoon of my exorcism party, my Texas friend Don Stone gave me a massage. He was a lawyer who had moved east to work for Exxon, which then dumped him in one of its many fits of downsizing, and he had taken up massage, singing, counseling, and a little Japanese, along with the stock market and some teaching to pay the bills. For years Don and his wife Annette had been part of my family, so they came from Connecticut to celebrate my release.

Three weeks later, they were driving through with a friend and offered me another massage. Don said, "You can have just me, like before, or you can have all three of us working on you at the same time." Inspired by my conviction that less is *not* more, and whoever said it was must have been sitting in a Victorian parlor, I said "All three." When Don asked, "Would you be comfortable taking off all your clothes?" I said, "May I keep on my underpants?"

Dusk was falling when we took the massage table out the back door to the patio, where our privacy was protected by an eight-foot fence on two sides and a carriage house on the third. Then I brought out all my candlesticks and improvised several more, lining the sides with little gleams of flickering light. The fireflies were out when I climbed onto the table; Mozart was playing softly; and three caring people trained in Esalen techniques began to work on my body. The underpants lasted maybe fifteen minutes, and at the end of an hour, as I was lying on my stomach with my head in the cradle, I began to cry.

For some time longer I lay there with tears I made no effort to stop falling softly onto the paving stones. Strong, tender hands were unlocking the pain and anger from the deep places, and I felt cherished. Finally, when the candles guttered and Mozart fell silent, I sat up slowly, washed my face, embraced my friends, and moved into a new place in my life.

Two months later, I was staying in New York with Speed and Martha Carroll, friends from the University of Texas whose home on West 11th Street had given me back my beloved city. Speed was now a brilliantly successful Wall Street lawyer who'd once taken a six-month sabbatical to work in Los Angeles as a massage therapist. He had studied in Japan as well as at Esalen; he could do Swedish massage, visceral manipulation, Shiatsu, cranial-sacral therapy, and things I couldn't even pronounce, much less spell. And as he piled up the towels and uncorked the oil for a birthday massage, he said, "This is for you. Talk or stay quiet, cry if you feel like it." I told him what had happened earlier but said, "Somehow I don't think I'll need to cry this time." Two hours later, with dry, happy eyes, and limbs that felt like Raggedy Ann's, I knew I had left a heavy weight behind forever.

The financial burden was more intractable, and for two years I paid the bills by doing a variety of things; I did some ghostwriting for the Women's Research and Education Institute, organized a couple of conferences, wrote some reports, and put together a blue-ribbon advisory committee for the National Abortion Rights Action League. Some of it a twenty-five-year-old could have done as handily, and none of it required a Ph.D., much less a book published by Harvard.

But in the process, I learned something about the way organizations operate and discovered how vacuous so much work is. I watched egos clash and well-laid plans shatter for reasons no more profound or sinister than that somebody forgot the butter or someone's kid got whooping cough. I came out of it marveling that anything ever got done since the human material was so mixed and volatile and the centrifugal forces so strong. And though I never stopped worrying about money, I could not kick the nutty habit of asking to review a book for fifty dollars that it might take me a week to read.

I rented my back two bedrooms to Kathy Bonk, one of the country's foremost feminist publicists, who stayed seven years. We got on so famously we never even had a tiff, and as our home became a gathering place for progressives in general and feminists in particular, I found myself part of a loose-knit group I had no husband to thank for. During the 1992 inaugural, we gave a brunch for Betsey Wright, without whom Bill Clinton could never have been governor of Arkansas, much less made it to the White House. And after looking around at some of the most effective women in Washington and then up at the photographs of our heroic predecessors—Fanny Wright, Virginia Woolf, Sojourner Truth, Elizabeth Cady Stanton, Margaret Sanger, and Eleanor Roosevelt— I said with a laugh but real conviction: "They're looking down on us today, and they are very, very happy!" Once when Pat Spearman was up from North Carolina, she stood in the kitchen and commented cheerfully, "You know, that exorcism really worked!"

In the years to come, friends from all over the country would drop in for a few hours, a few days, and on occasion for weeks at a time. At least once a year Diana Kealey would come from England. And more often than not we would have some sort of gathering—a Sunday brunch, perhaps, or a dinner—and around the long oval table would sit a voluble collection of interesting people: actors, lawyers, sculptors, architects, members of Congress, writers, deans, college presidents, scholars, psychotherapists, preachers, economists, Cabinet members, organizers, financiers, film makers, activists of every possible variety. One Thanksgiving a guest toasted to the spirit of happy anarchy, while after another, a friend who found the lively atmosphere more than a little unnerving complained that I had no "system." In fact our dinners usually teetered on the edge of chaos, but, as they were always a group project, we invariably pulled them off in the end. And though the noise level was sometimes daunting, nobody ever again whispered on leaving, "I don't see how you can stand it!"

And finally I stopped drinking. To nobody's surprise—at least not to mine—the horror I had gone through with Bob and his family had rocked my resolve, and I had broken the promise to David I had felt to be just short of sacred. So I had to start over.

The first time I tried Alcoholics Anonymous, I had called the number listed in the telephone book and asked where I might find a women's meeting, and the person said, "Just go to one that's convenient, and someone will have a booklet called *Where and When* that gives the times and places of meetings in the area." I told him where I was, he gave me some options, and that evening I walked into a room with about forty gay men and one other woman.

I stood there thinking, "Oh Good Lord!" But by now I was desperate enough to resist the urge to back out, and so I took a seat in the corner. It was the sort of meeting where everybody introduces himself and says something, and my turn didn't come for maybe forty-five minutes. When it did, I said this was my first time, to which they responded with shouts and applause. And then I confessed that I had hoped to find a group of women and was about to go on when a guy from the far corner said, "Lady, you got the next best thing!" And everybody dissolved in laughter.

For a while I persisted in trying to find a meeting where the people looked more like me, and then I would go for a few months thinking I could handle it alone. But some crisis or another would send me back to the bottle, and as Abraham Lincoln put it, many times I was driven to my knees because I had nowhere else to go. Finally I got Larry L. King to tell me about the group that had helped him kick his formidable habit, and for another few months, I let myself drink occasionally while going to this one meeting to see if I trusted it to help me too.

At last I decided to do a kind of ritual "goodbye to all that"—to the pleasures and even thrills of my life with alcohol—and took a trip to England with an old friend. He had never been abroad, and introducing someone I was fond of to so many places I loved was very wonderful. We drank nice wines at dinner, and then one glorious evening in London, after seeing *A Little Night Music,* we dined and danced at the Ritz, where our waiter brought me a little black cigar to go with my cognac.

A few weeks later, Diana came over from Manchester, and on Halloween, the night before David's thirtieth birthday, we drank a bottle of champagne and then an exquisite Beaujolais to accompany a fine steak dinner. And that was it. I had ended a turbulent phase of my life with a woman who is like my sister and in honor, so to speak, of my son.

My lifelong problems with "the God bit" were resolved, practically speaking, by a man who said simply, "Whoever God may be, I'm not it." In the years to come I would find myself in twelve-step meetings with women who had slept in the sewers of Paris and drunk mouthwash for the buzz. With ex-cons who had spent years on every drug I'd heard of and some I hadn't. With women who lived in shelters and men who lived on the street. With a guy who said, "I spent fifteen years drivin' without a license, but I figured it didn't matter 'cause I was usually drivin' stolen cars." With Vietnam vets who woke up in a sweat at night and an arthritic black man missing several front teeth who carried himself with towering dignity and died in an ice storm while trying to get the homeless into shelters. With a woman who said of her drinking days, "I had a lot of husbands, but none of them was mine." With another who told us wistfully, "Now I have problems in areas where I didn't even have areas before." With a choleric Italian who spent two years seething in a corner, but whose temper cooled as the time passed and whose wit and balance the rest of us came to count on. With senators, actors, elevator operators, maintenance men, and lots of ordinary people like me. Sometimes I even found myself sitting beside a Republican. Many told stories so harrowing it seemed a miracle the teller had survived, and I knew I had to "keep coming back."

While facing a disease that is "cunning, baffling, and powerful"—a disease that according to some authorities kills more than 90 percent of those who have it—we laugh a lot. And the whole thing works, I think, because we have all come up against our human frailty. Like the people in the early Church, we come together because we need the sustenance we draw from one another. When I feel myself wavering, I picture someone in those rooms and remember the story that goes with the face, and then a second person's and a third's, and I tell myself that if they can do it, so can I. Once more, I feel blessed by the healing power of friendship and laughter.

After about two years in those rooms, I had a new word to describe myself: happy. Not simply excited, or on an emotional high—but quietly, genuinely happy. Despite all that tight-lipped, stoic heritage, I had learned to look at the sky and the birds and flowers, I could dance through a beautiful morning. Humiliation had led at last to grace, and as everyday things took on a luminous quality, I began to suspect that at heart I was a druid.

I no longer needed a powerful man to secure my place in a group I treasured, for the world had changed and so had I. Best of all, I had learned, with the French novelist George Sand, that what I had always counted on but now cherished would take me to the end: "the sweetest of all human emotions, the one that is nourished by calamities and mistakes as well as by greatness and heroic acts, the one that spans every stage of life, that begins to develop in us from our very first sensation of being, and that endures as long as we do, the one that parallels and actually lengthens our life, that is reborn from its ashes and that reties itself as tightly and just as firmly after being broken; that emotion, alas! is not love . . . but friendship."

CHAPTER TWENTY-THREE

*I*n the summer of 1990 I had another moment of truth: I would fly to Texas and write about Ann Richards running for governor of the state that sets the national standard for macho. I had a huge debt, little available cash, and no book contract, but a woman who quipped that the cowboy was a guy who kissed the horse instead of the girl before he rode off into the sunset was worth the risk. Since my agent said I'd be more likely to get a publisher if I added Dianne Feinstein, I blithely said "Why not?"

I knew a lot about Texas, but nothing of California apart from my ten months in Palo Alto and my friendship with Phil and Sala Burton, both of whom were now dead. But my marriages had left me with a wealth of information and some insight into politics, and writing this book felt like a way of salvaging years of my life.

So I wrote a proposal that Ellen Levine and I faxed back and forth until we were both satisfied, and Betty Dooley commissioned me to write on the elections for the Women's Research and Education Institute. (This gave me a certain authority that might persuade people to take me seriously, while allowing contributions to the project to be tax-deductible.) I bought a round-trip ticket based on my plan to return from Austin two days after the November election simply because it would cost more to fly in a triangle and come back from Los Angeles. By late summer, the received wisdom was that Feinstein would win and Richards would lose, and I expected to stay for the victory celebration in LA, leave the next day for Austin, and the day after that, fly home.

So on a sweltering day in the last week of August, Ray Farabee met my plane in Austin and said over lunch that he would not only lend me a car for the duration but contribute a portable computer to my project. So I walked into the Richards for Governor headquarters a little off balance but terrifically pleased with the way things were going, and said, "When can I travel with Ann?"

Bill Cryer, her press secretary, suggested a Labor Day dove shoot in Kaufman County, and I said, "You've got to be crazy." I think killing beautiful creatures for sport is disgusting, and Kaufman County, where my mother was born, was about two hundred miles away. Besides, it was too hot to go outside for anything short of an emergency, and I said he would have to come up with something better.

In the next few days, while I shopped for computers, I pestered Cryer, who kept saying "doves," until I shot back irritably, "You can sucker a Yankee into doing that, but I'm not about to stand around with a bunch of loonies when it's 110 in the shade." And waited for him to get the picture.

Then one morning, while Ray's assistant Atelia Clarkson, a genius with computers, was installing my new word processing program, Jean Marshall called to say, "A woman from Massachusetts who's volunteered in Ann's campaign wants to go to the dove shoot but doesn't want to drive alone. Why don't you go with her?" I said no thanks for at least the third time, but as I put down the phone, Atelia looked over and said, "You really ought to go." And suddenly I knew they were right—the dove shoot, after all, was a hoary folk ritual in Texas—so I phoned Jeanie back to say, "Tell her okay."

So at about 10 A.M. the next morning we were standing under the kind of sun that makes squiggles run in the middle distance. I was surrounded by a brace of reporters who'd been wisecracking for the past couple of hours when Ann and her party gave up on the doves and came down from their little hill. She got about ten feet away before I said, "Happy birthday, Ann," and she looked over, stopped abruptly, and said, "What in the world are *you* doing here?" I said, "I'm writing a book about your race and Feinstein's."

We were friendly acquaintances rather than friends. (Otherwise, I couldn't have done the book.) She had even less idea what might come of this than I did, and I suspected that she would not be thrilled by a situation she could not control. We ambled over to a press tent; she dropped onto the table a couple of birds everyone was pretending she had shot; and when I sat down next to her, she said under her breath, "I want to talk to you."

Then she launched into a masterful performance, and I sat there enjoying the show while watching a couple of reporters who were mesmerized by the way she was matter-of-factly plucking the birds. By the time she got down to the skin, they looked vaguely ill—for the scrawny creatures *were* revolting—and when she noticed the reporters standing with their mouths agape, she said, "Mah daddy told me if you were gonna shoot 'em, you had to eat 'em. And if you're gonna eat 'em, you gotta clean 'em first." And with that, she got up smartly and went off to chat up the guys with the money.

Later that afternoon, Ann was to open her campaign headquarters in five adjacent counties, and at one stop, after working the crowd, she came over and said thoughtfully, "I don't know whether anybody'd want to buy that book." And I said, "They will if you win," and that's the way we left it.

Surrounded that day by all those sardonic reporters, I'd had a wonderful time, and from it came everybody's favorite chapter. I got yet another lesson in the virtue of listening to others, and it grounded me once more in the distinctive tone and rhythms of Texas.

For the next few weeks, the far-flung pieces of my life seemed to come together. My years with Willie had taught me not only a good deal about state politics but also about how a journalist does her business. My ties to the *Observer* gave me people to call whose insights I trusted. My experience with Texas Women for the '80s had taught me to walk into a stranger's office and ask for what I needed. Tom Wicker put me in touch with Dave McNeely of the *Austin American-Statesman,* who not only gave me a persuasive read on the governor's race but showed me how to use a tape recorder properly.

And then Ellen came through; after I'd been in Texas several weeks, she called to say that Scribner's would publish the book and give me an advance that might at least cover expenses. (A few days earlier, Barbara Grossman, who would become my editor, had phoned to ask if I could *really* get the manuscript in by January 1—a due date that must have been Ellen's idea. So off the top of my head, I said, "Not if you want footnotes," and she said, "I'll get back to you.") The gamble was paying off.

So I got back to work with even greater zest. Marriage to Bob had introduced me to Bill and Diana Hobby, who virtually turned over to me their third floor in Houston. Since Bill had been lieutenant governor for sixteen years, I asked for an interview that in the interstices of our schedules I ended up doing in curlers and dressing gown just after breakfast.

Ruth Bowers, who had said so memorably, "I have a plane," organized a luncheon in San Antonio with several pro-choice Republican women trapped between loyalty to their party and a commitment to reproductive freedom for women. ("Those *horrible* people," one of them complained of the Religious Right, "came out of *your* party into *our* party, and we want you to take them back!") And while I was staying with Ruth, she gave a fund raiser for Ann where I heard the candidate telling her hardcore supporters about the compromises she had to make in order to be a viable candidate. That night I said to myself, "Oh get real, this is my place and these are my people, and win or lose, this is where I want to be on November 6, 1990." And called for a round-trip ticket to Los Angeles, returning to Austin the Sunday before the election.

I spent a day traveling with Ann that taught me a lot about the stresses and indignities of running for high office — and incidentally, of working as a journalist. After going through the equivalent of doctoral orals before the editorial board of the *Houston Chronicle,* she had to fight off an obnoxious television journalist who stuck a microphone in her face and asked, "What do you think about the latest polls that show you fifteen points behind?" and "What do you think about the twelve black sheriffs who've endorsed your opponent?" (Did this horrid woman, I wondered, expect her to say, "Why, I think all that's just dandy"?)

After a luncheon speech, she and her party were almost shoved out the rear of the convention center so that her opponent Clayton Williams, who was expected to win, wouldn't have to see her. (This precaution would turn out to be shrewd on his part, for when they did meet face to face some weeks later, he would disgrace himself and lose the election.) Then we spent a couple of hours with the president, trustees, and students of Texas Southern University, the historically black college where my friend Taunya had taught. By now, I had heard many politicians hold forth on many different subjects. But after listening to Ann Richards talk about why that college had been founded and what it had meant, about the African American struggle and the ways she could help them, I knew she was tapping into her soul when she spoke on race and justice.

And suddenly I realized that not one single person had said anything nice to Ann Richards the entire day. So as we were shifting from one audience to the next, I beckoned and called, "Ann, I want to tell you something." When she came over, I said, "You were sensational just now! Absolutely sensational!" I had been moved to tears and I think my voice actually cracked, and she was so surprised she stared for a second before she asked, "Really?" And stared at me a few seconds more before moving on to her next audience.

Two hours later I was bumped off her plane for the singer Jerry Jeff Walker, and I was so angry I spent fifteen minutes in the Houston airport telling Bill Cryer why they were going to lose and how it served them right.

With the blessings of Don Edwards, the dean of California's congressional delegation, and Henry Waxman, one of Phil Burton's disciples in the wizardry of power, I then flew off to Los Angeles. For more than a month, I stayed in Santa Monica with friends from the University of Texas, and through a Washington reporter, I met several women at the *Los Angeles Times* who told me where to go and whom to see.

Of these, Kay Mills was the most insistent; among other things, she wanted me to talk to some key Republican women in San Diego. When I whined, "Kay, I'm focusing on the Democrats," she kept after me until I finally agreed, and these interviews helped me understand how different Texas is from California and why Pete Wilson was so formidable a candidate.

Wicker got me an interview with Willie Brown, the Speaker of the California Assembly who had taught me at Phil Burton's memorial service that it is possible to be funny at a funeral. In keeping with Willie's style, we met in the glamorous Redwood Room of the Clift Hotel in San Francisco, where he was so irreverent, sharp, and to the point that I'd have wagered he could hold his own with Faust's Mephistopheles. Through a friend of Mildred Wurf's, I interviewed Cecil Williams, the minister of Glide Memorial Church whose regard for Feinstein was the best thing I heard about her.

But I never got to talk personally with Feinstein or a member of her family, as I had with Ann Richards and hers. My marriages had taught me that politicians need journalists as much as journalists need them, so

I knew that even if what I wrote would not affect this election, her schedule was never too tight to squeeze in an interview. And being kept at arm's length not only dampened whatever enthusiasm I might have worked up for her candidacy, but also helped me understand people whose claims were more immediate when they complained bitterly about rebuffs they'd suffered at her hands or her staff's.

My biggest breakthrough came quite by chance when I was flying back to LA from San Francisco, where I had interviewed Hadley Roth, who'd been Feinstein's chief of staff when she was mayor. After propping my computer on my lap, I'd put the sheet with my questions on the armrest when the woman next to me noticed the name at the top of the page and said, "Hadley Roth—he's such a dear man! How do you know him?"

As it turned out, this woman had worked for Feinstein for the eight years she'd been mayor and agreed to talk to me if I would *not* use her name. So down went the computer and out came the tape recorder. All the way to Los Angeles, she told me fascinating tales about Dianne Feinstein—her temper, generosity, laziness, perfectionism—and sketched a background that illuminated the enigmatic comments I had gotten from members of her staff.

Eventually, I told all this to a San Francisco reporter who said "Ah ha!" and printed out five or six newspaper stories from the last decade that made similar points—giving me sources I *could* quote. And when a man high up in the campaign said teasingly, "I'll tell you the whole story when we're old and gray and the statute of limitations has run out," I could say: "You might as well tell me now because I know it already." So he did.

This meant I was not unduly cast down as Feinstein's chances of beating Pete Wilson slowly narrowed while I watched from the peripheries, or on the Sunday before the election, when I read in the *Los Angeles Times* on the plane to Austin that all the experts predicted she would lose. On the other hand, for the past two weeks my Texas friends had been calling in a frenzy, for Richards's poll numbers were climbing steadily. Clayton Williams had refused to shake her hand when their paths had crossed a couple of weeks earlier, and since Texas gentlemen are expected to treat ladies courteously, he was in trouble, for the cameras had caught this moment for posterity.

I had bought the round-trip ticket to Austin as the cheapest of the alternatives, but what had been a matter of economy was now turning into the chance of a lifetime: to be on hand when my native state elected a woman governor in her own right for the first time. So the next night, Ray Farabee and I joined an airport crowd so excited that everyone seemed ready to levitate. We watched a small white plane taxi in, and Richards come out to stand at the top of the stairs and, with a voice almost gone, give the best stump speech I expect ever to hear.

And I was there at the Hyatt on election night when the guys with the wires coming out of their ears moved in to mount guard over Texas' new governor as she gave the thumbs-up sign to a room packed with people on the thin edge of riot. I was at the state capitol the next morning at the press conference when she explained how they had pulled off what looked like a political miracle. And best of all, I was at her campaign headquarters that afternoon when she gave what I called her Ann-at-Agincourt speech, thanking the people who had stuck by her and kept the faith when the gurus had written her off and told them they were crazy.

She talked that afternoon about going to her Alcoholics Anonymous meeting the night before and said, "the reason those twelve-step programs work is that they not only teach you how *not* to indulge in whatever your addiction is, but they teach you a way of life. And that way of life is to live one day at a time." She continued: "But the other thing that this program teaches us is that we must let go and let God. . . . And in a sense . . . *you are God to me*. . . . Do you understand that? That the dynamics put together by a group of people working intensely and cohesively together—there is nothing more omnipotent or powerful than that. . . . for me, I *did* let go and let God! We won this race because of you, not because of me. We were a part of the whole."

Days like these teach you why politicians do it: why they put up with the insults and indignities, the heat and cold, the lousy food and dreary speeches, their well-meaning friends as well as their enemies, the stress, the boredom, the pain. One guy had said Ann had a little bit of Elvis in her, and not only had she put on a spectacular show, but she'd taught me something about how to live.

Two days after the election, I flew home to put a manuscript together. Along the way, I had transcribed almost two hundred interviews, many of them between an hour and two hours long, and done most of the research. Now I had seven weeks to do the interviews that remained, analyze the exit polls, and write a three-hundred-page book.

In early December I put a Christmas tree at the far end of my computer table, and for a month it twinkled at me from the minute I got up in the morning to the time I fell into bed. As Kathy Bonk put it, I bonded with that tree, which became my companion. On Christmas Day I worked until five, pausing only to talk to David, who had flown back that morning from Germany with his partner, Susanne Dietzel. I went to a neighbor's for holiday turkey and, after two hours, came home and worked until midnight.

The last weeks were the best, for I was caught up in the drama, and every day or so brought an insight that made the story sharper and better. Sculptors must feel the same as they watch a shape emerge from the stone. Painters, when they stand back, looking at the canvas, and see that the harmonies are almost right: a few lines here, a touch of ochre or cerulean blue there. . . .

I overshot the deadline by ten days or so, but despite a computer that broke twice, a printer that died, and all the muck, confusion, and dree that attend a task so ambitious, I did it. And in mid-January, when I boarded the train at Union Station to deliver the manuscript to Scribner's, I felt like I'd just had the most exciting six months of my life.

CHAPTER TWENTY-FOUR

*W*hen *Storming the Statehouse* was published more than a year later, it got a starred review in *Publishers Weekly* that objected only to my not making Dianne Feinstein as interesting as Ann Richards—which prompted me to pop off with, "Neither did God!" My favorite response, however, came from Barbara Jordan, who wrote, "Celia Morris's book made me feel proud." When I read that sentence I wept, for because of our peculiar history, nothing anyone else could say—black or white, male or female—could move me more deeply.

When I was young I had wanted to fight racism, but since conscience—or just plain cussedness—had kept me from working through the Church, the only way I had known to go about it was to marry a man who would engage in the battle and then to help him do it. Now I wasn't holding someone else's coat while he did the fighting; I was doing it my own way.

For American politics at the end of the twentieth century was preoccupied with race, though the language was often coded, and in writing about women who struggled for their equal measure of power, I was also engaging racism with the weapons at my disposal—my education, my experience, whatever gift I had with words. Fanny Wright, Ann Richards, and Dianne Feinstein had all been immersed in tangled issues of race, and recounting their experiences meant dramatizing and dissecting those issues in all their complexity.

But by the time *Statehouse* came out, I was well into another book

265

whose origins in race went even deeper, for shortly after Nina Totenberg had announced on National Public Radio that an Oklahoma law professor was charging Supreme Court nominee Clarence Thomas with sexual harassment, Taunya Banks had called to say she knew Anita Hill.

Taunya was one of my closest African American friends, and I had known her since 1983, when she took on a handful of women who were trying to make Texas Women for the '80s into their own fiefdom. On that memorable October morning, she said of Hill, "She's conservative, religious, and intensely protective of her privacy, and if she says this, I believe her. For it would make sense of something I've never been able to understand: why a woman with a law degree from Yale and a great job in Washington would move back to Oklahoma to teach at Oral Roberts University!" Taunya trusted Anita Hill, I trusted Taunya, and so by the end of that day we were both involved in the fight to make the Senate Judiciary Committee take Hill's story seriously.

Over the next few weeks, television allowed American women a collective experience they had never had before. Matters of race were inextricably tangled in the Hill-Thomas story with messages about the power imbalance between men and women. While we had a national teach-in on sexual harassment, as Ofra Bikel of PBS put it, all of us—whether we were women of color or white—watched some the country's most powerful men treat a woman who testified with breathtaking dignity as though she might be Salome or Mata Hari. As we saw them abusing their power in ways that were painfully familiar, many of us felt a shock of recognition that led, in my case, to another moment of truth: In order to explore the power imbalance between the sexes, I would find a cross section of American women whose memories had been ignited by the Hill-Thomas hearings and listen to their stories.

For I had spent years struggling with the fact that although I'd had as privileged a life as any woman could hope for, too many men I'd loved and trusted had abused the power our culture gave them over me, and in the months to come, I realized how deeply those experiences had changed me. Thirty years earlier, nobody would have dreamed of telling me a story like those I would hear, and I would never have asked them to. Now, however, I felt the power of those ancient words: "Behold, I have refined thee in the furnace of affliction!"

So I put out the word and, once again, friends scattered about the country did what they could to help. One day, for instance, Susan Ford

Wiltshire called from Nashville to say, "Some women here want to start a local version of EMILY's List, and I wonder if you'd come tell us how we won Texas?" Susan, who was chair of the classics department at Vanderbilt University, had grown up in Lubbock, where she knew my Aunt Bernice, and then had been a prize student of John Sullivan's at the University of Texas. I'd met her when I lectured at Vanderbilt in 1985, and together we'd heard "the cosmic click."

I told Susan nothing would give me more pleasure and asked if we could combine two things: "Can you set it up so that I can also talk to some women about the Hill-Thomas hearings and then invite them to tell me their own stories?" Susan called Nancy Ransom, who ran Vanderbilt's Women's Center, and Nancy put out a flyer saying, in effect, Celia Morris is going to be here on x day for a brown-bag lunch to discuss the Hill-Thomas hearings.

One Saturday morning a few weeks later, then, I talked about Ann Richards's race to more than a hundred determined women who showed up to form what became Women in the Nineties (WIN). And on the following Monday, thirty-odd women and one man came to the Women's Center on the Vanderbilt campus. We had a lively discussion, and after that, until well into the evening, I sat in an upstairs room with my tape recorder listening to a string of poignant, disturbing, even frightening stories. I cried once and three of the storytellers wept, two of them bitterly.

These interviews were different from those I had done for *Statehouse*. For more than a year, my job was not primarily to ask questions and then to analyze and interpret the answers; it was to listen respectfully to a piece of a woman's life. Whenever I traveled, I found a way to hear at least one more story, and ultimately I tape-recorded and transcribed almost 150 from all over the country.

Some few stories were worthless. As I sat at Pat Spearman's in Raleigh, for example, listening to a woman who was rancid with rage and self-pity, I remember thinking: "This isn't harassment; it's garden-variety adultery. She got sexually involved with her boss because she thought he'd get her out of a stale marriage." Later I climbed a hill in southern California with a woman I soon decided might be literally crazy. I met one or two for whom even Mother Teresa would have been hard-pressed to feel compassion.

But many stories were persuasive, and listening was almost always emotionally demanding. For I found a remarkable range of gutsy, touching, wounded, baffled, fighting, striving, and yes, ultimately heroic women. One, for instance, was a young woman about whom I would write that if Huck Finn had been a girl, he'd have been Tammy Miller. Tammy was a maintenance worker in her late twenties at a power plant in Indiana when a couple of guys wrestled her to the floor and a supervisor bit her on the rear so hard she bled through her jeans. She wanted the company to acknowledge that somebody had done something wrong. (The line that threads through her story is "That ain't right!") But the resistance was so fierce and the cover-up so determined that in a fit of despair she swallowed a handful of pills and went up in a crane with a CB radio over which she kept saying, "What's the matter? Can't you find me?" By the time they did, all her internal systems were down, and Tammy came as near to dying as you can get and still come out whole.

The single most dramatic story I heard was that of Jean Underwood, who claimed to have been harassed by her boss, the mayor of a medium-sized city in California. I sat in a friend's study in Oakland listening to what seemed an ordinary tale when I began to feel an awful sense of dread. Shirley Jackson's story "The Lottery" flashed through my mind—a story where a cluster of mundane details suddenly takes on a nightmarish quality and you know that something horrible is about to happen. And as I listened to Jean, sure enough, these minor instances of harassment plunged us deeper and deeper into what turned out to be a tale of incest.

Tammy and Jean were so precarious emotionally when they told me their stories that I was awed by their courage and moved by their confidence in me. Subsequently, we talked several times by phone as I followed the progress of their cases and listened as they grew stronger. Like so many others who talked to me, they came to have a deep investment in the book and I, to see that I was writing it for their sakes as well as mine—and the future's.

The book that became *Bearing Witness: Sexual Harassment and Beyond—Everywoman's Story,* then, was grounded in a collection of stories from a cross section of American women; ultimately I chose forty-seven of the most telling from women of every class, race, age, and ethnic background. Here were human faces and voices to help us understand *in a feeling way* what the statistics told us abstractly about male sexual coercion of women: that, at the very least, two out of five will be harassed at least once in their lifetimes; that according to the FBI, a woman is battered every fifteen seconds and, in 1992, a rape was reported every five minutes (a more conservative estimate suggested that one in ten American women will be raped); that six women in the United States are killed every day by their partners.

Looking at the stories together and plumbing them for meaning engaged me more profoundly than any other piece of work I had done. Arranging them to show the connections between sexual harassment and other forms of male violence against women, I argued that the power imbalance between the sexes was bad for both and could be changed. I made it clear that every woman was vulnerable to some form of harassment or abuse—neither class, education, nor skin color offering any sure protection. I showed that individual women could not effectively fight this power imbalance alone, but that women working together at many levels had already done a great deal to change it. And hoping for a future "in which women control their own sexuality and men share power rather than impose it," I concluded by saying, "It is a future that matters profoundly for our sons' sakes as well as for our daughters'. And so we reach out and touch. We laugh. We love again. And all the while, we organize."

My experience with both books was mixed. The editing was hard, if not as hard as it had been with Harvard, and neither got the attention I'd hoped for. Women I thought should have reviewed them did not. And as far as I know, no African Americans reviewed *Bearing Witness,* though the women's movement was regularly slammed for slighting blacks, and here a white woman was putting the sexual abuse of black women during slavery at the heart of her analysis of contemporary problems between men and women, and whites and blacks.

Statehouse, however, was reviewed on the front page of the *Los Angeles Times Book Review,* as *Fanny* had been, and *Kirkus Reviews* called *Witness* a "groundbreaking book." Writing them was exhilarating, and talking about them all over the country made me feel like part of a community working for justice. I met good people and eventually got tough enough to handle hostile questions without wanting to hide in the back of a closet.

A talk show host from Phoenix, Arizona, for instance, began our interview by saying, "I'm six foot seven and weigh 260 pounds, and nobody's equal to me," and for the next hour and a half, every dart within a hundred-mile radius of Phoenix was aimed at me. One man called, however, to say that he'd been listening to talk radio for fifteen years and this was the first time he'd called in, but he just *had* to say, "I agree with her: women really are equal to men." So they picked on him until they got tired and then refocused on me. (Blessedly, I was doing that interview by telephone from a friend's home in Chicago, and my hosts cushioned the shock.)

One of my most memorable experiences came with Governor Ann Richards, whose response to *Statehouse* I heard about first from a mutual friend who called to say "I saw Ann at a press conference and she said, 'Have you seen Celia's book? I read it from cover to cover, and it's intensely painful.'" Since the review in *Publishers Weekly* had said, "Ann Richards won not only with the electorate but with the author," I knew her reaction was skewed. Still, I was not wholly surprised; like most politicians, she had wanted to tell the story *her* way, and before *Statehouse* came out, she'd been giving speeches to the effect that since the election's outcome was never in doubt, she had never been worried. I had presented her, on the contrary, as a woman who had despaired, flown into rages, been hurt, made mistakes—had pierced one aide after another with her rapier wit—in short, as a fallible, if gutsy and admirable human being.

Virtually every morning TV talk show had told my publicist they would be happy to have me if Ann Richards were part of the package, but the governor had always found a reason to refuse. When I was in Texas, she managed *not* to come to two big book parties when she had little more to do than walk across the street. But she asked to see me in her office thirty minutes before my book party was scheduled to begin at the Scholz Beer Garten in Austin and I agreed.

Before coming into the anteroom with the pizzazz and charm for which she is famous, she kept me waiting for half an hour, and as soon as she shut the door behind us, she turned and said, "I'm sure you know this book was intensely painful for me; I'd put it all behind me, but here it was again in black and white, and I had to read it in a confined space."

By this time we were sitting across from one another, and so I said, "Ann, I, *as a person,* would like to say to you *as a person* that I am very, very sorry for the pain. But I, *as a writer,* want to say to you *as a politi-*

cian: this book is very good for you. I think it's a modern day *Pilgrim's Progress:* Pilgrim starts out for the Promised Land, and then she's beset by fire, flood, boils, snakes, earthquakes, tornadoes, hurricanes, but pushes on, and in the end she triumphs! And that's the way I talk about it." She looked at me thoughtfully and went on to something else before she circled back to ask, "Do you think you'll sell that book at the Democratic National Convention? After all, we *are* both Democrats." So we ended our time together chatting happily.

However, she had made me thirty minutes late to my own book party, and I woke up the next morning with a black eye. I had never had a black eye, and since I was quite sober now, I knew I had not run into a door or fallen down the stairs. So I decided this woman had occult powers, and all I could do was hope that now she felt even.

Books take a long time to produce, and by the time *Bearing Witness* hit the stores, media fads had shifted, and a book my publisher had expected to be another *Backlash* seemed to slip from public view before it came into focus. Michael Crichton's *Disclosure* had swept to the top of the bestseller list with its tale of a hapless guy preyed upon by a shrewish female boss who lured him into a sexual trap and then accused him of harassment. The new cry became "Women do it too!" and if women were no better than men and would use power similarly, why fret over the status quo?

A smart, erudite, self-confessed exhibitionist, Camille Paglia insisted that women like being shoved around and, suggesting that she knew what she was talking about, appeared in décolletage on the cover of a slick magazine with two glowering black guys in leather and chains. Women who called themselves feminists began tut-tutting over the "cult of victimhood" and suggesting that feminism had gone astray: surely some of these coeds who cried "rape" must be exaggerating! Surely women could take a little pornography. . . .

Again the media had a new line and younger faces to feature. Some of their points were well taken, though hardly new, and they helped undermine the public's capacity for sympathy, much less outrage. Then, too, people were tired of hard stories; even friends now and again grimaced and said, "Oh, your book is so painful!" and I had to admit it didn't have *Statehouse*'s laughs and light moments.

Still, I had thought everyone would open their hearts to the extraordinary women in *Bearing Witness* who had so much in common with the frontier women I held in awe. Dr. Frances Conley, for instance, had forced the powers-that-be at Stanford University to withdraw the nomination of a man to be dean of the medical school because he treated women disgustingly. Dr. Jean Jew had triumphed over the University of Iowa, which had argued in court: "This isn't sexual harassment; it's the way of the world!"

Seven of the forty-seven women in my book, in fact, had turned to the law, and *all* had won their cases or settled out of court, after taking on powerful people in their communities. They had been ridiculed and reviled; they had lost friends and, in some cases, their families; their privacy had been invaded and they'd gone into debt. And still they had persisted. Senator Bob Packwood, for instance, would finally be forced to resign his seat after twenty-four women simply refused to shut up. And from then on, stories about sexual harassment and abuse appeared regularly in newspapers that a decade earlier had not seemed to know the phenomenon existed. But the women whose stories I told were not only taking on men with real power over their lives but breaking silences enjoined on women for millennia. And this you do *not* do with impunity.

The second wave of American feminism had long since peaked, and the nature of the third was unclear. I had devoted a chapter in *Bearing Witness* to women's attacks on other women, and now the movement itself was divided. Even more discouraging, most women did not want to know that the struggle for equality might still be hard, or the goal elusive.

Men I had respected and even loved had fought as hard as they could against the second wave. Willie, for example, had published Irving Howe's irate review of Kate Millett's groundbreaking *Sexual Politics* and then an awful piece by Norman Mailer called "Prisoner of Sex." Though generally supportive on paper, Bob Eckhardt had voted against the extension of the Equal Rights Amendment. Men struggling with their own set of problems didn't want to believe they had unfair advantages. Men who knew better accused me of man-hating, and too many women acted as if the fight were over.

By now I knew something about the rhythms of political and cultural change, however—and how hard and relentlessly people fight against it—and so I was let down rather than flattened. We were up against disparities of power between men and women that had lasted for millennia, and the slow times had their place. The experience of writing the book had been immensely rewarding: I had watched women take hold of their lives and helped a handful like Tammy Miller and Jean Underwood as they became strong, proud people. Apart from a few fuzzy sentences, there was nothing I'd like to alter, and the book would be there to use again when the times were ripe and occasion called for it.

CHAPTER TWENTY-FIVE

*B*ut the time felt ripe *now* for those of us on the verge of turning sixty, so in the spring of 1995, I called several women I
loved, all of whom I'd met first at the University of Texas, to propose
that we come together and take stock. And after the necessary amount
of haggling and a handful of logistical nightmares, five contemporaries
from all over the country—Pat Spearman, Shirley Garner, Sydney Seaver,
Madeline Moore, and I—gathered in San Francisco for fun and reflection.

Most of our grandparents had come from a class and generation that
worked hard simply to survive—or, as William Faulkner put it, to endure; our parents, from a generation that had worked hard to prosper;
while we had represented the generation that was slated to enjoy the
blessings that accrued to all that accumulated labor. The same arc has
been transcribed by millions of families throughout the country, though
not necessarily in so neat a time frame, for it represents what we call the
American Dream.

Between us, however, we had eight divorces and thirteen children,
two current husbands, and more lovers than we could even remember,
much less would admit to. (At least two of Madeline's had been women.)
Obviously things hadn't gone quite the way we had expected, or our
parents and grandparents had expected for us. By now, we had broken
more taboos than we had known existed when we got to Austin in the
1950s, for we'd come there as middle-class white girls who'd been brought

up to take our rightful places alongside our husbands among the people who were going to rule Texas. But as we gathered to toast what we hoped would be at least another quarter century, we and our worlds had changed utterly.

Individual women had earlier gone through many of the personal struggles we had, but changes in technology and the economy, along with a social revolution, had made ours the first generation where large numbers of women all over the country had gradually become different kinds of people. While struggling for fullness and integrity in our personal lives, we'd had to redefine everything we had been raised to call virtue. We had marched alongside one another and petitioned for laws that treat women equally and give them a fair chance. We had sued and read and met and talked endlessly. We had fought for space within our professions and welcomed Gloria Steinem's remark that we could declare victory when a mediocre woman could rise as far and as fast as a mediocre man. That time hadn't come yet, and no doubt wouldn't in our lifetimes, but for us the struggle had been worth it—largely because we had done it together.

We gathered initially at the 11 o'clock service on a Sunday morning in Glide Memorial Church, and by the time we were all together, everybody in the big room was clapping and shouting and bouncing around like Tina Turner. For though the mercury had already shot past 90 degrees—record-breaking for San Francisco, even in August—nobody at Glide lets the weather dull the spirit.

A large African American woman in a shiny black pants suit was directing the choir with big, swooping gestures. Behind the mike, a man with an earring played a hot electric guitar, while the guy next to him wearing a red satin shirt with three gold chains went into a trance with a couple of gourds. While the windows rattled, we wondered, along with the rest of the congregation, if the mortar would hold.

Forty years earlier, we wouldn't have dreamed of going to a place like Glide, down in the heart of San Francisco's Tenderloin District, where you can find pimps, prostitutes, drug addicts, and scores of the homeless and desolate at any time of the day or night. But the 110-person choir singing "Do Not Pass Me By" was more than half white and middle class, and you knew you were in for something fine when the African American minister, Cecil Williams, leapt onto the dais. Wearing a white surplice and a black robe embroidered with a wide band of African kinte cloth, he shouted, "Good morning, good morning! Let us all stand and hold hands with our next-door friend, or spouse, or mate, or stranger. Hold hands! Listen, listen!" And then he began to pray.

"Some of us are trying to understand what we can *do* with ourselves and with our brothers and sisters. And some of us are trying to find a way to get out of the mess we're in. Some of us are feeling the stress and strain of life, and we don't know what to do, Lord. But we've come here to find the way. . . . Some way, somehow, You have stretched Your arms so much that You've included us all: no matter who we are, no matter where we've been, no matter what we've been through. . . . You've included us all! And You keep rocking us! Rocking us in your bosom, Lord! Thank you! We're truly blessed! Now we can say Amen! Hallelujah! Right on! Shalom!"

The congregation shouted after him, "Thank you! Amen! Hallelujah! Right on! Shalom!" And then those of us who were trying to figure out how to get out of the messes we were in started clapping and bopping around again as the guitars and drums and the piano got going and we all sang "The Battle Hymn of the Republic" with Cecil's voice soaring above the choir's and the congregation's: "Hallelujah! God's truth is marching on. . . . "

I'd first met Cecil Williams in 1990, when I was doing the book on Ann Richards and Dianne Feinstein and people in San Francisco told me to sound him out. When I did, I discovered that he'd grown up in San Angelo, Texas, where Pat Spearman had lived during her first marriage. In the world we'd known then, it had been unthinkable that a black man and a white woman might sit down together and have a useful, much less a pleasant conversation. But I was so taken with Cecil and Glide, which feeds thousands of needy people every day, that I'd said, "I think of myself as a pagan, or maybe a druid, but whenever I get to San Francisco, I plan on coming to your church."

USA Today has described Sunday morning at Glide as part revival, part gospel sing-along, and part talk show confessional, and there I was again, five years later, at the church the poet Maya Angelou calls home, with four women I'd loved for more than half a lifetime. And when the rousing "Battle Hymn of the Republic" wound down and Cecil called out, "Now turn around and embrace each other! Embrace your brothers and sisters!" we leaned over, hugging black men and women in the pews in front and behind, doing something that forty years earlier would have been flatly impossible. We had come here looking for wisdom from a black man, whom our 1950s culture had taught us to shun, and we were having a wonderful time.

Sydney, who'd been my sophomore roommate, was standing next to me in platform shoes and wearing a sarong-like, sleeveless dress with a pattern of brilliantly colored cockatoos. At twenty, she'd looked like Shirley Temple but now was a ringer for Jessica Lange, though she'd had five children—two sets of twins—and had just spent forty-eight hours taking care of three grandchildren. I had expected her to look at least more frazzled, and while we fanned ourselves and sang "The Angel Keeps Watching Over Me," I glanced at her and thought, "Oh, Lord, if You'd told me when I was thirty that this morning would come, it all would have been a lot easier."

In Cecil's sermon, he talked about a man named Dwayne Garrett, a political high-roller who had jumped off the Golden Gate Bridge the week before. Garrett had once given him a big check and told him that Glide was the only church he'd do that for. "Here was a person who had completely moved away from religion and spirituality," Cecil said, "yet he found it in a place like this." But still Garrett had suffered from profound depression.

Going on to distinguish between the good and the bad pride, Cecil said you needed some "pride and dignity" to find the true self. "You gotta have a self if you're gonna have life! You can't just squash yourself, you can't just push yourself away!" You had to be "realistic about the self you need and the self you have."

These were words so plain the five of us hadn't suspected they might be revolutionary until we'd had to break our lives apart to live in their spirit. For we had grown up in a culture that taught women to suppress themselves in the name of a higher good that too often turned out to be indistinguishable from another's convenience, and women we loved had died of that suppression, or lived on in corrosive rage and bitterness.

After decades of skepticism, I began to think about actually joining Glide's "community of compassion" along with Sydney. (Belonging to a church on the opposite side of the continent from where I live, I thought, might create *just* the right distance between me and the institutional church, which had, for the most part, opposed the great fights against slavery and segregation, and for women's rights.) When Cecil ended his sermon, we all sang "We Shall Overcome" with our arms around each other's waists—people of every color, hue, and shade of belief swaying from side to side—and then we poured out into a brilliant summer Sunday.

An hour later, at Greens Restaurant in the park at Ft. Mason overlooking San Francisco Bay, the five of us were laughing so hard that people at nearby tables had begun to twist in their chairs to stare and the waitress held back our lunches because she didn't want to interrupt the fun. The big room was filled with summer light that flooded in from a long wall of windows that stretched almost from floor to ceiling, and Sydney regaled us with tales of bringing up five children alone on forty acres in the Napa Valley in a house she had fashioned out of window screens— a house that for seven years had had no electricity or running water.

She now spent part of each year in Hawaii and part in a tiny garage apartment about twenty miles from the nine-bedroom Maybeck and White mansion in Marin County where she had lived with her first husband. Bringing her saga to a close, she commented that after more than two decades of monogamy and a few years of sexual experimentation, she now saw a man she loved unconditionally but had no desire to marry. A great big "Aaaaah" went around the table, eyebrows shot up with glee, and as I looked out on multicolored sails vivid in the middle distance and puffy little clouds drifting through the russet towers of the Golden Gate Bridge, I marveled happily that five white, middle-class Texas women had come to this.

For we had all known the blackest despair. In the late sixties, Shirley had called me one grim day from Palo Alto to say with a thin voice I could barely hear that the man she loved had hanged himself—and timed it so that she was bound to find him just hours before her doctoral orals at Stanford. Pat had had what she called a "breakdown/breakthrough" when she sued the Duke University Law School for sexual discrimination in not giving her tenure. Madeline's brother had committed suicide a few weeks after her third daughter was born, and a therapist she turned to had seduced her.

Almost every day for two months in 1988, Pat had counseled me through the kind of divorce that makes you question everything you ever believed in and had soothed my lawyer when I furiously nominated him ASSHOLE OF THE YEAR. (With a big laugh that has a manic cast to it, Pat has the habit of pointing out to me, "Celia, I *told* you not to do that!")

But here we sat, Shirley with her merry blue eyes and sleek gray-blonde pageboy looking rather like a burgher Frans Hals might have painted. Pat had the bold, fresh-faced look of a woman on good terms with plants and flowers, her thick, wavy hair now a stunning gray streaked with black. Sydney was so clearly attuned to the earth and natural rhythms that her second husband had boasted that he'd finally taught her to use an indoor toilet. Madeline had a mobile face with dark blue eyes that could flash alarm, as they had the day our tenth grade Latin teacher charged up the aisle and lifted the trot from inside her copy of Caesar's *Gallic Wars,* but now those eyes were crinkling at the corners.

For if anybody had asked Madeline or me at sixteen what and where we expected to be at sixty, a scene like this would never have occurred to us. After all, we'd worn ruffled tulle evening gowns over hoop skirts in the annual Lamar High School May Fetes, and I have pictures of us with large bouquets in our outstretched hands as we smiled broadly and bowed low to a friendly audience.

In fact, I have snapshots of each of us on the verge of becoming women, often at very proper meetings of some organization or other, but now and again wearing an outlandish costume to a fraternity party, or decked out in strapless ball gowns and cocktail dresses. Sydney in harlequin glasses with a ridiculous feather boa around her neck. Shirley in a frilly pinafore. Madeline dressed like a New Orleans madam. Pat in shorts with flour all over her face during a sorority free-for-all. Me in a suit and hat waving from the back of an open convertible with a sign on the door that reads "Celia Buchan: Sweetheart of the University of Texas, 1957."

Though high on energy and ambition, the five of us had not been strikingly different from our peers, and when Madeline leaned over to ask in a throaty stage whisper, "Did you think that pimply guy who sat next to you in algebra was better than you?" we all laughed wildly, though we knew by now that the world had assumed the laugh would be on us.

All of us had married men we admired and thought we loved whose lives we expected to be interesting and valuable. Pat had married the co-editor of the *Texas Law Review* whose office she shared. (She said, "We're either going to kill each other or get married" and chose the latter.) Madeline had wed a lawyer/politician; Sydney, an architect; Shirley, a Ph.D. geologist; I, a crusading journalist and Rhodes scholar.

And something in the frontier spirit *had* worked in our favor, for our ebullience and stamina were not put on for show. All of us knew how to work and worked hard. And all had become professional women: Shirley was a Shakespeare scholar and now served as chair of the English department at the University of Minnesota; Pat had been a domestic court judge and had recently retired after more than twenty years teaching at North Carolina Central Law School, a historically black college; Madeline was an expert on Virginia Woolf and a professor of English at the University of California at Santa Cruz, where she had started their women's studies program; among other things, Sydney had worked as a massage therapist until repetitive stress injuries forced her to change professions, and at fifty-six she had set up her own consulting firm on ergonomics; and I was a writer who took strong women as her primary subjects. Like Sydney, we all had a category that could be labeled "among other things," and we knew that some of the items might well have shocked our more staid contemporaries.

After Sydney told her raising-the-five-children (two-sets-of-twins) story, which makes Robinson Crusoe look like a couch potato, we kept the conversation light for upwards of an hour until I changed directions by saying, more or less abruptly, "You know, my mother drank herself to death."

Forks stopped in midair. Madeline's eyes and then Sydney's rounded like Olive's in Popeye, and their collective "Oh, Celia!" caught the next table's attention. Sydney had seen my mother gamely climb the three flights of stairs at Littlefield dormitory with armloads of clothes. Madeline had known her as a matter-of-fact, gray-haired matron who helped us roll back the living room rug to dance.

After decades of silence on painful, intimate subjects, suddenly the air was swirling with revelation: Shirley's mother had left her father before she was born, she said, and she has only sketchy memories of seeing him occasionally as a child. Their first real talk came when she was nineteen, after his cancerous vocal cords had been removed, so the conversation had been labored and minimal.

Not long after Madeline's brother killed himself, she had plunged into the murk of their past in search of explanations and had found far more than she'd bargained for.

Sydney had been sexually molested at five by her cousin. For her first decade, she'd been raised by devoted but silent grandparents, with few toys and no playmates, and she'd thought she was illegitimate. The whole family was so taciturn she didn't even *ask* about her father until after her mother died, but on beginning therapy at thirty-five, she started tracking him down. Five years later, when she finally reached him by phone and said, "Joe, this is your daughter, Sydney Dawn," he replied, "Well hello, Sweets!" When she asked, "What do you think about my calling you after all this time?" he said, "Well, it would have been foolish not to."

Pat's father had died when she was eleven, but her brother and sister, who were eleven and twelve years older, had been wonderfully supportive. "My *real* traumas began," she said, "after I got engaged."

We had *never* talked about such things at the university, and though as the 1950s receded, we learned to be more open with one another, some of these stories I was hearing now for the first time. And as a direct result of this learning to open up, as well as to take risks, each of us was convinced that we were *much* happier people than our own mothers had been. Because we'd lived at a different time, we had a wealth of choices they hadn't even dreamed of, and if the price we'd paid was far higher than we'd suspected it might be, so had been the rewards. With the stimulus of a political movement and rigorous bouts of personal therapy, we had come to know ourselves and build second, third, and sometimes even fourth lives we could enjoy and respect. We had put the lie to Scott Fitzgerald's melancholy dictum that there *are* no second acts in American lives.

As we rose for a walk in Golden Gate Park, we felt giddy with pleasure in each other's company—and incredibly lucky. In a century that has been very terrible—with country after country ravaged by wars, massacres, and famine, with huge populations crippled by disease and wretched poverty—our own lives had been unusually privileged. And since we had always wanted to use that privilege well, we seemed to be thinking along the same lines, for as we climbed into Sydney's van, Madeline burst out, "I miss the early days of the movement!" and sighed. All of us had been dismayed and frustrated as the second American women's movement weakened and splintered, for while transforming our own lives, it had taught us how much it takes to change a culture.

Shirley agreed: "I hate this vicious infighting!" Before becoming chair of the English department, she had headed Advanced Feminist Studies at Minnesota, and now she threw out a case in point: "A woman who calls herself a feminist—she's thirty-five, maybe forty—published a book last year trashing the 'homely' women in Women's Studies and saying they just preach anti-male, anti-sex sermons to get back at the beautiful girls."

In the nineteenth century, the women who did that sort of thing hadn't called themselves feminists, and I wondered aloud when the dialogue had shifted back to blaming the victim. It was vexing: if you tried to live with your heart and spirit open, and then woke to discover you'd been suckered, a chorus of voices mocked you for having been naive—instead of coming down hard on those who'd taken unfair advantage.

Shirley called from the backseat: "Celia, how did that quote go? You know, the one from the woman who stood up for Fanny Wright and talked about 'scaffolds' and 'executioners'"? The woman who had defended Fanny, Paulina Wright Davis, had been speaking at a women's rights convention in the 1870s, twenty years after Fanny died. Shirley and Pat liked to tease me about that quote because I could forget my doctor's name and my own phone number, but more than ten years after Harvard published the book, I could still recite it without notes, as I did now: "Women joined in the hue and cry against her, little thinking that men were building the gallows and making them the executioners. Women have crucified in all ages the redeemers of their own sex, and men mock them with the fact. It is time now that we trample beneath our feet this ignoble public sentiment that men have made for us; and if others are to be crucified before we can be redeemed, let men do the cruel, cowardly act; but let us learn to hedge womanhood round with generous, protecting care and love."

They gave me a little round of applause, and then Pat said: "These young women are falling for the same line we did—that they can do it all themselves. How sickening that history may have to repeat itself!"

Sydney's van had been winding up the hill, and now she pulled over and we all piled out at the top of a ledge overlooking San Francisco Bay and began to wander along a path under the immense evergreens. Pausing now and again to look out over dark blue water with patches of green and little lines of feathery breakers that twinkled in the sun, we talked about our part in a fight that would go on long past our lifetimes. The air was freighted with eucalyptus—a soft breeze cutting into the oppressive heat high up on the bluffs in this lovely park that Phil Burton had strong-armed Congress into creating. As we walked idly around a gigantic boulder, I looked over at Shirley and remembered Irving's confiding once that he didn't think Shirley would make it and didn't know whether I would. And though I marveled at how blind even the best of our male mentors had sometimes been, the struggle *had* been terrifically hard. Still, here we were, so far from where we'd come from but so intact, and for the moment, the ease of our communing was its own reward.

Wandering along the paths in shifting groups of two or three, we rang the changes on "Do you remember . . . ?" "Have you read . . . ?" and "Just wait till I tell you about. . . . " From time to time, tears fell and heads turned away. Long arms circled bent shoulders. Hoots of laughter startled owls, barks of indignation flushed small red squirrels and once a covey of guinea hens.

In the course of the afternoon, we ran through the arsenal of contemporary labels that had been pinned on us when we presumed to try to do things differently. We remembered the way our self-respect had been called self-regard. The way we were labeled unfeminine and/or inept if we shrank from manipulating men in the time-honored fashion. Or called whiny and ungrateful when we were taken aback to see people looking through us toward our husbands. Or made out to be unfeeling mothers when we tried to find substantive work that engaged some of our other faculties. Blamed for being depressed or demoralized. Called misguided for wanting a different world, since, our critics would insist tirelessly, we were up against human nature.

A burst of laughter came from over my shoulder as I heard Shirley say, "Nobody thinks women like us have stories to tell," and as I whirled around, Pat tripped over a root and Madeline ran into a tree. Suddenly we found ourselves drawn up in a jagged circle, for we discovered that we had all been so haunted by the gulf between the world we expected and the world we found, and so troubled by the resurgence of ideas we had spent our lifetimes outgrowing, that most of us had thought about writing something down.

None of us, to be sure, had discovered the cure for some intractable disease, or broken a genetic code, or written a latter-day *Iliad*. We hadn't flown in space, or run a call-girl ring, or taken over a Fortune 500 company, or done anything altogether grand as the world judges it. *We'd simply had chances millions of other women pine for, only to discover that the animating vision was something of a cheat.*

And most of us wanted to talk about it. Sydney confessed wistfully, "I've tried off and on, talking into a tape recorder." Madeline said, "My novel, *As You Desire,* is semi-autobiographical, and I'm starting another." Years earlier I had read fifty pages of a memoir Shirley had begun, and when I looked over pointedly, she reassured me: "I'll get back to it eventually."

Then Pat said, "Celia, how about it?" I had already written three books about strong women and their struggles to do work they loved and were well suited for. About the boxes women had been squeezed into that were far too small to contain their hearts, minds, and spirits. And in my keynote to the first Texas Women's Scholars conference, I'd glanced at the novels of the best male Texas writers of our generation and pointed out that their female characters were nothing like us or our closest friends.

So four vibrant women stood in the waning California sunlight looking hard and expectantly at me. And I stood looking at each in turn, wondering if the time had finally come for me to write openly about what I knew best. No more than two weeks later, as I was walking back from my weekly twelve-step meeting, I had the latest of my pagan mystical experiences and decided to try reconstructing my own life—and by extension, the lives of so many women in my generation.

CHAPTER TWENTY-SIX

For years, Shirley has taught a course called "Breaking Silences," and she warned me. But writing it down was still harder than I had expected, and in the early versions of my manuscript I slighted the pain. The joy and relief were easy enough—and thrilling—but you cannot tell about heartbreak in the language we inherited. Anyone who listens to Ann Richards and Molly Ivins can tell you that "good-old-girl" works wonderfully for politics and social satire, but for laying the soul bare, I found it very nearly useless. Virginia Woolf and Henry James, on the other hand, are grand models for plumbing the inner life, but if you try to picture either at a dinner table on Buffalo Speedway in Houston, Texas, or a political rally in the Eighth District, you get some hint of my dilemma.

The very breadth of our generation's experiences posed the problem, for lost love turned out not to be the end—arguably it was not even the most important part—of what we'd lived and had to account for. Then, too, my cast of characters was far too big for even sympathetic readers to follow, and cutting out so many people who have graced my life felt less like ingratitude than primal sin.

But now that I have told the basic story as best I can—and in enough detail to show how a generation's challenge played itself out in one woman's life—let me go back to sundown that day in San Francisco, when the five of us ended up around an oak table in a little coffee bar in North Beach where Shirley and I had gone now and again when we

285

were at Stanford. With its dark wood paneling, lace curtains, and shiny brass fixtures, it looked much the same, though a few more ferns dangled from the ceiling and the people around us seemed much younger than they had in the early sixties—and more representative of a mixed human family. As for us, we were both the same and very different.

Earlier that day, as we'd wandered through Golden Gate Park, each of us had played riffs on her individual experiences, and now we fell into something like a jazz session. From the African American experience that had contained so much pain and found such joy had come this rich art form that could express a whole spectrum of feelings, from the deepest melancholy to the heights of exhilaration. In this, as in so many things, we had learned from black people, and as the evening went on, we were struggling together to shape a composition, to make a statement. The theme around which our improvisations and solos swirled was a question: after all the turmoil, the work, the pain, the terror, the pride, the pleasure, what had we learned that we want to pass on—to our sons as well as to our daughters?

For the first few minutes—three at the outside—we mulled over the commonplace notion that we were old fogies nobody would pay attention to. But if we'd been the sort to listen to nay-sayers—who'd after all been with us from the beginning, warning that we could *never* do whatever it was we were up to at the moment—we wouldn't have been sitting at that table in North Beach in the first place. Still, going against the grain is never easy unless you have contempt for others, which we did not. But finally we put those fears aside; the young would do as they chose, but our business for the evening was to come to some conclusions. Listening was someone else's challenge.

As we each took turns, telling stories that sometimes seemed to have no end, laughing, sighing, bristling with anger, we were searching for the *common* experiences. So we listened carefully to one another, interrupting now and then, distilling, summarizing, wandering off the point and finding our way back again, and by the time the lights flickered to signal the evening's end, we had found our messages.

Four, to be precise. Four clear and simple maxims that by the standards of the world in which we were raised are revolutionary. (We decided to skip good advice like "Learn karate!" and "Cultivate your sense of humor!" on the grounds that life itself teaches those lessons; our peculiar experience is not required.)

At least one of our four maxims is taken for granted now by our own children, but since the counter-pressures are and will be intense, we wanted to underscore what some will find obvious. As I list them one by one, I'll use them to tie up the loose ends and come to terms, finally, with the story I have told, hoping always that in the not-too-distant future, Pat, Shirley, Madeline, Sydney, and many more women of our generation will tell the common story in their own way. Call it now my own variations on a four-part theme.

First, we discovered that we had to make and control our own money. White women of our time and place had been brought up to do at least our share, but in the division of labor, our husbands were expected to see to the family's financial security. As somebody aptly put it, the husband brings home the flour, the wife bakes the bread. And though the economy has changed radically since we were in our twenties, the culture hasn't fully adapted to women's working outside the home, especially in the matter of child care, and for decades to come, women will need to insist—sometimes even to themselves.

My own experience showed, for instance, that counting on a husband for financial security was such folly that on this subject, my hard-won serenity can vanish and in a split second I can turn into a wild-eyed maniac wandering the streets in her bedroom slippers. In the past few years, Bob Eckhardt has seldom entered my thoughts or invaded my spirit except when my bank statement rubs in the hard truth: that while he brought a substantial debt into our marriage, he left it with a retreat in Houston and enough money to pay off a debt that had tripled and to buy a house in Austin, where he can sit in a tree drinking scotch and enjoying the sunset. I came into it with no mortgage, no debt, and a six-room New York apartment and left it with a hundred-thousand-dollar debt and an expensive house I own with the bank.

This was not what I'd had in mind at eighteen when I so presumptuously decided that being rich wasn't worth the candle. I had certainly intended to be solvent; I just wasn't taken with the twenty-carat-diamond-and-yacht crowd. And when Bob Wheeler pursued me around the Texas campus trying to shame me into spurning men who might be so crass as to make money, I hadn't known that he was living off a passel of oil wells and the grazing rights to half of two counties.

Since, as my friend Larry L. King puts it, "the world rates freelance writers on the socioeconomic scale somewhere between busboys and rodeo clowns," I would wrestle the debt down to a place that felt manageable, and then it would shoot up again. And as it soared for about the third time to what I fervently hoped would be its final peak, the magazine *Working Woman* published an issue on women's salaries. On the cover they asked two questions: "Do You Make What You're Worth?" and "Do You Know How To Get It?" displaying six women's pictures along with their annual salaries. Demi Moore, who played the harassing boss in the movie *Disclosure*, made $12.5 million; a business executive made $594,000; a doctor, $110,350. Mine that year was closest to Hillary Rodham Clinton's, which was $0, and for some of the same reasons. My answer to both questions was an emphatic "No!"

Though white women of our generation hadn't been expected to make their own living, then, we'd come to see that a woman's integrity and well-being depend on her ability to support herself. And in the end we concluded that any account of women's roles that fails to put economic self-sufficiency first—however much this may limit a woman's ability to nurture others and give herself emotionally—can torpedo her chances of living with self-respect.

Our second conclusion might seem of a different order, for it speaks to what it means to be a "good" woman—which is to say, it has to do with where sex and anger fit in. When we grew up, good women were chaste and forgiving, and the world reserved a special brand of scorn for one who was angry. (The Biblical injunction extends, of course, to men as well, and when we talk about the eternal soul rather than sociopolitical arrangements, we have to think long and deeply. But that is another discussion in which God, of course, gets the final word.) Although the sexual double standard, happily, is no longer taken for granted—and women can expect to take as much pleasure in sex as men do—the prohibition against anger clings.

During the bleakest days of my financial crisis, for instance, my beloved second mother, Thelma Hamrick, stung me by saying how awful it was that I hadn't forgiven Bob. For reasons of temperament and generation, Thelma doesn't take the justice part of the justice/mercy dialogue seriously, while my native obsession with fairness had only been strengthened by Irving Howe's influence and my years on New York's Upper West Side. For that matter, I'd come to believe that the old Catholic church had the formula right: first comes justice, and then comes mercy—for mercy without justice can be a formula for disaster. So I quoted from Salman Rushdie's *Satanic Verses:* "In all those years he was the beneficiary of the infinite generosity of women, but he was its victim, too, because their forgiveness made possible the deepest . . . sweetest corruption of all . . . the idea that he was doing nothing wrong."

The discussion didn't end there, of course, and the conflict was emotionally exhausting since, for as long as I could remember, Thelma had stood for the best in the world I came from. To use a wonderfully apt Victorian phrase, she was "the angel in the house." Her spirit had lightened my childhood, and often during the past decade we had done the things together that the closest mothers and daughters do. I'd lavished on her the affection I wish I could have given my own mother, so I both hated letting her down and could scarcely blame her for minding if I implied that her bountiful compassion might be used to bad ends. But by now I was convinced that in a world where "good" women always forgive men, justice will go on eluding us and, as a noted Washington psychotherapist puts it, men will remain narcissistic and women hysterical.

Our second lesson, then, is that anger is a potent weapon and should be used in the fight for justice. "Forgiveness" has propped up an unjust system, as it had during slavery, and women who swallowed their anger have done themselves—and often those around them—very grave harm. So we resolved to *channel* our anger and psychic energy into fighting for a world in which men and women have more nearly equal power—while reserving our own love and caring for those who can return them. Meanwhile the heart has its own mysterious rhythms—and both heals and forgives at its own pace.

Our third lesson was that few people are *merely* victims—certainly none of the women around the table in North Beach was—and that each has to take responsibility for her own life. We had no patience for those who blame all their troubles on somebody else, or for that matter, on "the system." So without bringing out the hair shirts or the switches, each of us had to come to terms with her own role in her miseries.

This meant that I had to grapple with a humiliating question: how had a reasonably intelligent, well-motivated woman ended up in two destructive marriages when the choice of a husband remains the single most important one she is likely to make? For in hindsight I knew that my ideal relationship to Willie Morris would have been as a grateful reader who dipped into *North Toward Home* every few years, and to Bob

Eckhardt as a campaign worker who dropped in for an hour or so every few months. Had I seen this earlier, my entire adult life would have looked quite different.

Of course, the easiest and most traditional answer for bad choices is that the person who makes them is a fool. Since roughly half my contemporaries have been divorced at least once, that category seems too large to be useful, and none of the women I looked at so fondly in the lamplight struck me as being so. Lest this answer be correct in my case, however, I now set *one* condition: a true friend must never—EVER—introduce me again to a liberal folk hero.

A psychoanalytic interpretation might suggest that since the first important man in my life had betrayed me at a critical moment, I'd chosen husbands who would repeat the pattern. And this of course is possible. Still, the three men seem far too different for me to dwell on a possibility so dire and inflexible; my father was seldom "not there" for me like my husbands—though he was regularly "not there" to his own wife—and he was much more reliable and generous than either. (Actually, as I struggled to understand my choices, I wondered if I hadn't kept marrying my *mother,* still trying to make her happy and still failing.)

The explanation I came to find most persuasive, however, was that World War II, the Holocaust, and the accelerating conflict in my home had thrown my soul into such a state of terror that I'd had to cling, psychologically speaking, to a man who seemed to stand against the tide. Hence David versus Goliath. The Holocaust had taught me what can happen when democracy fails, and so I'd married men who plunged directly and dramatically into the democratic process. But I'd carried a war and frontier psychology into a private world where it had no place, for these buried fears are the kinds that subconsciously shape us.

Of course, I had also been done in by a combination of bad timing and bad judgment, for after the fact I could see any number of clues I'd missed. If I'd stopped drinking before Bob Eckhardt came back into my life, for instance, I feel sure I'd have picked up on those clues much earlier. But luck and happenstance always play a role; no one ever has *all* the facts at her disposal, and a full life is impossible without trust.

The inescapable fact, however, is that the world of our young adulthood didn't encourage or even allow women to do the important things the men I married did. And since I never doubted that doing those things mattered, I was left to wonder, finally, whether it took so much psychic energy to gain the cultural space to act, much less to stand against the dominant social mores on matters like race, that my husbands simply had to appropriate *my* energy to bolster their own, leaving the disparity between the ideals they stood for and their ways of treating me.

In *A Room of One's Own,* while struggling to make sense of the ideas that undergirded "man's world, woman's place," Virginia Woolf had speculated that woman's subjugation had been necessary to man's "power to believe in himself": "Women have served all these centuries as looking-glasses possessing the magic and delicious power of reflecting the figure of man at twice its natural size. Without that power probably the earth would still be swamp and jungle."

Perhaps my husbands had needed a double dose of psychic energy to keep their grip on the world. But for me, the experience was like having a giant vacuum clamped onto my soul, sucking out a heart and mind and spirit I needed for other purposes.

So there it was: according to the fantasies my generation grew up with, I should have had a fairy-tale life, but instead I'd had what turned out to be a common experience. And when the periods of acute suffering passed, I could actually value what I had learned. Not that I romanticized the pain, or invited anyone else to, for no sane person who has lived for an hour, much less years, enduring the psychological equivalent of having her head held under water treasures the experience or wishes it on others. And if I dwelt on what I could have done with the time and energy I'd spent on marriages that self-destructed, I might fall to my knees and howl.

But my experience had taught me something about the way the world *really* works: in my two marriages together, I'd had the fundamental problems that surveys and studies tell us wives typically complain of, and that my four contemporaries in San Francisco shared—failures that have to do with sex, money, intimacy, and the need to be taken seriously. I'd learned that in the bosom of his family, a man could violate elementary canons of fair play and still be honored by the world he lives in. I'd learned that the world gives a husband far more power than a wife herself willingly gives him. And I'd come to understand that when a man stops his ears to what trustworthy women tell him, he is likely to screen out other key information as well.

For I was still convinced that Willie Morris and Bob Eckhardt had been sincere in hating injustice and fighting for the underdog. But with mothers who'd had to live through them and had therefore indulged them endlessly, they'd grown up with certain assumptions about a man's rights and privileges—his entitlement—and those assumptions had blinded them. Though they chose to marry women they knew wouldn't— they knew couldn't—fit into the narrow place tradition assigned them, they didn't know how to live *with,* they knew only how to live *over.* And though they may well have loved their wives, as they insisted so tirelessly, they didn't know how to *care* about them. They never learned to listen to what they found it unpleasant to hear, and since they were powerful men and often good company—since the excitement they generated made life alongside them seem more intense—people indulged them in their folly. Ultimately they destroyed not only the homes they said they wanted, but their careers as well.

More than a decade after our divorce, Willie moved back to Mississippi. Ten years later still, he remarried, and his last decade seems to have been his happiest. Without the pressure of an intensely demanding job, and with a Mississippi wife before whom he didn't feel compelled to tout the state's singular virtues, he became less defensive and, I'm told, even drank a bit less. But, in August, 1999, at the age of sixty-four, he collapsed in his study, and several hours later he died. On the afternoon he was being buried in Yazoo City, I was walking alone along the ocean beach at Wellfleet on Cape Cod, with the magnificent dunes on the one side and the vast, silent ocean on the other. Trudging with a leaden heart, I'd walked far beyond most people glorying in the sun on such a day, when suddenly I saw a woman with a cavorting black Lab almost exactly Ichabod's size, and I began to cry. It seemed a visit from a blessed spirit, and I was grateful through the tears and pain.

Willie had had a huge impact on my life, for better and for worse, and there had been a great deal of both. But the outpouring of grief and the many tributes to his generosity made me wonder if his long and oft-reported submersion in misery after both our marriage and his job at *Harper's* ended hadn't taught him something fine at last, hadn't made him better and kinder. Though I had no independent knowledge, since he'd rarely broken his self-imposed ban on talking with me, David had said he seemed almost a different person. Several of the many reports of his death quoted David as saying he had long been alienated from his father, but they had worked through their problems and nothing remained to be said at the end. For me, there was little left to ask for.

I also had two of the most outstanding male mentors anyone could want—John Silber and Irving Howe—and in both instances we were so fond of one other that I don't shrink from calling that feeling love. (So great was Irving's power over my imagination that I didn't realize for years that the title of his best-selling book, *The World of Our Fathers,* left somebody important out—someone rather like me.) Both were brilliant, iconoclastic, deeply cultured men. Yet they were capable of belittling me and other women at crucial moments, largely, I suspect, because of ideas about sexual difference so deeply ingrained that they didn't even realize they were irrational, much less that they might be false.

Our fourth and final lesson, then, had to do with politics, for as the twentieth century came to its end, those same ideas about sexual difference that had so twisted our lives provided the underpinnings for the battle raging over "family values." "The family" had become every politician's synonym for virtue and a kind of dumping ground for the problems that society could not seem to handle.

While evidence of domestic violence and sexual abuse within the home soared and the term "dysfunctional family" became a cliché, Democrats vied with Republicans to swear undying commitment to "family values"—which is now little more than a code word in a sound-bite world for a conservative economic and social philosophy. But the promise implied by waving the "family values" wand is profoundly misleading, for virtually any family whose members are reasonably content will stay together without politicians urging them to.

To the artistic or religious imagination, on the other hand, the idea of "family" is altogether different: for it it alludes to the eternal human dilemma, which Christian tradition calls "original sin." Adam and Eve first violate God's commandment; then Cain kills Abel; and a string of Old Testament atrocities follow until God's own Son is crucified, after which the hideous cycle continues unabated. Nor had the Greeks before them any illusions about blood ties, for sons destroy fathers in Greek mythology and literature, as wives do husbands, and vice versa: Oedipus murders his father and marries his mother; Agamemnon sacrifices his daughter; Clytemnestra kills her husband, Orestes his mother, Medea her children, and so on.

Contemporary families may be rather less bloody without invariably being models of human caring. Those of us who met at Glide Memorial Church that memorable Sunday were convinced that we knew as much as we needed to know about them, for we had been typical products of the outgoing, barbecue-in-the-backyard, white Protestant America of our time and place, and so were the men we married. All of us had come from stable families, or what passed for them, and been loved as children. We had grown up with every essential advantage the culture offered and many frills as well.

But instead of *solving* all of life's problems, our intact families had *created* many that we ourselves would struggle with all our lives. And the "real" world that assumed male entitlement had crashed down on us sometime in our mid- to late twenties, after we'd had children. Straddling two eras with quite different expectations for them, women who enjoyed many more options than their mothers had been shocked to find that little had changed in the century since John Stuart Mill had written, "The generality of the male sex cannot yet tolerate the idea of living with an equal." Subsequently we had been grateful when the scholar and literary critic Carolyn Heilbrun wrote, "Power is the ability to take one's place in whatever discourse is essential to action and the right to have one's part matter," for here was the crux of the matter: we had discovered that a husband could flatly refuse to grant his wife that power.

In the end, my friends and I were forced to see that the traditional family—too often a breeding ground for rancor, cruelty, and despair—had *not* ministered to the profound human needs we were too young and inexperienced to recognize when we began creating our own. We'd had to come to terms with the fact that the world we grew up in had buried too many crucial truths. As Katherine Anne Porter put it, "human nature is not grounded in common sense . . . there is a deep place in it where the mind does not go, where the blind monsters sleep and wake, war among themselves, and feed upon death." By means of denial, alcohol, make-believe, or compulsiveness in its many forms, workaholism being perhaps the most common, the culture in which we'd come of age had obscured that deep place. Too often the will had been called upon to do the work of the heart and spirit and, not surprisingly, it had often failed.

Finally, then, we do *not* accept that traditional world, and together we'll fight the assumption that women are the second sex as if our lives depend on it—*which we're convinced they do*. For deeply imbedded in our hearts and psyches are so many cruel memories. My own mother, who drank herself to death in despair over her failure to find dignity in the role society had designed for her. Women we've loved and others we know of who died from investing their lives and souls in marriages that ultimately betrayed them. Both men and women whom we've watched cling to their marriages while fading into pale imitations of the people they might have become. Some, yes, who lost their very souls. With all those memories indelibly impressed, then, and sure we've given marriage more than a fair chance, we'll keep insisting on our four revolutionary ideas. And as Ann Richards said to the African American students at Texas Southern University, we don't care if insisting *is* too much trouble.

For myself, however, I am finally able to say "All's well that ends well" and to glory in the adage that the redeemed are more joyous than the elect. My parents' misery left ugly scars, yet they raised healthy children, gave them good public school educations, and taught them to work hard and keep going. I'd lived in a world where women like me were expected to be generous to their family, their friends, and their neighbors—and had been given the time and space to be. This expectation was so fruitful and so fine I think we should try extending it to everyone. Before foundering in irretrievable disaster, my marriages had taken me places I couldn't have gone on my own and had also given me experiences and precious friends I wouldn't have known otherwise. And my son has turned out to be a responsible, caring man with work he loves and does well.

Not long after that memorable San Francisco Sunday, I sat in Siena looking at the great *Maesta* that Duccio di Boninsegna painted in the early fourteenth century for the cathedral's high altar. In the midst of a room pulsing with glorious golds and reds and greens, I realized that the power of the Christian story relies on the fact that it refuses to skirt the horror. The slaughter of the innocents, the flight into Egypt, Judas's kiss of betrayal, Christ at Gethsemane, Christ crucified between the two thieves—all of it is there in pitiless detail. And I knew that you don't have to believe in the Virgin birth, or for that matter the Resurrection, to be shaken by this majestic Madonna and Child, for they move us so profoundly because we know how that story comes out. You look at a solemn Mother who can do nothing to avert Her Son's terrible fate, who will stand weeping at the foot of the Cross and then hold his lifeless body in her eternal embrace. For anyone who cares about social justice, the glass is always at least half empty, which means that pity, patience, and mercy may be the only responses we can ultimately make.

A year after the five of us gathered at Glide, I went there again with Sydney and joined its motley congregation. Cecil Williams had assured us that Jew, Buddhist, agnostic, Christian, atheist—all were welcome. Despite my lifelong problems with dogma, I believed in Grace—and, for that matter, sin and evil—and I wanted to celebrate the created world with its intoxicating sweetness and grandeur not only with my own friends but also in the company and rhythms I found in that sanctuary.

I also wanted their companionship when times were tough. Democratic politics, we'd discovered, requires far more time and effort than we had suspected. My pastor had said, "I have a feeling we're on a course toward the worst conditions we could face. I know I can't stop it, but I'm going to always have hope and faith. But you've got to go *through* something before you can get *to* something." In that spirit, my friends and I keep trying to do our share. As Studs Terkel puts it, we are less optimistic but still hopeful.

Furthermore, I needed solace as we faced our personal tragedies. One bleak afternoon Diana called from Manchester to say that our precious David Palmer had died suddenly. Not long afterward, John and Kathryn Silber's son David died of AIDS at age forty-one. Jayne Howell's beautiful daughter, my beloved Madeline, died horribly of uterine cancer at thirty-six, leaving two small children. Doris Meissner's husband Chuck died on the plane that crashed into a mountain in Croatia with Commerce Secretary Ron Brown and thirty-three others on board. Mike Hammond's twenty-nine-year-old son died suddenly of heart failure, not long after Mike found out that the pancreatic cancer he thought he'd beaten eight years earlier had reappeared. And one particularly fine Sunday morning, a man from my twelve-step meeting with whom I'd felt a keen rapport—whose wry smile and wickedly funny stories had tickled my spirit—leapt off a high bridge in Rock Creek Park and plummeted to the freeway below, where drivers braked frantically and cars swerved to miss what was left of the man for whom God's absence had at last become too overwhelming. Everywhere we looked, the beauty we found was shot through with mortality.

But the five of us who met at Glide had had the chance both to raise children we loved and to do work we believed in that stretched us. We had been wrenched from narrow, predictable lives and thrown into a much richer world when we plunged into the two most important civil rights struggles of our lifetimes—for the rights of both African Americans and women. We had loved without holding anything back, had known friendship at its best, and had experienced far more than our fair share of joy. We ended that long day when Madeline pulled out a copy of Yeats's Crazy Jane poems and read us one that had baffled us when we were young:

> *I met the Bishop on the road*
> *And much said he and I.*
> *"Those breasts are flat and fallen now,*
> *Those veins must soon be dry;*
> *Live in a heavenly mansion,*
> *Not in some foul sty."*
>
> *"Fair and foul are near of kin,*
> *And fair needs foul," I cried.*
> *"My friends are gone, but that's a truth*
> *Nor grave nor bed denied,*
> *Learned in bodily lowliness*
> *And in the heart's pride.*
>
> *"A woman can be proud and stiff*
> *When on love intent;*
> *But Love has pitched his mansion in*
> *The place of excrement;*
> *For nothing can be sole or whole*
> *That has not been rent."*

Now, at last, we understood.

Should I have the chance to be reincarnated, however, I would just as soon skip the *Sturm und Drang* altogether and come back as a cellist with masses of long frizzy hair who can write like Fran Lebowitz or Larry McMurtry.

CAST OF CHARACTERS

My Family

THE BUCHANS

Buchan, Emelia Reinke (Grandma): my paternal grandmother, a German-speaking frontier girl who moved to Galveston from central Texas just in time to experience the 1900 hurricane. She loathed Adolf Hitler but accepted almost everyone else, whatever their color or beliefs. Like Dilsey, she endured.

Buchan, Glenn: my brother, nine years younger.

Buchan, Inez Fix (Mama): my mother, who deserved better than she got.

Buchan, Mickey: Daddy's kid brother and my favorite uncle.

Buchan, Rudolph Carl (Daddy): my father, the delight and solace of my childhood.

Buchan, Teka: Mickey's wife and now my treasured aunt, who grew up in the Czech community of Dime Box, Texas, where they would retire.

THE PINSONS AND FIXES

Fix, Annie Pinson (Nana): my maternal grandmother, who turned her life over to me when I was thirteen.

Fix, Bernice (Aunt Bernice): my aunt the painter, who married Mama's brother Avery and who called herself, after her astrological sign, Leo Bernice Fix.

Fix, Grover Glenn (Dindaddy): my maternal grandfather, the sweetest of them all.

McKellar, Kate Pinson (Aunt Kate): Nana's younger sister and for decades my favorite aunt.

My Household(s)

Morris, Willie: a Mississippian who captured national attention as a crusading campus newspaper editor at the University of Texas; a Rhodes scholar; the youngest editor-in-chief in the history of *Harper's* magazine; author of *North Toward Home* and *New York Days;* my first husband.

Morris, David: my son, now a photographer in New Orleans.

Eckhardt, Bob: a Texas labor lawyer; state representative from Houston; member of Congress, 1965–80; recipient of Ralph Nader's award for being "the congressman with the most probity"; my second husband.

My Friends and Associates

Adame, Jayne Upton Howell: the outrageous girl who lived across the hall when we were freshmen and became one of my closest friends; a gifted teacher and mother of Madeline, Celia, and Rachel.

Arend, Larry: for ten years my step-son-in-law and subsequently my friend.

Arend, Orissa Eckhardt: Bob's eldest daughter.

Arend, Rebecca: for ten years my beloved step-granddaughter.

Arrowsmith, Bill: noted translator and influential professor of classics who came to the University of Texas in the middle of my time there.

Banks, Taunya: a black law professor whom I first met in Houston, where she fought off a palace coup in Texas Women for the '80s; a friend of Anita Hill's who called one fateful Sunday morning to say she was inclined to believe Hill's story about Clarence Thomas.

Bishop, Barry: a polio victim in an iron lung who became a special friend.

Black, Susan: my best friend in high school.

Bonk, Kathy: a feminist publicist and founder of the Communications Consortium who lived in the back of my Washington house for seven years.

Bowers, Ruth: the abortion-rights activist who largely paid the legal costs for *Roe vs. Wade*. She would contribute handsomely to Texas Women for the '80s and become a sister in spirit.

Brammer, Bill: a journalist and staff assistant to Senator Lyndon Johnson who won the Houghton Mifflin Literary Prize in 1961 for his novel *The Gay Place* and who taught me how to read Austin's liberal community in the early sixties.

Brammer, Nadine. *See* Eckhardt, Nadine Brammer

Brammer, Sydney: Bill and Nadine's elder daughter, an enchantress at three.

Burton, Phil: outrageous and outstanding congressman from San Francisco, who came within one vote of being Speaker of the House; informal leader of The Group, a bunch of dedicated liberal members in the late 1970s; mad genius of reapportionment.

Carroll, Speed: a college friend who became a high-powered Wall Street lawyer and gifted massage therapist and who, with his wife Martha, has often given me a bed in some corner of their New York brownstone.

Childres, Bob: an Ole Miss football star and Rhodes scholar whom I met on the *Queen Mary* in 1958 and who would play a peculiarly tortured role in several people's lives.

Childres, Clare: Bob's first wife.

Clark, Shirley. *See* Garner, Shirley Nelson Clark

Cleveland, Ceil: a native of Archer City, Texas, who grew up with Larry McMurtry and supposedly served as the model for Jacy in *The Last Picture Show*. We met in Cincinnati when I was researching the life of Fanny Wright and have gone through many tumultuous changes together.

Cochran, Gloria: a member of Bob Eckhardt's congressional staff from the beginning and a motherly woman who tried subsequently to bring order to his financial chaos.

Cowles, John: owner of *Harper's* magazine when Willie was editor-in-chief.

Cowles, Sage: wife of John and a former Merce Cunningham dancer.

Crouse, Stanley: the name I give my first analyst.

D'Arms, John: an American classicist at Oxford who hung out with the Rhodes bunch, married Evelyn Waugh's oldest daughter Theresa, and became a noted academic administrator.

D'Arms, Theresa Waugh: one of the rather intimidating young Englishwomen I met in my first months at Oxford.

Davis, Marian: University of Texas professor of art history and my first example of a superior female academic and teacher.

Dooley, Betty: a Texan who directed the Congressional Caucus for Women's Issues.

Dorsen, Norman: NYU law professor and in due time president of the American Civil Liberties Union.

Droshine, Sydney Fielder. *See* Seaver, Sydney Fielder Droshine

Dugger, Celia: my oldest namesake and beloved friend.

Dugger, Jean. *See* Sherrill, Jean(ie) Dugger Marshall

Dugger, Ronnie: editor of the *Daily Texan* who started the *Texas Observer*, a beacon for Texas liberals; an early inspiration and the father of Celia Dugger.

Eckhardt, Nadine Brammer: a hard-playing, sexy brunette I met in Austin before she divorced Bill Brammer and married the man who would in time become my second husband.

Eckhardt, Orissa: Bob Eckhardt's first wife and eldest daughter

Eckhardt, Rosalind: for ten years my cherished stepdaughter; mother of Robert Stanley Walker, the magical child.

Egerton, John: a writer from Nashville, Tennessee, who gave me the idea of doing the biography of Fanny Wright; winner of the Robert Kennedy award for his splendid book *Speak Now against the Day: The Generation before the Civil Rights Movement in the South.*

Farabee, Ray: the friend from my freshman year at the University of Texas who became a state senator and later a vice-chancellor of our alma mater.

Feinstein, Dianne: candidate for governor of California in 1990 and subject of my second book; subsequently a U.S. senator from California.

Fiedler, Herma: our landlady at South Lane House my first year in Oxford; the daughter of the German don who built the house fifty years earlier.

Fielder, Sydney. *See* Seaver, Sydney Fielder Droshine

Fischer, Betty: wife of Jack, who persuaded the Bank Street School to look seriously at David as a possible student and who may have thereby saved his life. We reconnected in my late fifties when she became a treasured friend.

Fischer, Jack: editor-in-chief of *Harper's* magazine who brought Willie to New York as a possible successor.

Foudraine, Claire: a psychotherapist and my first friend in Washington.

Garner, Shirley Nelson Clark: a member of my freshman study group and the first woman to become what I call a sister.

Goodwyn, Larry: a contentious writer for the *Texas Observer* who would become an authority on American Populism and whose editing suggestions rescued my Fanny Wright book from two years of oblivion.

Gray, Jocelyn: a member of Bob Eckhardt's Houston staff; treasurer of Texas Women for the '80s with whom I shared an Austin apartment for a year.

Gretton, Mary Sturge: our landlady during my second year at Oxford. She typically wrote "J.P., B. Litt, Oxon, widow, etc." after her name, even on her laundry tickets.

Hamilton, Carol. *See* Nicklaus, Carol Hamilton

Hammond, Michael: the most charismatic of Willie's Rhodes group. He lived with us for several months in Oxford and after a hiatus of years became again a close friend.

Hamrick, Thelma: Mama's college roommate, the blithe spirit of my early years, and since the late 1970s, my second mother.

Hamrick, Wendell, Sr. and Jr.: Thelma's husband and son.

Herskovits, Jean: a history student from Swarthmore whom I met at Oxford; daughter of the famous anthropologist Melville Herskovits; authority on Nigeria. For more than a decade she was like my sister.

Hinds, Pat. *See* Spearman, Pat Hinds Marschall

Hiss, Anna: Alger's sister and dean of women's sports at the University of Texas.

Howe, Irving: my principal graduate school adviser; a noted Jewish intellectual and socialist; brilliant teacher, inspiration, and beloved friend; winner of the Pulitzer Prize for *The World of Our Fathers;* recipient of a MacArthur "genius" award.

Howell, Jayne. *See* Adame, Jayne Upton Howell

Howell, Madeline: David's playmate and my beloved almost-daughter.

Howes, Joanne: director in 1983–84 of the National Women's Vote Project who invited me to join a book group made up largely of feminist activists.

Ichabod: our grand Labrador retriever.

Janeway, Elizabeth: author of *Man's World, Woman's Place* who became a mentor and friend.

Kealey, Diana: a friend of David Palmer's who came to the United States to do a master's degree in American studies and became my sister in spirit.

King, Larry L.: one of Willie's writing gang at *Harper's;* favorite drinking buddy; author of *The Best Little Whorehouse in Texas.*

Leach, Tom: an architect who built me a window seat; husband of Sally Sparks Leach.

Leach, Sally Sparks: member of my freshman study group and destined to become a sister in spirit.

Luckett, Ellie: a small, dimpled blond chosen University of Texas Sweetheart in 1952 during my first trip to Austin and soon my idol.

Maguire, Billie: social activist, especially on behalf of children; wife of John.

Maguire, John: a civil rights activist and college administrator who became president of SUNY–Old Westbury and then Claremont Graduate University; one of my most ebullient and supportive friends and a model of commitment to making a better world.

McComb, Dave: noted author and my swimming buddy on the Golfcrest team. I was the first girl he kissed, when he was fourteen and I, thirteen, and we've been friends ever since.

Marschall, Pat. *See* Spearman, Pat Hinds Marschall

Marshall, Jean. *See* Sherrill, Jean(ie) Dugger Marshall

Mitchell, Lillian: the black woman who sang at Daddy's funeral.

Moore, Madeline: a sassy friend from high school through college and beyond.

Nagle, Pat Tracy: a member of my original freshman study group and eventually my refuge in San Francisco.

Nelson, Shirley. *See* Garner, Shirley Nelson Clark

Newstead, Helaine: professor of medieval literature at the City University of New York and the second academic woman to show me how fine women can be as teachers.

Nicklaus, Carol Hamilton: a member of my freshman study group at the University of Texas and dauntless companion on my first trip to Europe.

Ooms, Van Doorn: the first Rhodes scholar I met at Oxford, who would become, for a time, my closest friend.

Painter, Roger: the name I gave my second analyst.

Palmer, David: a red-headed Englishman who introduced me to Oxford, helped me get to know Chaucer and Shakespeare, and filled my heart with gentle blessings.

Payne-Gaposchkin, Cecilia: world-famous astronomer at Harvard who controlled access to papers in the Houghton Library that were crucial for my biography of Fanny Wright.

Perkins, Alice: co-author of a 1939 biography of Fanny Wright.

Person, Peggy Rowland: student leader at the University of Texas who set a standard of political engagement, generosity of spirit, and grace under pressure that I'll always struggle to meet.

Pratt, Willis: director of Plan II, my freshman English professor, and ultimately my friend.

Ransom, Harry: English professor and graduate dean who hired me in 1957 to "interpret him to students and students to him," which made me one of "Harry's girls." ("Harry's boys," who were more numerous, included William Arrowsmith, John Silber, and Roger Shattuck.) In no very long time, Ransom would become president and then chancellor of the University of Texas. His passion for books, along with his vision, inspired what became the Harry Ransom Humanities Research Center, which now houses one of the world's most distinguished manuscript collections.

Richards, Ann: first woman elected governor of Texas in her own right and the celebrated subject of my second book.

Richardson, Nancy: mother of four and wife of a philosophy professor who lived in the Oxford flat under ours when David was born.

Richardson, Norman: Nancy's husband and longtime chair of the philosophy department at Gettysburg College. Both were the proverbial salt of the earth.

Rowland, Peggy. *See* Person, Peggy Rowland

Rudenstein, Neil: a Rhodes scholar from Princeton who'd already won a congratulatory first in English literature when I met him at the flat he shared with Mike Hammond and John D'Arms on Beaumont Street in Oxford. He would become president of Harvard.

Schiffrin, Andre: the publisher of Pantheon Books who occupied a penthouse in the New York apartment building where I lived for ten years. He and his wife Leina kept including me even after I left my famous first husband.

Schiffrin, Leina: a delightful eccentric of English and Spanish parentage who met Andre, happily, at Cambridge and, as the owner of penthouse A at 250 West 94th Street would become an integral, if intermittent, part of my life.

Seaver, Sydney Fielder Droshine: high-spirited sophomore roommate and mother of five, including two sets of twins.

Shattuck, Roger: distinguished professor of French literature and prize-winning author.

Sherrill, Jean(ie) Dugger Marshall: a dedicated teacher and Ronnie Dugger's first wife; mother of Celia Dugger; game companion in many adventures.

Silber, John: my University of Texas ethics professor; subsequently the dean of Arts and Sciences whom Board of Regents chairman Frank Irwin fired for over-reaching; finally president of Boston University and Democratic nominee for governor of Massachusetts in 1990. He became a close friend before our radical differences drove us to a painful schism, one that we have begun to mend.

Smith, Block: director of the University Y when I was a freshman at the University of Texas; a radical and courageous man I came to call a primitive Christian.

Snapp, E. A., Sr. and Jr.: my swimming coaches, father and son.

Sparks, Sally. *See* Leach, Sally Sparks

Spearman, Bob: native of North Carolina; Rhodes scholar; graduate of the Yale Law School; Democratic Party activist; second husband of Pat Hinds; genial companion both as host and guest.

Spearman, Pat Hinds Marschall: the first girl I met in Austin who was going to be a professional woman; ultimately a sister in spirit.

Spinks, Jeff: the carpenter I flew from Houston to Washington to build my kitchen.

Stegall, Lael: a social activist who asked me, memorably, whether I could raise $30,000 in three weeks; one of the original staff members for the Women's Political Caucus and member of my book group.

Stone, Don: a college friend, lawyer, massage therapist, on occasion my salvation.

Strum, Shirley: editor of the *Daily Texan* the year before Willie Morris and eventually the first president of SUNY at Stony Brook who wasn't a physicist named John.

Styron, Bill: the southern writer whose friendship Willie particularly coveted; author of *The Confessions of Nat Turner* and *Sophie's Choice*.

Styron, Rose: wife of Bill, gifted poet, writer of children's books, mother of four, gracious hostess; later a key board member of Amnesty International.

Sullivan, John: a British classicist and prolific scholar who won a starred double first at Cambridge and taught at Oxford before coming to Austin to edit the provocative journal *Orion*. His influence on my life remains incalculable.

Sylvester, Dick: a West Point Rhodes scholar who would leave the army and become an authority on Russian literature.

Terkel, Studs: Chicago talk-show host and interviewer par excellence; winner of the Pulitzer Prize for *Working,* along with many other prizes, including the president's humanities medal.

Theresa: the name I've given my closest friend from childhood, whose fate so terrified me.

Tobin, Mrs.: the name I give the Kappa Alpha Theta alumna tyrant.

Tracy, Pat. *See* Nagle, Pat Tracy

Underwood, Jean. *See* Wells, Jean Underwood

Upton, Jayne. *See* Adame, Jayne Upton Howell

Walker, Robert Stanley: for ten years my beloved step-grandson.

Wells, Jean Underwood: a California woman who told me a wrenching story for publication and thereby began transforming her own life.

West, Jim: one of Houston's most colorful multimillionaire oil men.

Wheeler, Bob: a law student and state legislator when I was a college freshman. He bullied me into political awareness and goaded me into marrying a liberal.

Wicker, Tom: reporter and columnist for the *New York Times* whom I met when he was covering the election to fill Lyndon Johnson's vacant U.S. Senate seat—an election in which more than seventy candidates registered for the primary.

Williams, Cecil: pastor of Glide Memorial Church in San Francisco.

Wilson, Jerry: president of the University of Texas student body when I was a freshman. We would eventually declare ourselves brother and sister.

Wiltshire, Susan Ford: native of Lubbock, Texas; former student of John Sullivan; chair of classics at Vanderbilt University in Nashville, Tennessee; political activist and writer whose life has interwoven with mine since the middle 1980s.

Wolfson, Theresa: co-author of the 1939 biography of Fanny Wright.

Woodward, C. Vann: dean of southern historians who taught me how beautifully history can be written and stayed in my life when it was no longer glamorous.

Wright, Fanny: a radical Scotswoman brought up in England who came to the United States in 1817 when she was twenty-three and spent about half her adult life fighting for her beliefs. She was the dazzling subject of my first book.

Wurf, Mildred: lifelong political activist and widow of Jerry Wurf, long-time president of AFSCME. Our friendship began with the women's vote project in 1983 and flourished after she began inviting me to her summer home in Wellfleet on Cape Cod.